Thinking in Bets

Thinking in Bets

MAKING SMARTER DECISIONS
WHEN YOU DON'T HAVE ALL THE FACTS

ANNIE DUKE

PORTFOLIO / PENGUIN

PORTFOLIO / PENGUIN
An imprint of Penguin Random House LLC
penguinrandomhouse.com

Most Portfolio books are available at a discount when purchased in quantity for sales promotions or corporate use. Special editions, which include personalized covers, excerpts, and corporate imprints, can be created when purchased in large quantities. For more information, please call (212) 572-2232 or e-mail specialmarkets@penguinrandomhouse.com. Your local bookstore can also assist with discounted bulk purchases using the Penguin Random House corporate Business-to-Business program. For assistance in locating a participating retailer, e-mail B2B@penguinrandomhouse.com.

Library of Congress Cataloging-in-Publication Data

Names: Duke, Annie, 1965- author.
Title: Thinking in bets : making smarter decisions when you don't have all the facts / Annie Duke.
Description: New York : Portfolio, 2018. | Includes bibliographical references and index.
Identifiers: LCCN 2017042666 | ISBN 9780735216358 (hardback) | ISBN 9780735216365 (epub)
Subjects: LCSH: Management games. | Decision making. | BISAC: BUSINESS & ECONOMICS / Decision-Making & Problem Solving. | PSYCHOLOGY / Cognitive Psychology. | BUSINESS & ECONOMICS / Strategic Planning.
Classification: LCC HD30.6 .D85 2018 | DDC 658.4/0353--dc23
LC record available at https://lccn.loc.gov/2017042666

First Portfolio / Penguin hardcover edition : February 2018
First Portfolio / Penguin trade edition : May 2019
Portfolio / Penguin trade paperback ISBN: 9780735216372

Printed in the United States of America
17th Printing

Book design by Daniel Lagin

To Lila and Henry Gleitman, generous of heart and intellect

CONTENTS

CHAPTER 3 | Bet to Learn: Fielding the Unfolding Future   75

CHAPTER 4 | The Buddy System   119

INTRODUCTION

Why This Isn't a Poker Book

When I was twenty-six, I thought I had my future mapped out. I had grown up on the grounds of a famous New Hampshire prep school, where my father chaired the English department. I had graduated from Columbia University with degrees in English and psychology. I had attended graduate school at the University of Pennsylvania, where I won a fellowship from the National Science Foundation, earning a master's and completing my doctoral course work in cognitive psychology.

But I got sick right before finishing my dissertation. I took a leave of absence, left Penn, got married, and moved to a small town in Montana. Not surprisingly, my NSF fellowship didn't cover my cross-country experiment in adulting, so I needed money. My brother Howard, a professional poker player who had already made the final table of the World Series of Poker by this time, suggested I check out the legal poker games in Billings. This suggestion wasn't as random as it might sound. I grew up in a competitive, games-playing family, and Howard had brought me out to Las Vegas a few times for vacations I couldn't otherwise afford on my stipend. I had watched him play, and played in a few low-stakes games myself.

I fell in love with poker right away. It wasn't the bright lights of Vegas that lured me in, but the thrill of playing and testing my skills in the basement of a Billings bar named the Crystal Lounge. I had a lot to learn, but I was excited to learn it. My plan was to earn some money during this break from school, stay on the academic path, and continue playing poker as a hobby.

My temporary break turned into a twenty-year career as a professional poker player. When I retired from playing in 2012, I had won a World Series of Poker gold bracelet, the WSOP Tournament of Champions, and the NBC National Heads-Up Championship, and earned more than $4 million in poker tournaments. Howard, meanwhile, went on to win two World Series bracelets, a pair of titles at the Hall of Fame Poker Classic, two World Poker Tour championships, and over $6.4 million in tournament prize money.

To say that I had strayed from the academic path might seem like an understatement. But I realized pretty quickly that I hadn't really left academics so much as moved to a new kind of lab for studying how people learn and make decisions. A hand of poker takes about two minutes. Over the course of that hand, I could be involved in up to twenty decisions. And each hand ends with a concrete result: I win money or I lose money. The result of each hand provides immediate feedback on how your decisions are faring. But it's a tricky kind of feedback because winning and losing are only loose signals of decision quality. You can win lucky hands and lose unlucky ones. Consequently, it's hard to leverage all that feedback for learning.

The prospect of some grizzled ranchers in Montana systematically taking my money at a poker table forced me to find practical ways to either solve this learning puzzle or go broke. I was lucky, early in my career, to meet some exceptional poker players and learn from them how they handled not only luck and uncertainty but also the relationship between learning and decision-making.

Over time, those world-class poker players taught me to understand what a bet really is: a decision about an uncertain future. The implications of treating decisions as bets made it possible for me to find learning opportunities in uncertain environments. Treating decisions as bets, I discovered, helped me avoid common decision traps, learn from results in a more rational way, and keep emotions out of the process as much as possible.

In 2002, thanks to my friend and super-successful poker player Erik Seidel turning down a speaking engagement, a hedge-fund manager asked me to speak to a group of traders and share some poker tips that might apply to securities trading. Since then, I have spoken to professional groups across many industries, looking inward at the approach I learned in poker, continually refining it, and helping others apply it to decisions in financial markets, strategic planning, human resources, law, and entrepreneurship.

The good news is that we can find practical work-arounds and strategies to keep us out of the traps that lie between the decisions we'd like to be making and the execution of those decisions. The promise of this book is that thinking in bets will improve decision-making throughout our lives. We can get better at separating outcome quality from decision quality, discover the power of saying, "I'm not sure," learn strategies to map out the future, become less reactive decision-makers, build and sustain pods of fellow truth-seekers to improve our decision process, and recruit our past and future selves to make fewer emotional decisions.

I didn't become an always-rational, emotion-free decision-maker from thinking in bets. I still made (and make) plenty of mistakes. Mistakes, emotions, losing—those things are all inevitable because we are human. The approach of thinking in bets moved me *toward* objectivity, accuracy, and open-mindedness. That movement compounds over time to create significant changes in our lives.

So this is not a book about poker strategy or gambling. It is, however, about things poker taught me about learning and decision-making. The practical solutions I learned in those smoky poker rooms turned out to be pretty good strategies for anyone trying to be a better decision-maker.

Thinking in bets starts with recognizing that there are exactly two things that determine how our lives turn out: the quality of our decisions and luck. Learning to recognize the difference between the two is what thinking in bets is all about.

CHAPTER 1

Life Is Poker, Not Chess

Pete Carroll and the Monday Morning Quarterbacks

One of the most controversial decisions in Super Bowl history took place in the closing seconds of Super Bowl XLIX in 2015. The Seattle Seahawks, with twenty-six seconds remaining and trailing by four points, had the ball on second down at the New England Patriots' one-yard line. Everybody expected Seahawks coach Pete Carroll to call for a handoff to running back Marshawn Lynch. Why wouldn't you expect that call? It was a short-yardage situation and Lynch was one of the best running backs in the NFL.

Instead, Carroll called for quarterback Russell Wilson to pass. New England intercepted the ball, winning the Super Bowl moments later. The headlines the next day were brutal:

- *USA Today*: "What on Earth Was Seattle Thinking with Worst Play Call in NFL History?"

- *Washington Post*: "'Worst Play-Call in Super Bowl History' Will Forever Alter Perception of Seahawks, Patriots"
- FoxSports.com: "Dumbest Call in Super Bowl History Could Be Beginning of the End for Seattle Seahawks"
- *Seattle Times*: "Seahawks Lost Because of the Worst Call in Super Bowl History"
- The *New Yorker*: "A Coach's Terrible Super Bowl Mistake"

Although the matter was considered by nearly every pundit as beyond debate, a few outlying voices argued that the play choice was sound, if not brilliant. Benjamin Morris's analysis on FiveThirtyEight.com and Brian Burke's on Slate.com convincingly argued that the decision to throw the ball was totally defensible, invoking clock-management and end-of-game considerations. They also pointed out that an interception was an extremely unlikely outcome. (Out of sixty-six passes attempted from an opponent's one-yard line during the season, zero had been intercepted. In the previous fifteen seasons, the interception rate in that situation was about 2%.)

Those dissenting voices didn't make a dent in the avalanche of criticism directed at Pete Carroll. Whether or not you buy into the contrarian analysis, most people didn't want to give Carroll the credit for having thought it through, or having *any* reason at all for his call. That raises the question: Why did *so* many people *so* strongly believe that Pete Carroll got it *so* wrong?

We can sum it up in four words: the play didn't work.

Take a moment to imagine that Wilson completed the pass for a game-winning touchdown. Wouldn't the headlines change to "Brilliant Call" or "Seahawks Win Super Bowl on Surprise Play" or "Carroll Outsmarts Belichick"? Or imagine the pass had been incomplete and the Seahawks scored (or didn't) on a third- or fourth-down running play. The headlines would be about those other plays. What Pete Carroll called on second down would have been ignored.

Carroll got unlucky. He had control over the quality of the play-call decision, but not over how it turned out. It was exactly because he didn't get a favorable result that he took the heat. He called a play that had a high percentage of ending in a game-winning touchdown or an incomplete pass (which would have allowed two more plays for the Seahawks to hand off the ball to Marshawn Lynch). He made a good-quality decision that got a bad result.

Pete Carroll was a victim of our tendency to equate the quality of a decision with the quality of its outcome. Poker players have a word for this: "resulting." When I started playing poker, more experienced players warned me about the dangers of resulting, cautioning me to resist the temptation to change my strategy just because a few hands didn't turn out well in the short run.

Pete Carroll understood that his universe of critics was guilty of resulting. Four days after the Super Bowl, he appeared on the *Today* show and acknowledged, "It was the worst *result* of a call ever," adding, "The call would have been a great one if we catch it. It would have been just fine, and nobody would have thought twice about it."

Why are we so bad at separating luck and skill? Why are we so uncomfortable knowing that results can be beyond our control? Why do we create such a strong connection between results and the quality of the decisions preceding them? How can we avoid falling into the trap of the Monday Morning Quarterback, whether it is in analyzing someone else's decision or in making and reviewing the decisions in our own lives?

The hazards of resulting

Take a moment to imagine your best decision in the last year. Now take a moment to imagine your worst decision.

I'm willing to bet that your best decision preceded a good result and the worst decision preceded a bad result.

That is a safe bet for me because resulting isn't just something we do from afar. Monday Morning Quarterbacks are an easy target, as are writers and bloggers providing instant analysis to a mass audience. But, as I found out from my own experiences in poker, resulting is a routine thinking pattern that bedevils all of us. Drawing an overly tight relationship between results and decision quality affects our decisions every day, potentially with far-reaching, catastrophic consequences.

When I consult with executives, I sometimes start with this exercise. I ask group members to come to our first meeting with a brief description of their best and worst decisions of the previous year. I have yet to come across someone who doesn't identify their best and worst *results* rather than their best and worst decisions.

In a consulting meeting with a group of CEOs and business owners, one member of the group identified firing the president of his company as his worst decision. He explained, "Since we fired him, the search for a replacement has been awful. We've had two different people on the job. Sales are falling. The company's not doing well. We haven't had anybody come in who actually turns out to be as good as he was."

That sounds like a disastrous result, but I was curious to probe into why the CEO thought the decision to fire his president was so bad (other than that it didn't work out).

He explained the decision process and the basis of the conclusion to fire the president. "We looked at our direct competitors and comparable companies, and concluded we weren't performing up to their level. We thought we could perform and grow at that level and that it was probably a leadership issue."

I asked whether the process included working with the president to understand his skill gaps and what he could be doing better. The company had, indeed, worked with him to identify his skill gaps. The CEO hired an executive coach to work with him on improving his leadership skills, the chief weakness identified.

In addition, after executive coaching failed to produce improved performance, the company considered splitting the president's responsibilities, having him focus on his strengths and moving other responsibilities to another executive. They rejected that idea, concluding that the president's morale would suffer, employees would likely perceive it as a vote of no confidence, and it would put extra financial pressure on the company to split a position they believed one person could fill.

Finally, the CEO provided some background about the company's experience making high-level outside hires and its understanding of the available talent. It sounded like the CEO had a reasonable basis for believing they would find someone better.

I asked the assembled group, "Who thinks this was a bad decision?" Not surprisingly, everybody agreed the company had gone through a thoughtful process and made a decision that was reasonable given what they knew at the time.

It sounded like a bad result, not a bad decision. The imperfect relationship between results and decision quality devastated the CEO and adversely affected subsequent decisions regarding the company. The CEO had identified the decision as a mistake solely because it didn't work out. He obviously felt a lot of anguish and regret because of the decision. He stated very clearly that he thought he should have known that the decision to fire the president would turn out badly. His decision-making behavior going forward reflected the belief that he made a mistake. He was not only resulting but also succumbing to its companion, hindsight bias. Hindsight bias is the tendency, after an outcome is known, to see the outcome as having been inevitable. When we say, "I should have known that would happen," or, "I should have seen it coming," we are succumbing to hindsight bias.

Those beliefs develop from an overly tight connection between outcomes and decisions. That is typical of how we evaluate our past decisions. Like the army of critics of Pete Carroll's decision to pass on the last play of the Super Bowl, the CEO had been guilty of resulting, ignoring his (and his company's) careful analysis and focusing only on the poor outcome. The decision didn't work out, and he treated that result as if it were an inevitable consequence rather than a probabilistic one.

In the exercise I do of identifying your best and worst decisions, I never seem to come across anyone who identifies a bad decision where they got lucky with the result, or a well-reasoned decision that didn't pan out. We link results with decisions even though it is easy to point out indisputable examples where the relationship between decisions and results isn't so perfectly correlated. No sober person thinks getting home safely after driving drunk reflects a good decision or good driving ability. Changing future decisions based on that lucky result is dangerous and unheard of (unless you are reasoning this out while drunk and obviously deluding yourself).

Yet this is exactly what happened to that CEO. He changed his behavior based on the quality of the result rather than the quality of the decision-making process. He decided he drove better when he was drunk.

Quick or dead: our brains weren't built for rationality

The irrationality displayed by Pete Carroll's critics and the CEO should come as no surprise to anyone familiar with behavioral economics. Thanks to the work of many brilliant psychologists, economists, cognitive researchers, and neuroscientists, there are a number of excellent books that explain why humans are plagued by certain kinds of irrationality in decision-making. (If you are unaware of these books, see the Selected Bibliography and Recommendations for Further Reading.) But here's a summary.

To start, our brains evolved to create certainty and order. We are uncomfortable with the idea that luck plays a significant role in our lives. We recognize the existence of luck, but we resist the idea that, despite our best efforts, things might not work out the way we want. It feels better for us to imagine the world as an orderly place, where randomness does not wreak havoc and things are perfectly predictable. We evolved to see the world that way. Creating order out of chaos has been necessary for our survival.

When our ancestors heard rustling on the savanna and a lion jumped out, making a connection between "rustling" and "lions" could save their lives on later occasions. Finding predictable connections is, literally, how our species survived. Science writer, historian, and skeptic Michael Shermer, in *The Believing Brain*, explains why we have historically (and prehistorically) looked for connections even if they were doubtful or false. Incorrectly interpreting rustling from the wind as an oncoming lion is called a type I error, a false positive. The consequences of such an error were much less grave than those of a type II error, a false negative. A false negative could have been fatal: hearing rustling and always assuming it's the wind would have gotten our ancestors eaten, and we wouldn't be here.

Seeking certainty helped keep us alive all this time, but it can wreak havoc on our decisions in an uncertain world. When we work backward from results to figure out why those things happened, we are susceptible to a variety of cognitive traps, like assuming causation when there is only a correlation, or cherry-picking data to confirm the narrative we prefer. We will pound a lot of square pegs into round holes to maintain the illusion of a tight relationship between our outcomes and our decisions.

Different brain functions compete to control our decisions. Nobel laureate and psychology professor Daniel Kahneman, in his 2011 best-selling *Thinking, Fast and Slow*, popularized the labels of "System 1" and "System 2." He characterized System 1 as "fast thinking." System 1 is what causes you to hit the brakes the instant someone jumps into the street in front of your car. It encompasses reflex, instinct, intuition, impulse, and automatic processing. System 2, "slow thinking," is how we choose, concentrate, and expend mental energy. Kahneman explains how System 1 and System 2 are capable of dividing and conquering our decision-making but work mischief when they conflict.

I particularly like the descriptive labels "reflexive mind" and "deliberative mind" favored by psychologist Gary Marcus. In his 2008 book, *Kluge: The Haphazard Evolution of the Human Mind*, he wrote, "Our thinking can be divided into two streams, one that is fast, automatic, and largely unconscious, and another that is slow, deliberate, and judicious." The first system, "the reflexive system, seems to do its thing rapidly and automatically, with or without our conscious awareness." The second system, "the deliberative system . . . deliberates, it considers, it chews over the facts." The differences between the systems are more than just labels. Automatic processing originates in the evolutionarily older parts of the brain, including the cerebellum, basal ganglia, and amygdala. Our deliberative mind operates out of the prefrontal cortex.

Colin Camerer, a professor of behavioral economics at Caltech and leading speaker and researcher on the intersection of game theory and neuroscience, explained to me the practical folly of imagining that we could just get our deliberative minds to do more of the decision-making work. "We have this thin layer of prefrontal cortex made just for us, sitting on top of this big animal brain. Getting this thin little layer to handle more is unrealistic." The prefrontal cortex doesn't control most of the decisions we make every day. We can't fundamentally get more out of that unique, thin layer of prefrontal cortex. "It's already overtaxed," he told me.

These are the brains we have and they aren't changing anytime soon.* Making more rational decisions isn't just a matter of willpower or consciously handling more decisions in deliberative mind. Our deliberative capacity is already maxed out. We don't have the option, once we recognize the problem, of merely shifting the work to a different part of the brain, as if you hurt your back lifting boxes and shifted to relying on your leg muscles.

Both deliberative and reflexive mind are necessary for our survival and advancement. The big decisions about what we want

---

* Technically, they are continually evolving, but not fast enough to do us any good in our lifetimes.

to accomplish recruit the deliberative system. Most of the decisions we execute on the way to achieving those goals, however, occur in reflexive mind. The shortcuts built into the automatic processing system kept us from standing around on the savanna, debating the origin of a potentially threatening sound while its source devoured us. Those shortcuts keep us alive, routinely executing the thousands of decisions that make it possible for us to live our daily lives.

We need shortcuts, but they come at a cost. Many decision-making missteps originate from the pressure on the reflexive system to do its job fast and automatically. No one wakes up in the morning and says, "I want to be closed-minded and dismissive of others." But what happens when we're focused on work and a fluff-headed coworker approaches? Our brain is already using body language and curt responses to get rid of them without flouting conventions of politeness. We don't deliberate over this; we just do it. What if they had a useful piece of information to share? We've tuned them out, cut them short, and are predisposed to dismiss anything we do pick up that varies from what we already know.

Most of what we do daily exists in automatic processing. We have habits and defaults that we rarely examine, from gripping a pencil to swerving to avoid an auto accident. The challenge is not to change the way our brains operate but to figure out how to work within the limitations of the brains we already have. Being aware of our irrational behavior and wanting to change is not enough, in the same way that knowing that you are looking at a visual illusion is not enough to make the illusion go away. Daniel Kahneman used the famous Müller-Lyer illusion to illustrate this.

MÜLLER-LYER ILLUSION

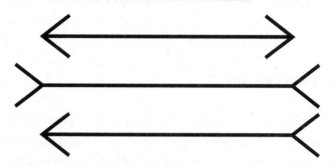

Which of these three lines is longest? Our brain sends us the signal that the second line is the longest, but you can see from adding the measurement lines that they are the same length.

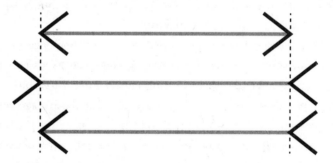

We can measure the lines to confirm they are the same length, but we can't make ourselves unsee the illusion.

What we can do is look for practical work-arounds, like carrying around a ruler and knowing when to use it to check against how your brain processes what you see. It turns out that poker is a great place to find practical strategies to get the execution of our decisions to align better with our goals. Understanding how poker players think can help us deal with the decision challenges that bedevil us in our workplaces, financial lives, relationships—even in deciding whether or not passing the ball was a brilliant play.

Two-minute warning

Our goal is to get our reflexive minds to execute on our deliberative minds' best intentions. Poker players don't need to know the underlying science to understand the difficulty of reconciling the two systems. Poker players have to make multiple decisions with significant financial consequences in a compressed time frame, and do it in a way that lassoes their reflexive minds to align with their long-term goals. This makes the poker table a unique laboratory for studying decision-making.

Every poker hand requires making at least one decision (to fold your starting cards or play them), and some hands can require up to twenty decisions. During a poker game in a casino card room, players get in about thirty hands per hour. An average hand of poker takes about two minutes to complete, including the time it takes for the dealer to gather, shuffle, and deal the cards between hands. Poker sessions typically last for several hours, with many decisions in every hand. This means a poker player makes hundreds of decisions per session, all of which take place at breakneck speed.

The etiquette and rules of the game discourage players from slowing down the game to deliberate, even when huge financial consequences ride on the decision. If a player takes extra time, another player can "call the clock" on them. This gives the deliberating player all of *seventy seconds* to now make up their mind. That is an eternity in poker time.

Every hand (and therefore every decision) has immediate financial consequences. In a tournament or a high-stakes game, each decision can be worth more than the cost of an average three-bedroom house, and players have to make those decisions more quickly than we decide what to order in a restaurant. Even at lower stakes, most or all of the money a player has on the table is potentially at stake in every decision. Poker players, as a result, must become adept at in-the-moment decision-making or they won't survive in the profession. That means finding ways to execute their best intentions (deliberated in advance) within the constraints of the speed expected at the table. Making a living at poker requires interpolating between the deliberative and reflexive systems. The best players must find ways to harmonize otherwise irresolvable conflicts.

In addition, once the game is over, poker players must learn from that jumbled mass of decisions and outcomes, separating the luck from the skill, the signal from the noise, and guarding against resulting. That's the only way to improve, especially when those same under-pressure situations will recur in a variety of forms.

Solving the problem of how to execute is even more important than innate talent to succeed in poker. All the talent in the world won't matter if a player can't execute; avoiding common decision traps, learning from results in a rational way, and keeping emotions out of the process as much as possible. Players with awe-inspiring talent clean up on their best nights but go broke plenty of other nights if they haven't confronted this challenge. The poker players who stand the test of time have a variety of talents, but what they share is the ability to execute in the face of these limitations.

We all struggle to execute our best intentions. Poker players have the same struggle, with the added challenges of time pressure, in-your-face uncertainty, and immediate financial consequences. That makes poker a great place to find innovative approaches to overcoming this struggle. And the value of poker in understanding decision-making has been recognized in academics for a long time.

Dr. Strangelove

It's hard for a scientist to become a household name. So it shouldn't be surprising that for most people the name John von Neumann doesn't ring a bell.

That's a shame because von Neumann is a hero of mine, and should be to anyone committed to making better decisions. His contributions to the science of decision-making were immense, and yet they were just a footnote in the short life of one of the greatest minds in the history of scientific thought. (And, not co-incidentally, he was a poker player.)

After a twenty-year period in which he contributed to prac-tically every branch of mathematics, this is what he did in the last ten years of his life: played a key role on the Manhattan Project, pioneered the physics behind the hydrogen bomb, developed the first computers, figured out the optimal way to route bombers and choose targets at the end of World War II, and created the concept of mutually assured destruction (MAD), the governing geopolitical principle of survival throughout the Cold War. Even after being diagnosed with cancer in 1955 at the age of fifty-two, he served in the first civilian agency overseeing atomic research and development, attending meetings, though in great pain, in a wheelchair for as long as he was physically able.

Despite all he accomplished in science, somehow von Neumann's legacy in popular culture is as one of the models for the title character in Stanley Kubrick's apocalyptic comedy, *Dr. Strangelove*: a heavily accented, crumpled, wheelchair-bound genius whose strategy of relying on mutually assured destruction goes awry when an insane general sends a single bomber on an unauthorized mission that could trigger the automated firing of all American and Soviet nuclear weapons.

In addition to everything else he accomplished, John von Neumann is also the father of game theory. After finishing his day job on the Manhattan Project, he collaborated with Oskar Morgenstern to publish *Theory of Games and Economic Behavior* in 1944. The Boston Public Library's list of the "100 Most Influential Books of the Century" includes *Theory of Games*. William Poundstone, author of a widely read book on game theory, *Prisoner's Dilemma*, called it "one of the most influential and least-read books of the twentieth century." The introduction to the sixtieth-anniversary edition pointed out how the book was instantly recognized as a classic. Initial reviews in the most prestigious academic journals heaped it with praise, like "one of the major scientific achievements of the first half of the twentieth century" and "ten more such books and the progress of economics is assured."

Game theory revolutionized economics, evidenced by at least eleven economics Nobel laureates connected with game theory and its decision-making implications, including John Nash (a student of von Neumann's), whose life story was chronicled in the Oscar-winning film *A Beautiful Mind*. Game theory has broad applications outside economics, informing the behavioral sciences (including psychology and sociology) as well as political science, biomedical research, business, and numerous other fields.

Game theory was succinctly defined by economist Roger

Myerson (one of the game-theory Nobel laureates) as "the study of mathematical models of conflict and cooperation between intelligent rational decision-makers." Game theory is the modern basis for the study of the bulk of our decision-making, addressing the challenges of changing conditions, hidden information, chance, and multiple people involved in the decisions. Sound familiar?

Fortunately, you don't need to know any more than this about game theory to understand its relevance. And the important thing for this book is that John von Neumann modeled game theory on a stripped-down version of poker.

Poker vs. chess

In *The Ascent of Man*, scientist Jacob Bronowski recounted how von Neumann described game theory during a London taxi ride. Bronowski was a chess enthusiast and asked him to clarify. "You mean, the theory of games like chess?"

Bronowski quoted von Neumann's response: "'No, no,' he said. 'Chess is not a game. Chess is a well-defined form of computation. You may not be able to work out the answers, but in theory there must be a solution, a right procedure in any position. Now, real games,' he said, 'are not like that at all. Real life is not like that. Real life consists of bluffing, of little tactics of deception, of asking yourself what is the other man going to think I mean to do. And that is what games are about in my theory.'"

The decisions we make in our lives—in business, saving and spending, health and lifestyle choices, raising our children, and relationships—easily fit von Neumann's definition of "real games." They involve uncertainty, risk, and occasional deception, prominent elements in poker. Trouble follows when we treat life decisions as if they were chess decisions.

Chess contains no hidden information and very little luck. The pieces are all there for both players to see. Pieces can't randomly appear or disappear from the board or get moved from one position to another by chance. No one rolls dice after which, if the roll goes against you, your bishop is taken off the board. If you lose at a game of chess, it must be because there were better moves that you didn't make or didn't see. You can theoretically go back and figure out exactly where you made mistakes. If one chess player is more than just a bit better than another, it is nearly inevitable the better player will win (if they are white) or, at least, draw (if they are black). On the rare occasions when a lower-ranked grand master beats a Garry Kasparov, Bobby Fischer, or Magnus Carlsen, it is because the higher-ranked player made identifiable, objective mistakes, allowing the other player to capitalize.

Chess, for all its strategic complexity, isn't a great model for decision-making in life, where most of our decisions involve hidden information and a much greater influence of luck. This creates a challenge that doesn't exist in chess: identifying the relative contributions of the decisions we make versus luck in how things turn out.

Poker, in contrast, is a game of *incomplete information*. It is a game of decision-making under conditions of uncertainty over time. (Not coincidentally, that is close to the definition of game theory.) Valuable information remains hidden. There is also an element of luck in any outcome. You could make the best possible decision at every point and still lose the hand, because you don't know what new cards will be dealt and revealed. Once the game is finished and you try to learn from the results, separating the quality of your decisions from the influence of luck is difficult.

In chess, outcomes correlate more tightly with decision quality. In poker, it is much easier to get lucky and win, or get unlucky and lose. If life were like chess, nearly every time you ran a red light you would get in an accident (or at least receive a ticket). If life were like chess, the Seahawks would win the Super Bowl every time Pete Carroll called that pass play.

But life is more like poker. You could make the smartest, most careful decision in firing a company president and still have it blow up in your face. You could run a red light and get through the intersection safely—or follow all the traffic rules and signals and end up in an accident. You could teach someone the rules of poker in five minutes, put them at a table with a world champion player, deal a hand (or several), and the novice could beat the champion. That could never happen in chess.

Incomplete information poses a challenge not just for split-second decision-making, but also for learning from past decisions. Imagine my difficulty as a poker player in trying to figure out if I played a hand correctly when my opponents' cards were never revealed. If the hand concluded after I made a bet and my opponents folded, all I know is that I won the chips. Did I play poorly and get lucky? Or did I play well?

If we want to improve in any game—as well as in any aspect of our lives—we have to learn from the results of our decisions. The quality of our lives is the sum of decision quality plus luck. In chess, luck is limited in its influence, so it's easier to read the results as a signal of decision quality. That more tightly tethers chess players to rationality. Make a mistake and your opponent's play points it out, or it is capable of analysis afterward. There is always a theoretically right answer out there. If you lose, there is little room to off-load losing to any other explanation than your inferior decision-making. You'll almost never hear a chess player say, "I was robbed in that game!" or, "I played perfectly and caught some terrible breaks." (Walk the hallways during a break in a poker tournament and you'll hear a lot of that.)

That's chess, but life doesn't look like that. It looks more like poker, where all that uncertainty gives us the room to deceive ourselves and misinterpret the data. Poker gives us the leeway to make mistakes that we never spot because we win the hand anyway and so don't go looking for them, or the leeway to do everything right, still lose, and treat the losing result as proof that we made a mistake. Resulting, assuming that our decision-making is good or bad based on a small set of outcomes, is a pretty reasonable strategy for learning in chess. But not in poker—or life.

Von Neumann and Morgenstern understood that the world doesn't easily reveal the objective truth. That's why they based game theory on poker. Making better decisions starts with understanding this: uncertainty can work a lot of mischief.

A lethal battle of wits

In one of the more famous scenes in *The Princess Bride*, the Dread Pirate Roberts (the love-besotted Westley) catches up to Vizzini, the mastermind who kidnapped Princess Buttercup. Having vanquished Fezzik the Giant in a battle of strength and having out-dueled swordsman Inigo Montoya, the Dread Pirate Roberts proposes he and Vizzini compete in a lethal battle of wits, which provides a great demonstration of the peril of making decisions with incomplete information. The pirate produces a packet of deadly iocane powder and, hiding two goblets of wine from view, he empties the packet, and puts one goblet in front of himself and the other in front of Vizzini. Once Vizzini chooses a goblet, they will both drink "and find out who is right and who is dead."

"It's all so simple," Vizzini scoffs. "All I have to do is deduce, from what I know of you, the way your mind works. Are you the kind of man who would put the poison into his own glass, or into the glass of his enemy?" He provides a dizzying series of reasons why the poison can't (or must) be in one cup, and then in the other. His rant accounts for cleverness, anticipating cleverness, iocane's origin (the criminal land of Australia), untrustworthiness, anticipating untrustworthiness, and dueling presumptions related to Westley defeating the giant and the swordsman.

While explaining all this, Vizzini diverts Westley's attention, switches the goblets, and declares that they should drink from the goblets in front of them. Vizzini pauses for a moment and, when he sees Westley drink from his own goblet, confidently drinks from the other.

Vizzini roars with laughter. "You fell victim to one of the classic blunders. The most famous is 'Never get involved in a land war in Asia,' but only slightly less well known is this: 'Never go in against a Sicilian when death is on the line.'"

In the midst of laughing, Vizzini falls over, dead. Buttercup says, "To think, all that time it was your cup that was poisoned."

Westley tells her, "They were both poisoned. I've spent the last two years building up immunity to iocane powder."

Like all of us, Vizzini didn't have all the facts. He considered himself a genius without equal: "Let me put it this way. Have you ever heard of Plato, Aristotle, Socrates? *Morons.*" But, also like all of us, he underestimated the amount and effect of what he didn't know.

Suppose someone says, "I flipped a coin and it landed heads four times in a row. How likely is that to occur?"

It feels like that should be a pretty easy question to answer. Once we do the math on the probability of heads on four consecutive 50-50 flips, we can determine that would happen 6.25% of the time (.50 × .50 × .50 × .50).

That's making the same mistake as Vizzini. The problem is that we came to this answer without knowing anything about the coin or the person flipping it. Is it a two-sided coin or three-sided or four? If it is two-sided, is it a two-headed coin? Even if the coin is two-sided (heads and tails), is the coin weighted to land on heads more often than tails (but maybe not always)? Is the flipper a magician who is capable of influencing how the coin lands? This information is all incomplete, yet we answered the question as if we had examined the coin and knew everything about it. We never considered that both goblets might be poisoned. ("Inconceivable" would have been Vizzini's term, had he been able to comment on his own death.)

Now if that person flipped the coin 10,000 times, giving us a sufficiently large sample size, we could figure out, with some certainty, whether the coin is fair. Four flips simply isn't enough to determine much about the coin.

We make this same mistake when we look for lessons in life's results. Our lives are too short to collect enough data from our own experience to make it easy to dig down into decision quality from the small set of results we experience. If we buy a house, fix it up a little, and sell it three years later for 50% more than we paid, does that mean we are smart at buying and selling property, or at fixing up houses? It could, but it could also mean there was a big upward trend in the market and buying almost any piece of property would have made just as much money. Or maybe buying that same house and not fixing it up at all might have resulted in the same (or even better) profit. A lot of previously successful

house flippers had to face that real possibility between 2007 and
2009.

When someone asks you about a coin they flipped four times,
there is a correct answer: "I'm not sure."

"I'm not sure": using uncertainty to our advantage

Just as we have problems with resulting and hindsight bias, when
we evaluate decisions solely on how they turn out, we have a mirror-
image problem in making prospective decisions. We get only one
try at any given decision—one flip of the coin—and that puts great
pressure on us to feel we have to be certain before acting, a certainty that necessarily will overlook the influences of hidden information and luck.

Famed novelist and screenwriter William Goldman (who
wrote *The Princess Bride*, as well as *Misery* and *Butch Cassidy and
the Sundance Kid*) reflected on his experiences working with actors like Robert Redford, Steve McQueen, Dustin Hoffman, and
Paul Newman at the height of their successful careers. What did
it mean to be a "movie star"? He quoted an actor who explained
the type of characters he wanted to play: "I don't want to be the
man who learns. I want to be the man who *knows*."

We are discouraged from saying "I don't know" or "I'm not
sure." We regard those expressions as vague, unhelpful, and even
evasive. But getting comfortable with "I'm not sure" is a vital step
to being a better decision-maker. We have to make peace with *not
knowing*.

Embracing "I'm not sure" is difficult. We are trained in
school that saying "I don't know" is a bad thing. Not knowing in

school is considered a failure of learning. Write "I don't know" as an answer on a test and your answer will be marked wrong.

Admitting that we don't know has an undeservedly bad reputation. Of course, we want to encourage acquiring knowledge, but the first step is understanding what we don't know. Neuroscientist Stuart Firestein's book *Ignorance: How It Drives Science* champions the virtue of recognizing the limits of our knowledge. (You can get a taste of the book by watching his TED Talk, "The Pursuit of Ignorance.") In the book and the talk, Firestein points out that in science, "I don't know" is not a failure but a necessary step toward enlightenment. He backs this up with a great quote from physicist James Clerk Maxwell: "Thoroughly conscious ignorance is the prelude to every real advance in science." I would add that this is a prelude to every great decision that has ever been made.

What makes a decision great is not that it has a great outcome. A great decision is the result of a good process, and that process must include an attempt to accurately represent our own state of knowledge. That state of knowledge, in turn, is some variation of "I'm not sure."

"I'm not sure" does not mean that there is no objective truth. It means that we treat our beliefs as works in progress, as under construction. Firestein's point is, in fact, that acknowledging uncertainty is the first step in executing on our goal to get closer to what is objectively true. To do this, we need to stop treating "I don't know" and "I'm not sure" like strings of dirty words.

What if we shifted our definition of "I don't know" from the negative frame ("I have no idea" or "I know nothing about that," which feels like we lack competence or confidence) to a more neutral frame? What if we thought about it as recognizing that, although we might know something about the chances of some event occurring, we are still not sure how things will turn out in any given instance? That is just the truth. If we accept that, "I'm not sure" might not feel so bad.

What good poker players and good decision-makers have in common is their comfort with the world being an uncertain and unpredictable place. They understand that they can almost never know exactly how something will turn out. They embrace that uncertainty and, instead of focusing on being sure, they try to figure out how *unsure* they are, making their best guess at the chances that different outcomes will occur. The accuracy of those guesses will depend on how much information they have and how experienced they are at making such guesses. This is part of the basis of all bets.

To be sure, an experienced poker player is more likely to make a better guess than a novice player at determining the chances they will win or lose a hand. The experienced player knows the math better and is better able to narrow down what their opponents' cards might be based on how players behave with certain types of hands. They will also be better at figuring out the choices their opponents are likely to make with those cards. So, yes, more experience will allow the player to narrow down the possibilities. None of that experience, however, makes it possible for a poker player to know how any given hand will turn out.

This is true in any field. An expert trial lawyer will be better than a new lawyer at guessing the likelihood of success of different strategies and picking a strategy on this basis. Negotiating against an adversary whom we have previously encountered gives us a better guess at what our strategy should be. An expert in any field will have an advantage over a rookie. But neither the veteran nor the rookie can be sure what the next flip will look like. The veteran will just have a better guess.

It is often the case that our best choice doesn't even have a particularly high likelihood of succeeding. A trial lawyer with a tough case could be choosing among strategies that are all more likely to fail than to succeed. The goal of a lawyer in that situation is to identify the different possible strategies, figure out their best guess of the chance of success for each unpromising alternative, and pick the least awful one to maximize the quality of the outcome for their client. That's true in any business. Start-ups have very low chances of succeeding but they try nonetheless, attempting to find the best strategy to achieve the big win, even though none of the strategies is highly likely to create success for the company. This is still worthwhile because the payoff can be so large.

There are many reasons why wrapping our arms around uncertainty and giving it a big hug will help us become better decision-makers. Here are two of them. First, "I'm not sure" is simply a more accurate representation of the world. Second, and related, when we accept that we can't be sure, we are less likely to fall into the trap of black-and-white thinking.

Imagine you're stepping on a traditional medical scale. It has two weight bars, one with notches at fifty-pound intervals and the other with notches at one-pound intervals. This allows the user to measure their weight down to the pound. What would happen if your doctor used a scale with only one bar with just two notches, one at fifty pounds and one at five hundred pounds, with no way to measure anything in between? Good luck getting medical advice after the person weighing you writes one or the other on your chart. You could only be morbidly obese or severely underweight. It would be impossible to make good decisions about your weight with such a poor model.

The same holds true for just about all of our decisions. If we misrepresent the world at the extremes of right and wrong, with no shades of grey in between, our ability to make good choices—choices about how we are supposed to be allocating our resources, what kind of decisions we are supposed to be making, and what kind of actions we are supposed to be taking—will suffer.

The secret is to make peace with walking around in a world where we recognize that we are not sure and that's okay. As we learn more about how our brains operate, we recognize that we don't perceive the world objectively. But our goal should be to *try*.

Redefining wrong

When I attend charity poker tournaments, I will often sit in as the dealer and provide a running commentary at the final table. The atmosphere at these final tables is fun and raucous. Everyone running the event has had a long night and is breathing a sigh of relief. There is typically a big crowd around the table including friends and families of the players, rooting them on (or vocally rooting against them). If people have been drinking, then . . . people have been drinking. Everyone is having a good time.

When players have put all their chips in the pot, there is no more betting on the hand. After an all-in situation, the players in the hand turn their cards faceup on the table so that everyone can see them before I deal the remaining cards. This makes it fun for the audience, because they get to see each player's position in the hand and the drama mounts. With the cards faceup, I can determine the likelihood each player will win the hand, and announce the percentage of the time each hand will win in the long run.

At one such tournament, I told the audience that one player

would win 76% of the time and the other would win 24% of the time. I dealt the remaining cards, the last of which turned the 24% hand into the winner. Amid the cheers and groans, someone in the audience called out, "Annie, you were wrong!"

In the same spirit that he said it, I explained that I wasn't. "I said that would happen 24% of the time. That's not zero. You got to see part of the 24%!"

A few hands later, almost the same thing happened. Two players put all of their chips in the pot and they turned their cards faceup. One player was 18% to win and the other 82% to win the hand. Again, the player with the worse hand when they put in their chips hit a subsequent lucky card to win the pot.

This time that same guy in the crowd called out, "Look, it was the 18%!" In that aha moment, he changed his definition of what it meant to be wrong. When we think in advance about the chances of alternative outcomes and make a decision based on those chances, it doesn't automatically make us wrong when things don't work out. It just means that one event in a set of possible futures occurred.

Look how quickly you can begin to redefine what it means to be wrong. Once we start thinking like this, it becomes easier to resist the temptation to make snap judgments after results or say things like "I knew it" or "I should have known." Better decision-making and more self-compassion follow.

The public-at-large is often guilty of making black-and-white judgments about the "success" or "failure" of probabilistic thinking. When the UK voted to leave the European Union ("Brexit") in July 2016, it was an unlikely result. Betting shops had set odds heavily favoring a vote for Remain. That does not mean the betting shops had an opinion that Remain would win the day. The goal of the bookmaker is to make sure the amount of money bet on either side is equal, so that the losers essentially pay the winners while the bookmaker just takes their fee. They aim to have no stake in the outcome and adjust the odds accordingly. The bookmaker's odds reflect the market's view, essentially our collective best guess of what is fair.

That didn't stop even sophisticated people from resulting, declaring after the vote came in Leave that the bookmakers made a mistake. The chief strategist at one Swiss bank told the *Wall Street Journal*, "I can't remember any time when the bookies were so wrong." One of America's most famous lawyers and professors, Alan Dershowitz, made this same error. Asserting in September 2016 that the Clinton-Trump election was too difficult to make any predictions about, he said, "Think about the vote on Brexit. Virtually all the polls—including exit polls that asked voters how they voted—got it wrong. The financial markets got it wrong. The bookies got it wrong."

Just like my spectator, Dershowitz missed the point. Any prediction that is not 0% or 100% can't be wrong solely because the most likely future doesn't unfold. When the 24% result happened at the final table of the charity tournament, that didn't reflect inaccuracy about the probabilities as determined before that single outcome. Long shots hit some of the time. Blaming the oddsmakers or the odds themselves assumes that once something happens, it was bound to have happened and anyone who didn't see it coming was wrong.

The same thing happened after Donald Trump won the presidency. There was a huge outcry about the polls being wrong. Nate Silver, the founder of FiveThirtyEight.com, drew a lot of that criticism. But he never said Clinton was a sure thing. Based on his aggregation and weighting of polling data, he had Trump between 30% and 40% to win (approximately between two-to-one and three-to-two against) in the week before the election. An event predicted to happen 30% to 40% of the time will happen a lot.

Being a poker player, I've played out more two-to-one shots in my tournament career than I could possibly count. A lot of those have been situations where the tournament was on the line for me. If I lose the hand, I'm out of the tournament. If I win, I earn a huge pot, maybe even winning the entire tournament. I know viscerally how likely 60–40 and 70–30 favorites are to lose (and, of course, the opposite). When people complained that Nate Silver did his job poorly because he had Clinton favored, I thought, "Those people haven't gotten all their chips in a pot with a pair against a straight draw and lost." Or, more likely, they've had those things happen throughout their lives and didn't realize that's what 30% or 40% feels like.

Decisions are bets on the future, and they aren't "right" or "wrong" based on whether they turn out well on any particular iteration. An unwanted result doesn't make our decision wrong if we thought about the alternatives and probabilities in advance and allocated our resources accordingly, as my client the CEO and Pete Carroll both did. It would be absurd for me, after making a big bet on the best possible starting hand (a pair of aces) and losing, to spend a lot of time thinking that I was wrong to make the decision to play the hand in the first place. That would be resulting.

When we think probabilistically, we are less likely to use adverse results alone as proof that we made a decision error, because we recognize the possibility that the decision might have been good but luck and/or incomplete information (and a sample size of one) intervened.

Maybe we made the best decision from a set of unappealing choices, none of which were likely to turn out well.

Maybe we committed our resources on a long shot because

the payout more than compensated for the risk, but the long shot didn't come in this time.

Maybe we made the best choice based on the available information, but decisive information was hidden and we could not have known about it.

Maybe we chose a path with a very high likelihood of success and got unlucky.

Maybe there were other choices that might have been better *and* the one we made wasn't wrong or right but somewhere in between. The second-best choice isn't wrong. By definition, it is more right (or less wrong) than the third-best or fourth-best choice. It is like the scale at the doctor's office: there are a lot more choices other than the extremes of obesity or anorexia. For most of our decisions, there will be a lot of space between unequivocal "right" and "wrong."

When we move away from a world where there are only two opposing and discrete boxes that decisions can be put in—right or wrong—we start living in the continuum between the extremes. Making better decisions stops being about wrong or right but about calibrating among all the shades of grey.

Redefining wrong is easiest in situations where we know the mathematical facts in advance. In the charity-tournament final-table example with the players' cards faceup, or when I get all my chips in with the best possible starting hand, the hidden information is removed. We can make a clear calculation. If we have that unquestionably right and make an allocation of resources (a bet) on the calculation, we can more naturally get to "I wasn't wrong just because it didn't turn out well and I shouldn't change my behavior." When the chances are known, we are tethered more tightly to a rational interpretation of the influence of luck. It feels a little more like chess that way.

There is no doubt it is harder to get there when we add in hidden information on top of the influence of luck. Untethered from seeing what the coin actually looks like, we are more likely to anchor ourselves to the way things turned out as the sole signal for whether we were right or wrong. We are more likely to declare, "I told you so!" or "I should have known!" When we start doing that, compassion goes out the window. Just ask Pete Carroll.

Redefining wrong allows us to let go of all the anguish that comes from getting a bad result. But it also means we must redefine "right." If we aren't wrong just because things didn't work out, then we aren't right just because things turned out well. Do we win emotionally to making that mindset trade-off?

Being right feels really good. "I was right," "I knew it," "I told you so"—those are all things that we say, and they all feel very good to us. Should we be willing to give up the good feeling of "right" to get rid of the anguish of "wrong"? Yes.

First, the world is a pretty random place. The influence of luck makes it impossible to predict exactly how things will turn out, and all the hidden information makes it even worse. If we don't change our mindset, we're going to have to deal with being wrong a lot. It's built into the equation.

Poker teaches that lesson. A great poker player who has a good-size advantage over the other players at the table, making significantly better strategic decisions, will still be losing over 40% of the time at the end of eight hours of play. That's a whole lot of wrong. And it's not just confined to poker.

The most successful investors in start-up companies have a majority of bad results. If you applied to NASA's astronaut program or the NBC page program, both of which have drawn thousands of applicants for a handful of positions, things will go your way a minority of the time, but you didn't necessarily do anything wrong. Don't fall in love or even date anybody if you want only positive results. The world is structured to give us lots of opportunities to feel bad about being wrong if we want to measure ourselves by outcomes. Don't fall for it!

Second, being wrong hurts us more than being right feels good. We know from Daniel Kahneman and Amos Tversky's work on loss aversion, part of prospect theory (which won Kahneman the Nobel Prize in Economics in 2002), that losses in general feel about two times as bad as wins feel good. So winning $100 at blackjack feels as good to us as losing $50 feels bad to us. Because being right feels like winning and being wrong feels like losing, that means we need two favorable results for every one unfavorable result just to break even emotionally. Why not live a smoother existence, without the swings, especially when the losses affect us more intensely than the wins?

Are you ready to really wrap your arms around uncertainty, like great decision-makers do? Are you ready to embrace this redefinition of wrong, and to recognize you are always guessing and that those guesses drive how you place your resources? Getting comfortable with this realignment, and all the good things that follow, starts with recognizing that you've been betting all along.

CHAPTER 2

Wanna Bet?

Thirty days in Des Moines

During the 1990s, John Hennigan, an eccentric gambler who had been making a living by his wits and skills in poker and pool for several years, moved from Philadelphia to Las Vegas. His reputation and nickname, "Johnny World," preceded him, due to his already exceptional skills and willingness to bet on anything. His talent has stood the test of time: he is a legendarily successful player in high-stakes games, and in major poker tournaments has earned five World Series of Poker bracelets, a World Poker Tour championship, and more than $8 million in prize money.

John was a perfect match for Las Vegas. He arrived already in rhythm with the town: sleeping all day and spending all night in poker games, pool halls, bars, and restaurants with adventurous, like-minded peers. He quickly found a group of professional gamblers with similar interests, many from the East Coast.

Although John and Vegas seemed made for each other, he had a love-hate relationship with the lifestyle. Playing poker for a living has the allure of giving you the freedom to make your own schedule but, once it boils down to your per-hour net advantage, you are tethered to putting in the hours. You're "free" to play or not play whenever you want, but you can feel compelled to punch a clock. Worse, the best games are at night, so you're working the graveyard shift. You get out of rhythm with the rest of the world, never see the sun, and your workplace is a smoke-filled room where you can't even see outside. John felt this keenly.

One night, John was in a high-stakes poker game and the talk between hands somehow included the state capitol of Iowa, Des Moines. John had never been there or seen much of the Midwest, so he was curious about what life in Des Moines might be like—a "normal" life that increasingly seemed foreign to him, waking up in the morning and living in the daylight hours. This led to some good-natured ribbing as the other players in the game imagined the prospect of a nocturnal action junkie like John in a place that seemed, to them at least, like the opposite of Las Vegas: "There's no gambling action." "The bars close early." "You'd hate it there." Over the course of the evening, the discussion shifted to whether Hennigan could even live in such an unfamiliar place.

As is often the case with poker players, a conversation about a hypothetical turned into an opportunity to propose a wager. What would the stakes have to be for Hennigan to get up from the table, catch a flight, and relocate to Des Moines? If he took such a bet, how long would he have to live there?

John and the others landed on a month in Des Moines—a real commitment but not a permanent exile. When he seemed willing to, literally, walk out of a poker game and move 1,500 miles to a place he had never been, the other players added a diabolical condition to the negotiation: he would have to confine himself to one street in Des Moines, a street with a single hotel, restaurant, and bar, where everything closed at 10 p.m. That enforced idleness would be a challenge for anyone, regardless of the location. But for someone like John, a young, single, high-stakes gambler, this might actually count as torture. John said he would take such a challenge if they made one concession: he could practice and play at a nearby golf course.

After agreeing on the conditions, they still had to negotiate the size of the bet. The other players needed a number that was large enough to entice John to accept the wager, but not so large that it would entice John to stay even if he really hated it in Iowa. As one of the most successful cash-game players in Las Vegas, a month in Des Moines could cost John, potentially, six figures. On the other hand, if they offered him too large of an upside to stay in Des Moines, he would certainly endure the discomfort and boredom.

They settled on $30,000.

John considered two distinct and mutually exclusive alternatives: taking the bet or not taking the bet. Each came with new risks and new reward potentials. He could win or lose $30,000 if he took the bet (or win or lose greater dollar amounts at the poker table if he turned it down). He could also win to the decision to move to Des Moines long after the bet was over, if he used the golf-practice time to improve his chances gambling at high-stakes golf. He could further his reputation of being willing to bet on anything and being capable of anything, a profitable asset for professional gamblers. He also had to think about the other, less quantifiable things he might value. How much might he like the pace of life? How would he value taking a break from the action? Would he become more relaxed experiencing the more traditional schedule? Was the break worth it to take the big pay cut from not being able to play poker for a month? And then there were the real unknowns. He might just meet the love of his life on that one street in Iowa. He had to weigh all of this against the opportunity costs of leaving Vegas—money from lost earning opportunities, nights missing doing the things he enjoyed, and even perhaps *missing* meeting the love of his life at the Mirage during that month.

Johnny World moved to Des Moines.

Was a month of detox away from the nightly life of a high-stakes Vegas pro going to be a blessing or a curse?

It took just two days for him to realize that it was a curse. From his hotel room in Des Moines, John called one of his friends on the other side of the bet and tried to negotiate a settlement. Just as parties in commercial lawsuits often settle before trial, in the gambling world negotiated settlements are common. What was particularly funny about John's call was that his opening offer was that the others *pay him* $15,000 to spare them the cost and indignity of losing the whole amount. He argued that since he was already in Des Moines, he was clearly capable of waiting out the month to get the full amount.

The other bettors, literally, were not buying it. After all, John made this offer *after only two days*. That was a pretty strong signal that not only would they likely win the bet, but they might earn a return (in fun) by needling John while he served out his sentence.

Within a few days, John agreed to *pay* $15,000 to get out of the bet and return to Vegas. John proved, in spectacular fashion, that the grass is always greener.

WANNA BET! | 41

We've all been to Des Moines

The punch line of the John Hennigan–Des Moines story—"after two days, he *begged* to get out of it"—made it part of gambling folklore. That punch line, however, obscures how *usual* the underlying analysis about whether to move was. The only real difference between Johnny World's decision to move to Des Moines and anyone else's decision to relocate or take a job was that he and the poker players made explicit that the decision was a bet on what would most improve their quality of life (financial, emotional, and otherwise).

John considered two distinct and mutually exclusive alternative futures: taking the bet and living for a month in Des Moines, or not taking the bet and staying in Las Vegas. Any of us thinking about relocating for a new job has this same choice between moving, with the potential to earn the money being offered, or staying where we are and maintaining the status quo. How does the new job pay compared to what we have now? There are plenty of things we value in addition to money; we might be willing to make less money to move to a place we imagine we would like a lot better. Will the new job have better opportunities for advancement and future gains, independent of short-term gains in compensation? What are the differences in pay, benefits, security, work environment, and the kind of work we'd be doing? What are we giving up by leaving our city, colleagues, and friends for a new place?

We have to inventory the potential upside and downside of taking the bet just like Hennigan did. That his $30,000 wasn't a sure thing doesn't make his decision distinct from other job or relocation decisions. People take jobs all the time where a large portion of the compensation is contingent. In many businesses, compensation includes bonuses, stock options, or performance-based pay. Even though most people don't have to consider losing $30,000 when they take a job, every decision has risks, regardless of whether we acknowledge them. Even a set salary is still not "guaranteed." We could get laid off or hate the job and quit (as John Hennigan did), or the company could go out of business. When we take a job, especially one promising big financial re-wards, the commitment to work can cost us time with our family and affect those relationships, a costly if not losing compromise.

In addition, whenever we choose an alternative (whether it is taking a new job or moving to Des Moines for a month), we are automatically rejecting every other possible choice. All those re-jected alternatives are paths to possible futures where things could be better or worse than the path we chose. There is poten-tial opportunity cost in any choice we forgo.

Likewise, the players on the other side of that bet, risking $30,000 to see if John would live a month in Des Moines, thought about similar factors that employers consider in making job of-fers or spending money to create enticing workplace environ-ments. The poker players had to strike a fine balance in offering that bet to Hennigan: the proposition had to be good enough to entice him to take the bet but not so good that it would be guar-anteed to cost them the $30,000.

Although employers aren't trying to entice employees to quit, their goal is similar in arriving at a compensation package to get the prospect to accept the offer and stay in the job. They must balance offering attractive pay and benefits with going too far and impairing their ability to make a profit. Employers also want em-ployees to be loyal, and work long, productive hours, and maintain morale. An employer might or might not offer on-premises child care. That could encourage someone to work more hours . . . or scare off a prospective employee because it implies they may be expected to sacrifice aspects of their non-work lives. Offering paid vacation leave makes a job more attractive but, unlike offering free dining and exercise facilities, encourages them to spend time away from work.

Hiring an employee, like offering a bet, is not a riskless choice. Betting on hiring the wrong person can have a huge cost (as the CEO who fired his president can attest). Recruitment costs can be substantial, and every job offer has an associated opportunity cost. This is the only person you can offer *this* opportunity. You might have dodged the cost of hiring Bernie Madoff, but you might have lost the benefit of hiring Bill Gates.

The John Hennigan story seems so unusual because it started with a discussion about what Des Moines was like and ended with one of the people in the discussion moving there the next day. That happened, though, because when you are betting, you have to back up your belief by putting a price on it. You have to put your money where your mouth is. To me, the ironic thing about a story that seems so crazy is how the underlying analysis was actually very logical: a difference of opinion about alternatives, consequences, and probabilities.

By treating decisions as bets, poker players explicitly recognize that they are deciding on alternative futures, each with benefits and risks. They also recognize there are no simple answers. Some things are unknown or unknowable. The promise of this book is that if we follow the example of poker players by making explicit that our decisions are bets, we can make better decisions and anticipate (and take protective measures) when irrationality is likely to keep us from acting in our best interest.

All decisions are bets

Our traditional view of betting is very narrow: casinos, sporting events, lottery tickets, wagering against someone else on the chance of a favorable outcome of some event. The definition of "bet" is much broader. *Merriam-Webster's Online Dictionary* defines "bet" as "a *choice* made by thinking about *what will probably happen*," "to *risk* losing (something) when you try to do or achieve something" and "to make *decisions* that are based on the *belief* that something will happen or is true." I have emphasized the broader, often overlooked, aspects of betting: choice, probability, risk, decision, belief. We can also see from this definition that betting doesn't have to take place in a casino or against somebody else.

No matter how far we get from the familiarity of betting at a poker table or in a casino, our decisions are always bets. We routinely decide among alternatives, put resources at risk, assess the likelihood of different outcomes, and consider what it is that we value. Every decision commits us to some course of action that, by definition, eliminates acting on other alternatives. Not placing a bet on something is, itself, a bet. Choosing to go to the movies means that we are choosing to not do all the other things with our time that we might do during that two hours. If we accept a job offer, we are also choosing to foreclose all other alternatives: we aren't sticking with our current job, or negotiating to get a better deal in our current job, or getting or taking other offers, or changing careers, or taking some time away from work. There is always opportunity cost in choosing one path over others.

The betting elements of decisions—choice, probability, risk, etc.—are more obvious in some situations than others. Investments are clearly bets. A decision about a stock (buy, don't buy, sell, hold, not to mention esoteric investment options) involves a choice about the best use of financial resources. Incomplete information and factors outside of our control make all our investment choices uncertain. We evaluate what we can, figure out what we think will maximize our investment money, and execute. Deciding not to invest or not to sell a stock, likewise, is a bet. These are the same decisions I make during a hand of poker: fold, check, call, bet, or raise.

We don't think of our parenting choices as bets but they are. We want our children to be happy, productive adults when we send them out into the world. Whenever we make a parenting choice (about discipline, nutrition, school, parenting philosophy, where to live, etc.), we are betting that our choice will achieve the future we want for our children more than any other choice we might make given the constraints of the limited resources we have to allocate—our time, our money, our attention.

Job and relocation decisions are bets. Sales negotiations and contracts are bets. Buying a house is a bet. Ordering the chicken instead of the steak is a bet. Everything is a bet.

Most bets are bets against ourselves

One of the reasons we don't naturally think of decisions as bets is because we get hung up on the zero-sum nature of the betting that occurs in the gambling world; betting *against somebody else* (or the casino), where the gains and losses are symmetrical. One person wins, the other loses, and the net between the two adds to zero. Betting includes, but is not limited to, those situations.

In most of our decisions, we are not betting against another person. Rather, we are betting against *all the future versions of ourselves that we are not choosing*. We are constantly deciding among alternative futures: one where we go to the movies, one where we go bowling, one where we stay home. Or futures where we take a job in Des Moines, stay at our current job, or take some time away from work. Whenever we make a choice, we are betting on a potential future. We are betting that the future version of us that results from the decisions we make will be better off. At stake in a decision is that the return to us (measured in money, time, happiness, health, or whatever we value in that circumstance) will be greater than what we are giving up by betting against the other alternative future versions of us.

Have you ever had a moment of regret after a decision where you felt, "I knew I should have made the other choice!"? That's an alternative version of you saying, "See, I told you so!"

When Pete Carroll called for a pass on second down, he didn't need an inner voice second-guessing him. He had the collective cry of the Seahawks fans yelling, "When you called for Wilson to pass, you bet on the wrong future!"

How can we be sure that we are choosing the alternative that is best for us? What if another alternative would bring us more happiness, satisfaction, or money? The answer, of course, is we can't be sure. Things outside our control (luck) can influence the result. The futures we imagine are merely *possible*. They haven't happened yet. We can only make our best guess, given what we know and don't know, at what the future will look like. If we've never lived in Des Moines, how can we possibly be sure how we will like it? When we decide, we are betting whatever we value (happiness, success, satisfaction, money, time, reputation, etc.) on one of a set of possible and uncertain futures. That is where the risk is.

Poker players live in a world where that risk is made explicit. They can get comfortable with uncertainty because they put it up front in their decisions. Ignoring the risk and uncertainty in every decision might make us feel better in the short run, but the cost to the quality of our decision-making can be immense. If we can find ways to become more comfortable with uncertainty, we can see the world more accurately and be better for it.

Our bets are only as good as our beliefs

In an episode of the classic sitcom *WKRP in Cincinnati*, called "Turkeys Away," the radio station's middle-aged manager, Mr. Carlson, tries to prove he can stage a successful promotion for the rock-and-roll station. He sends his veteran news reporter, Les Nessman, to a local shopping center and tells him to report, live, on a turkey giveaway he is about to unleash.

The station's DJ, Johnny Fever, cuts from his show to a live "man on the scene" report from Nessman. Nessman fills time, describing a helicopter overhead. Then something comes out of the helicopter. "No parachutes yet . . . Those can't be skydivers. I can't tell what they are but—oh, my God! They're turkeys! . . . One just went through the windshield of a parked car! This is terrible! . . . Oh, the humanity! . . . The turkeys are hitting the ground like sacks of wet cement!" Nessman has to flee amid an ensuing riot. He returns to the studio and describes how Mr. Carlson tried to land the helicopter and free the remaining turkeys, but they waged a counterattack.

Carlson enters, ragged and covered with feathers. "As God is my witness, I thought turkeys could fly."

We bet based on what we believe about the world. Pete Carroll's Super Bowl decision to pass on the Patriots' one-yard line was driven by his beliefs—his beliefs about quarterback Russell Wilson's likelihood of completing the pass, of having the pass intercepted, of getting sacked (or scrambling for a touchdown). He had data on and experience about all these things, and then had to apply that to this unique situation, considering his beliefs about the Patriots' defense and how their coach, Bill Belichick, would set up the defense for a likely running play on the goal line. He then made a choice about the best play to call based on these beliefs. He bet on a pass play.

The CEO who suffered all that anguish over firing the president did what he did based on his beliefs. He made his decision based on his beliefs about how the company was doing compared with competitors, what he thought the president did that contributed to or detracted from that, the likelihood he could get the president's performance to improve, the costs and benefits to splitting the job between two people, and the likelihood he could find a replacement. He bet on letting the president go.

John Hennigan had beliefs about how he would adapt to Des Moines. Our beliefs drive the bets we make: which brands of cars better retain their value, whether critics knew what they were talking about when they panned a movie we are thinking about seeing, how our employees will behave if we let them work from home.

This is ultimately very good news: part of the *skill* in life comes from learning to be a better belief calibrator, using experience and information to more objectively update our beliefs to more accurately represent the world. The more accurate our beliefs, the better the foundation of the bets we make. There is also skill in identifying when our thinking patterns might lead us astray, no matter what our beliefs are, and in developing strategies to work with (and sometimes around) those thinking patterns. There are effective strategies to be more open-minded, more objective, more accurate in our beliefs, more rational in our decisions and actions, and more compassionate toward ourselves in the process.

We have to start, however, with some bad news. As Mr. Carlson learned in *WKRP in Cincinnati*, our beliefs can be way, way off.

Hearing is believing

When I speak at professional conferences, I will occasionally bring up the subject of belief formation by asking the audience a question: "Who here knows how you can predict if a man will go bald?" People will raise their hands, I'll call on someone, and they'll say, "You look at the maternal grandfather." Everyone nods in agreement. I'll follow up by asking, "Does anyone know how you calculate a dog's age in human years?" I can practically see audience members mouthing, "Multiply by seven."

Both of these widely held beliefs aren't actually accurate. If you search online for "common misconceptions," the baldness myth is at the top of most lists. As *Medical Daily* explained in 2015, "a key gene for baldness is on the X chromosome, which you get from your mother" but "it is not the only genetic factor in play since men with bald fathers have an increased chance of going bald when compared to men whose fathers have a full set of hair. . . . [S]cientists say baldness anywhere in your family may be a sign of your own impending fate."

As for the dog-to-human age ratio, it's just a made-up number that's been circulating with no basis, yet with increasing weight through repetition, since the thirteenth century. Where did we get these beliefs? And why do they persist, despite contrary science and logic?

We form beliefs in a haphazard way, believing all sorts of things based just on what we hear out in the world but haven't researched for ourselves.

This is how *we think* we form abstract beliefs:

(1) We hear something;
(2) We think about it and vet it, determining whether it is true or false; only after that
(3) We form our belief.

It turns out, though, that we *actually* form abstract beliefs this way:

(1) We hear something;
(2) We believe it to be true;
(3) Only sometimes, later, if we have the time or the inclination, we think about it and vet it, determining whether it is, in fact, true or false.

Harvard psychology professor Daniel Gilbert, best known for his book *Stumbling on Happiness* and his starring role in Prudential Financial commercials, is also responsible for some pioneering work on belief formation. In a 1991 paper in which he summarized centuries of philosophical and scientific study on the subject, he concluded, "Findings from a multitude of research literatures converge on a single point: People are credulous creatures who find it very easy to believe and very difficult to doubt. In fact, believing is so easy, and perhaps so inevitable, that it may be more like involuntary comprehension than it is like rational assessment."

Two years later, Gilbert and colleagues demonstrated through a series of experiments that our default is to believe that what we hear and read is true. Even when that information is clearly presented as being false, we are still likely to process it as true. In these experiments, subjects read a series of statements about a criminal defendant or a college student. These statements were color coded to make it clear whether they were true or false. Subjects under time pressure or who had their cognitive load increased by a minor distraction made more errors in recalling whether the statements were true or false. But the errors weren't random. The subjects were not equally likely to ignore some statements labeled "true" as they were to rely on some statements labeled "false." Rather, their errors went in one direction: under any sort of pressure, they presumed all the statements were true, regardless of their labeling. This suggests our default setting is to believe what we hear is true.

This is why we believe that baldness is passed down from the maternal grandfather. If you, like me until I looked it up for this book, held that belief, had you ever researched it for yourself? When I ask my audiences this question, they generally say it is just something they heard but they have no idea where or from whom. Yet they are very confident that this is true. That should be proof enough that the way we form beliefs is pretty goofy.

As with many of our irrationalities, how we form beliefs was shaped by the evolutionary push toward efficiency rather than accuracy. Abstract belief formation (that is, beliefs outside our direct experience, conveyed through language) is likely among the few things that are uniquely human, making it relatively new in the scope of evolutionary time. Before language, our ancestors could form new beliefs only through what they directly experienced of the physical world around them. For perceptual beliefs from direct sensory experience, it's reasonable to presume our senses aren't lying. Seeing is, after all, believing. If you see a tree right in front of you, it would generally be a waste of cognitive energy to question whether the tree exists. In fact, questioning what you see or hear can get you eaten. For survival-essential skills, type I errors (false positives) were less costly than type II errors (false negatives). In other words, better to be safe than sorry, especially when considering whether to believe that the rustling in the grass is a lion. We didn't develop a high degree of skepticism when our beliefs were about things we directly experienced, especially when our lives were at stake.

As complex language evolved, we gained the ability to form beliefs about things we had not actually experienced for ourselves. And, as Gilbert pointed out, "nature does not start from scratch; rather, she is an inveterate jury rigger who rarely invents a new mechanism to do splendidly what an old mechanism can be modified to do tolerably well." In this case, the system we already had was (1) experience it, (2) believe it to be true, and (3) maybe, and rarely, question it later. We may have more reasons to question this flood of secondhand information, but our older system is still in charge. (This is a very simple summary of a great deal of research and documentation. For some good overviews, I highly recommend Dan Gilbert's *Stumbling on Happiness*, Gary Marcus's *Kluge*, and Dan Kahneman's *Thinking, Fast and Slow*, listed in the Selected Bibliography and Recommendations for Further Reading.)

A quick Google search will show that many of our commonly held beliefs are untrue. We just don't get around to doing Google searches on these things. (Spoiler alerts: (1) Abner Doubleday had nothing to do with inventing the game of baseball. (2) We use all parts of our brain. The 10% figure was made up to sell self-improvement books; neural imaging and brain-injury studies disprove the fabrication. (3) Immigrants didn't have their names Americanized, involuntarily or otherwise, at Ellis Island.)

Maybe it's no big deal that some of these inconsequential common beliefs are clearly false. Presumably, people aren't using a bogus dog-age calculator to make medical decisions for their pets, and veterinarians know better. But this is our general belief-formation process, and it applies in areas that can have significant consequences.

In poker, this belief-formation process can cost players a lot of money. One of the first things players learn in Texas Hold'em is a list of two-card starting hands to play or fold, based on your table position and actions from players before you.* When Texas Hold'em first developed in the sixties, some expert players innovated deceptive plays with middle cards consecutive in rank and of the same suit (like the six and seven of diamonds). In poker shorthand, such cards are called "suited connectors."

Suited connectors have the attraction of making a powerful,

---

*The deal in Texas Hold'em begins with two cards, facedown, to each player. Following an initial round of betting, all additional cards are community cards, dealt faceup. If there are two or more players remaining after the conclusion of the betting rounds, the winner is the player who makes the highest hand from a combination of their two hidden cards and the community cards dealt during the hand.

When players make their initial betting decision, there are still three more betting rounds and five community cards to be dealt. Even with so many cards yet to be dealt, there is a significant advantage to having a strong two-card combination. The best starting hand, of course, would be two aces. The worst is a seven and a two of different suits.

camouflaged straight or a flush. Expert players might choose to play these types of hands in a very limited set of circumstances, namely where they feel they could fold the hand at a small loss; successfully bluff if it doesn't develop; or extract maximum value in later betting rounds by trapping a player with conventionally stronger starting cards when the hand does develop favorably.

Unfortunately, the mantra of "win big or lose small with suited connectors" filtered down over the years without the subtlety of the expertise needed to play them well or the narrow circumstances needed to make those hands profitable. When I taught poker seminars, most of my students strongly believed suited connectors were profitable starting cards under pretty much any circumstances. When I asked why, I would hear "everyone knows that" or "I see players cleaning up with suited connectors all the time on TV." But no one I asked had kept a P&L on their experience with suited connectors. "Do that," I'd say, "and report back what you find." Lo and behold, players who came back to me discovered they were net losers with suited connectors.

The same belief-formation process led hundreds of millions of people to bet the quality and length of their lives on their belief about the merits of a low-fat diet. Led by advice drawn, in part, from research secretly funded by the sugar industry, Americans in one generation cut a quarter of caloric intake from fat, replacing it with carbohydrates. The U.S. government revised the food pyramid to include six to eleven servings of carbohydrates and advised that the public consume fats sparingly. It encouraged the food industry (which enthusiastically followed) to substitute starch and sugar to produce "reduced-fat" foods. David Ludwig, a Harvard Medical School professor and doctor at Boston Children's Hospital, summarized the cost of substituting carbs for fats in the *Journal of the American Medical Association*: "Contrary to prediction, total calorie intake increased substantially, the prevalence of obesity tripled, the incidence of type 2 diabetes increased many-fold, and the decades-long decrease in cardiovascular disease plateaued and may reverse, despite greater use of preventive drugs and surgical procedures."

Low-fat diets became the suited connectors of our eating habits.

Even though our default is "true," if we were good at updating our beliefs based on new information, our haphazard belief-formation process might cause relatively few problems. Sadly, this is not the way it works. We form beliefs without vetting most of them, and maintain them even after receiving clear, corrective information. In 1994, Hollyn Johnson and Colleen Seifert reported in the *Journal of Experimental Psychology* the results of a series of experiments in which subjects read messages about a warehouse fire. For subjects reading messages mentioning that the fire started near a closet containing paint cans and pressurized gas cylinders, that information (predictably) encouraged them to infer a connection. When, five messages later, subjects received a correction that the closet was empty, they still answered questions about the fire by blaming burning paint for toxic fumes and citing negligence for keeping flammable objects nearby. (This shouldn't be a surprise to anyone recognizing the futility of issuing a retraction after reporting a news story with a factual error.)

Truthseeking, the desire to know the truth regardless of whether the truth aligns with the beliefs we currently hold, is not naturally supported by the way we process information. We might think of ourselves as open-minded and capable of updating our beliefs based on new information, but the research conclusively shows otherwise. Instead of altering our beliefs to fit new information, we do the opposite, altering our interpretation of that information to fit our beliefs.

"They saw a game"

As a college football season is about to close, all eyes are fixed on a fierce rivalry. The favorite, playing at home, has a twenty-two-game winning streak and is on the verge of completing a second consecutive undefeated season. The most emotional reception will be for Dick Kazmaier, the offensive star. One of the school's all-time athletic heroes, he made the cover of *Time* and is in contention for All-American and other postseason honors. The visitors, however, have no intention of going down to defeat quietly. Although their record this season has been only average, they have a reputation for playing hard. Pulling off a stunning upset would be an unexpected treat.

Welcome to Princeton's Palmer Stadium, November 23, 1951. The Dartmouth-Princeton football game became famous: part of a historic rivalry, the end of an epoch in Ivy League sports, and the subject of a groundbreaking scientific experiment.

First, the game. Princeton won, 13–0. The outcome was not in much doubt, but it was nevertheless a dirty, violent, penalty-laden game. Dartmouth received seventy yards in penalties, Princeton twenty-five. A fallen Princeton player got kicked in the ribs. One Dartmouth player broke a leg, and a second also suffered a leg injury. Kazmaier exited the game in the second quarter with a concussion and a broken nose. (He returned for the final play, earning a victory lap on his teammates' shoulders. A few months later he became the last player from the Ivy League to win the Heisman Trophy.)

Surprised by the ferocity of the editorials in both schools' newspapers after the game, a pair of psychology professors saw the occasion as an opportunity to study how beliefs can radically alter the way we process a common experience. Albert Hastorf of Dartmouth and Hadley Cantril of Princeton collected the newspaper stories, obtained a copy of the game film, showed it to groups of students from their schools, and had them complete questionnaires counting and characterizing the infractions on both sides. Their 1954 paper, "They Saw a Game," could have been called "They Saw Two Games" because students from each school, based on their questionnaires and accounts, seemed to be watching different games.

Hastorf and Cantril collected anecdotal evidence of this in the lively accounts and editorials of the Dartmouth-Princeton game in local newspapers. The *Daily Princetonian* said, "Both teams were guilty but the blame must be laid primarily on Dartmouth's doorstep." The *Princeton Alumni Weekly* called out Dartmouth for a late hit on the play that ended Kazmaier's college career and for kicking a prone Princeton player in the ribs. Meanwhile, an editorial in the *Dartmouth* placed heavy blame on Princeton coach Charley Caldwell. After the injury to the "Princeton idol," "Caldwell instilled the old see-what-they-did-go-get-them attitude into his players. His talk got results," the editorial asserted, referring to the pair of Dartmouth players suffering leg injuries in the third quarter. In the next issue of the *Dartmouth*, the paper listed star players from the opposing team that Princeton had stopped by a similar "concentrated effort."

When the researchers showed groups of students the film of the game and asked them to fill out the questionnaires, the same difference of opinion about what they had seen appeared. Princeton students saw Dartmouth commit twice as many flagrant penalties and three times the mild penalties as Princeton. Dartmouth students saw each team commit an equal number of infractions.

Hastorf and Cantril concluded, "We do not simply 'react to' a happening. . . . We behave according to what we bring to the occasion." Our beliefs affect how we process all new things, "whether the 'thing' is a football game, a presidential candidate, Communism, or spinach."

A study in the 2012 *Stanford Law Review* called "They Saw a Protest" (the title is a homage to the original Hastorf and Cantril experiment) by Yale professor of law and psychology Dan Kahan, a leading researcher and analyst of biased reasoning, and four colleagues reinforces this notion that our beliefs drive the way we process information.

In the study, two groups of subjects watched a video of police action halting a political demonstration. One group was told the protest occurred outside an abortion clinic, aimed at protesting legalized abortion. Another group was told it occurred at a college career-placement facility, where the military was conducting interviews and protestors were demonstrating against the then-existing ban on openly gay and lesbian soldiers. It was the same video, carefully edited to blur or avoid giving away the subject of the actual protest. Researchers, after gathering information about the worldviews of the subjects, asked them about facts and conclusions from what they saw.

The results mirrored those found by Hastorf and Cantril nearly sixty years before: "Our subjects all viewed the same video. But what they *saw*—earnest voicing of dissent intended only to persuade, or physical intimidation calculated to interfere with the freedom of others—depended on the congruence of the protest-ors' positions with the subjects' own cultural values." Whether it is a football game, a protest, or just about anything else, our pre-existing beliefs influence the way we experience the world. That those beliefs aren't formed in a particularly orderly way leads to all sorts of mischief in our decision-making.

The stubbornness of beliefs

Flaws in forming and updating beliefs have the potential to snowball. Once a belief is lodged, it becomes difficult to dislodge. It takes on a life of its own, leading us to notice and seek out ev-idence confirming our belief, rarely challenge the validity of confirming evidence, and ignore or work hard to actively dis-credit information contradicting the belief. This irrational, cir-cular information-processing pattern is called *motivated reasoning*. The way we process new information is driven by the beliefs we hold, strengthening them. Those strengthened beliefs then drive how we process further information, and so on.

During a break in a poker tournament, a player approached me for my opinion about how he played one of those suited-connector hands. I didn't witness the hand, and he gave me a very abbreviated description of how he stealthily played the six and seven of diamonds to make a flush on the second-to-last card but "had the worst luck" when the other player made a full house on the very last card.

We had only a minute or two left in the break, so I asked what I thought to be the most relevant question: "Why were you playing six-seven of diamonds in the first place?" (Even a brief explanation, I expected, would fill in details on many of the areas that determine how to play a hand like that and whether it was a profitable choice, such as table position, pot size, chip stack sizes, his opponent's style of play, how the table perceived his style, etc.)

His exasperated response was, "That's not the point of the story!" Motivated reasoning tells us it's not really the point of anyone's story.

It doesn't take much for any of us to believe something. And once we believe it, protecting that belief guides how we treat further information relevant to the belief. This is perhaps no more evident than in the rise in prominence of "fake news" and disinformation. The concept of "fake news," an intentionally false story planted for financial or political gain, is hundreds of years old. It has included such legendary practitioners as Orson Welles, Joseph Pulitzer, and William Randolph Hearst. Disinformation is different than fake news in that the story has some true elements, embellished to spin a particular narrative. Fake news works because people who already hold beliefs consistent with the story generally won't question the evidence. Disinformation is even more powerful because the confirmable facts in the story make it feel like the information has been vetted, adding to the power of the narrative being pushed.

Fake news isn't meant to change minds. As we know, beliefs are hard to change. The potency of fake news is that it entrenches beliefs its intended audience already has, and then amplifies them. The Internet is a playground for motivated reasoning. It provides the promise of access to a greater diversity of information sources and opinions than we've ever had available, yet we gravitate toward sources that confirm our beliefs, that agree with us. Every flavor is out there, but we tend to stick with our favorite.

Making matters worse, many social media sites tailor our

Internet experience to show us more of what we already like. Author Eli Pariser developed the term "filter bubble" in his 2011 book of the same name to describe the process of how companies like Google and Facebook use algorithms to keep pushing us in the directions we're already headed. By collecting our search, browsing, and similar data from our friends and correspondents, they give users headlines and links that cater to what they've divined as our preferences. The Internet, which gives us access to a diversity of viewpoints with unimaginable ease, in fact speeds our retreat into a confirmatory bubble. No matter our political orientation, none of us is immune.

The most popular websites have been doing our motivated reasoning for us.*

Even when directly confronted with facts that disconfirm our beliefs, we don't let facts get in the way. As Daniel Kahneman pointed out, we just want to think well of ourselves and feel that the narrative of our life story is a positive one. Being *wrong* doesn't fit into that narrative. If we think of beliefs as only *100% right* or *100% wrong*, when confronting new information that might contradict our belief, we have only two options: (a) make the massive shift in our opinion of ourselves from 100% right to 100% wrong, or (b) ignore or discredit the new information. It feels bad to be wrong, so we choose (b). Information that disagrees with us is an assault on our self-narrative. We'll work hard to swat that threat away. On the flip side, when additional information agrees with us, we effortlessly embrace it.

How we form beliefs, and our inflexibility about changing our beliefs, has serious consequences because we bet on those

*In fairness, after the 2016 presidential election, Facebook is attempting to address this, as are some other sites.

beliefs. Every bet we make in our lives depends on our beliefs: who we believe will make the best president, if we think we will like Des Moines, if we believe a low-fat diet will make us healthier, or even if we believe turkeys can fly.

Being smart makes it worse

The popular wisdom is that the smarter you are, the less susceptible you are to fake news or disinformation. After all, smart people are more likely to analyze and effectively evaluate where information is coming from, right? Part of being "smart" is being good at processing information, parsing the quality of an argument and the credibility of the source. So, intuitively, it feels like smart people should have the ability to spot motivated reasoning coming and should have more intellectual resources to fight it.

Surprisingly, being smart isn't a defense, and can actually make bias worse. Let me give you a different intuitive frame: the smarter you are, the better you are at constructing a narrative that supports your beliefs, rationalizing and framing the data to fit your argument or point of view. After all, people in the "spin room" in a political setting are generally pretty smart for a reason.

In 2012, psychologists Richard West, Russell Meserve, and Keith Stanovich tested the blind-spot bias—an irrationality where people are better at recognizing biased reasoning in others but are blind to bias in themselves. Overall, their work supported, across a variety of cognitive biases, that, yes, we all have a blind spot about recognizing our biases. The surprise is that blind-spot bias is greater the smarter you are. The researchers tested subjects for seven cognitive biases and found that cognitive ability did not attenuate the blind spot. "Furthermore, people who were aware of their own biases were not better able to overcome them." In fact, in six of the seven biases tested, "more cognitively sophisticated participants showed *larger* bias blind spots." (Emphasis added.) They have since replicated this result.

Dan Kahan's work on motivated reasoning also indicates that smart people are not better equipped to combat bias—and may be even more susceptible. He and several colleagues looked at whether conclusions from objective data were driven by subjective pre-existing beliefs on a topic. When subjects were asked to analyze complex data on an experimental skin treatment (a "neutral" topic), their ability to interpret the data and reach a conclusion depended, as expected, on their numeracy (mathematical aptitude) rather than their opinions on skin cream (since they really had no opinions on the topic). More numerate subjects did a better job at figuring out whether the data showed that the skin treatment increased or decreased the incidence of rashes. (The data were made up, and for half the subjects, the results were reversed, so the correct or incorrect answer depended on using the data, not the actual effectiveness of a particular skin treatment.)

When the researchers kept the data the same but substituted "concealed-weapons bans" for "skin treatment" and "crime" for "rashes," now the subjects' opinions on those topics drove how subjects analyzed the exact same data. Subjects who identified as "Democrat" or "liberal" interpreted the data in a way supporting their political belief (gun control reduces crime). The "Republican" or "conservative" subjects interpreted the same data to support their opposing belief (gun control increases crime).

That generally fits what we understand about motivated reasoning. The surprise, though, was Kahan's finding about subjects with differing math skills and the same political beliefs. He discovered that the *more numerate* people (whether pro- or anti-gun) made *more mistakes* interpreting the data on the emotionally charged topic than the less numerate subjects sharing those same beliefs. "This pattern of polarization . . . does not abate among high-Numeracy subjects. Indeed, it *increases*." (Emphasis in original.)

It turns out the better you are with numbers, the better you are at spinning those numbers to conform to and support your beliefs.

Unfortunately, this is just the way evolution built us. We are wired to protect our beliefs even when our goal is to truthseek. This is one of those instances where being smart and aware of our capacity for irrationality alone doesn't help us refrain from biased reasoning. As with visual illusions, we can't make our minds work differently than they do no matter how smart we are. Just as we can't unsee an illusion, intellect or willpower alone can't make us resist motivated reasoning.

So far, this chapter has mainly been bad news. We bet on our beliefs. We don't vet those beliefs well before we form them. We stubbornly refuse to update our beliefs. Now I've piled on by telling you that being smart doesn't help—and can make it worse.

The good news starts here.

Wanna bet?

Imagine taking part in a conversation with a friend about the movie *Citizen Kane*. Best film of all time, introduced a bunch of new techniques by which directors could contribute to story-telling. "Obviously, it won the best-picture Oscar," you gush, as part of a list of superlatives the film unquestionably deserves.

Then your friend says, "Wanna bet?"

Suddenly, you're not so sure. That challenge puts you on your heels, causing you to back off your declaration and question the belief that you just declared with such assurance. When someone challenges us to bet on a belief, signaling their confidence that our belief is inaccurate in some way, ideally it triggers us to vet the belief, taking an inventory of the evidence that informed us.

- How do I know this?
- Where did I get this information?
- Who did I get it from?
- What is the quality of my sources?
- How much do I trust them?
- How up to date is my information?
- How much information do I have that is relevant to the belief?
- What other things like this have I been confident about that turned out not to be true?
- What are the other plausible alternatives?
- What do I know about the person challenging my belief?
- What is their view of how credible my opinion is?
- What do they know that I don't know?
- What is their level of expertise?
- What am I missing?

Remember the order in which we form abstract beliefs:

(1) We hear something;
(2) We believe it;

(3) Only sometimes, later, if we have the time or the inclination, we think about it and vet it, determining whether or not it is true.

"Wanna bet?" triggers us to engage in that third step that we only sometimes get to. It reminds us that our beliefs are works in progress. Being asked if we are willing to bet money on it makes it much more likely that we will examine our information in a less biased way, be more honest with ourselves about how sure we are of our beliefs, and be more open to updating and calibrating our beliefs. The more objective we are, the more accurate our beliefs become. And the person who wins bets over the long run is the one with the more accurate beliefs.

Of course, in most instances, the person offering to bet isn't actually looking to put any money on it. They are just making a point—a valid point that perhaps we overstated our conclusion or made our statement without including relevant caveats. Most people aren't like poker players, around whom there is always the potential that someone might propose a bet and they will mean it.

Next thing you know, someone moves to Des Moines and there's $30,000 at stake.

It's a shame the social contract for poker players is so different than for the rest of us in this regard because a lot of good can result from someone saying, "Wanna bet?" Offering a wager brings the risk out in the open, making explicit what is already implicit (and frequently overlooked). The more we recognize that we are betting on our beliefs (with our happiness, attention, health, money, time, or some other limited resource), the more we are likely to temper our statements, getting closer to the truth as we acknowledge the risk inherent in what we believe.

Expecting everyone starting to throw the gauntlet down, challenging each other to bet on any opinion, is impractical if you aren't hanging out in a poker room. (Even in poker rooms, this generally happens only among players who know each other well.) I imagine that if you went around challenging everyone with "Wanna bet?" it would be difficult to make friends and you'd lose the ones you have. But that doesn't mean we can't change the framework for ourselves in the way we think about our decisions. We can train ourselves to view the world through the lens of "Wanna bet?"

Once we start doing that, we are more likely to recognize that there is always a degree of uncertainty, that we are generally less sure than we thought we were, that practically nothing is black and white, 0% or 100%. And that's a pretty good philosophy for living.

Redefining confidence

Not much is ever certain. Samuel Arbesman's *The Half-Life of Facts* is a great read about how practically every fact we've ever known has been subject to revision or reversal. We are in a perpetual state of learning, and that can make any prior fact obsolete. One of many examples he provides is about the extinction of the coelacanth, a fish from the Late Cretaceous period. A mass-extinction event (such as a large meteor striking the Earth, a series of volcanic eruptions, or a permanent climate shift) ended the Cretaceous period. That was the end of dinosaurs, coelacanths, and a lot of other species. In the late 1930s and independently in the mid-1950s, however, coelacanths were found alive and well. A species becoming "unextinct" is pretty common. Arbesman cites the work of a pair of biologists at the University of Queensland who made a list of all 187 species of mammals declared extinct in the last five hundred years. More than a third of those species have subsequently been rediscovered.

Given that even scientific facts can have an expiration date, we would all be well-advised to take a good hard look at our beliefs, which are formed and updated in a much more haphazard way than those in science. If we take an honest look at the things we believed strongly when we were younger, we can see we have the capability of updating our beliefs. What forty-year-old thinks everything they believed at twenty is still correct?

We need to recognize that what we believe *now* is also subject to change. We don't need someone challenging us to an actual bet to do this. We can think like a bettor, purposefully and on our own, like it's a game even if we're just doing it ourselves.

We would be better served as communicators and decision-makers if we thought less about whether we are confident in our beliefs and more about *how* confident we are. Instead of thinking of confidence as all-or-nothing ("I'm confident" or "I'm not confident"), our expression of our confidence would then capture all the shades of grey in between.

When we express our beliefs (to others or just to ourselves as part of our internal decision-making dialogue), they don't generally come with qualifications. What if, in addition to expressing what we believe, we also rated our level of confidence about the accuracy of our belief on a scale of zero to ten? Zero would mean we are certain a belief is not true. Ten would mean we are certain that our belief is true. A zero-to-ten scale translates directly to percentages. If you think the belief rates a three, that means you are 30% sure the belief is accurate. A nine means you are 90%

sure. So instead of saying to ourselves, "*Citizen Kane* won the Oscar for best picture," we would say, "I think *Citizen Kane* won the Oscar for best picture but I'm only a six on that." Or "I'm 60% that *Citizen Kane* won the Oscar for best picture." That means your level of certainty is such that 40% of the time it will turn out that *Citizen Kane* did not win the best-picture Oscar. Forcing ourselves to express how sure we are of our beliefs brings to plain sight the probabilistic nature of those beliefs, that what we believe is almost never 100% or 0% accurate but, rather, somewhere in between.

In a similar vein, the number can reflect several different kinds of uncertainty. "I'm 60% confident that *Citizen Kane* won best picture" reflects that our knowledge of this past event is incomplete. "I'm 60% confident the flight from Chicago will be late" incorporates a mix of our incomplete knowledge and the inherent uncertainty in predicting the future (e.g., the weather might intervene or there might be an unforeseen mechanical issue).

We can also express how confident we are by thinking about the number of plausible alternatives and declaring that range. For example, if I am stating my belief about what age Elvis died, I might say, "Somewhere between age forty and forty-seven." I know he died in his forties and I remember that it was his earlier forties, so for me this is the range of plausible alternatives. The more we know about a topic, the better the quality of information we have, the tighter the range of plausible alternatives. (When it comes to predictions, the plausible range of outcomes would also be tighter when there is less luck involved.) The less we know about a topic or the more luck involved, the wider our range.

We can declare how sure we are whether we are thinking about a particular fact or set of facts ("dinosaurs were herd animals"), a prediction ("I think there is life on other planets"), or how the future will turn out given some decision we might make ("I think I will be happier if I move to Des Moines than I am where I live now" or "I think the company will be better off if we fire the president"). These are all beliefs of differing sorts.

Incorporating uncertainty into the way we think about our beliefs comes with many benefits. By expressing our level of confidence in what we believe, we are shifting our approach to how we view the world. Acknowledging uncertainty is the first step in measuring and narrowing it. Incorporating uncertainty in the way we think about what we believe creates open-mindedness, moving us closer to a more objective stance toward information that disagrees with us. We are less likely to succumb to motivated reasoning since it feels better to make small adjustments in degrees of certainty instead of having to grossly downgrade from "right" to "wrong." When confronted with new evidence, it is a very different narrative to say, "I was 58% but now I'm 46%." That doesn't feel nearly as bad as "I thought I was right but now I'm wrong." Our narrative of being a knowledgeable, educated, intelligent person who holds quality opinions isn't compromised when we use new information to calibrate our beliefs, compared with having to make a full-on reversal. This shifts us away from treating information that disagrees with us as a threat, as something we have to defend against, making us better able to truthseek.

Treating decisions as bets helps the uncertainty bubble to the surface. Making explicit that we aren't sure makes us want to reduce our uncertainty. That makes us hungry for information to fill in the gaps of our knowledge. It makes us grateful for opposing viewpoints. Instead of looking for ways to confirm we're right, we're more likely to ask, "Why am I wrong?"

When we work toward belief calibration, we become less judgmental of ourselves. Incorporating percentages or ranges of alternatives into the expression of our beliefs means that our personal narrative no longer hinges on whether we were wrong or right but on how well we incorporate new information to adjust the estimate of how accurate our beliefs are. There is no sin in finding out there is evidence that contradicts what we believe. The only sin is in not using that evidence as objectively as possible to refine that belief going forward.

Declaring our uncertainty in our beliefs to others makes us more credible communicators. We assume that if we don't come off as 100% confident, others will value our opinions less. The opposite is usually true. If one person expresses a belief as absolutely true, and someone else expresses a belief by saying, "I believe this to be true, and I'm 80% on it," who are you more likely to believe? The fact that the person is expressing their confidence as less than 100% signals that they are trying to get at the truth, that they have considered the quantity and quality of their information with thoughtfulness and self-awareness. And thoughtful and self-aware people are more believable.

Expressing our level of confidence also invites people to be our collaborators. As I said, most of us don't live our lives in poker rooms, where it is more socially acceptable to challenge a peer who expresses an opinion we believe to be inaccurate to a wager. Outside of the poker room, when we declare something as 100% fact, others might be reluctant to offer up new and relevant information that would inform our beliefs for two reasons. First, they might be afraid they are wrong and so won't speak up, worried they will be judged for that, by us or themselves. Second, even if they are very confident their information is high quality, they might be afraid of making us feel bad or judged. By saying, "I'm 80%" and thereby communicating we aren't sure, we open the door for others to tell us what they know.

They realize they can contribute without having to confront us by saying or implying, "You're wrong." Admitting we are not sure is an invitation for help in refining our beliefs, and that will make our beliefs much more accurate over time as we are more likely to gather relevant information.

Expressing our beliefs this way also serves our listeners. We know that our default is to believe what we hear, without vetting the information too carefully. If we communicate to our listeners that we are not 100% on what we are saying, they are less likely to walk away having been infected by our beliefs. Expressing the belief as uncertain signals to our listeners that the belief needs further vetting, that step three is still in progress.

When scientists publish results of experiments, they share with the rest of their community their methods of gathering and analyzing the data, the data itself, and their confidence in that data. That makes it possible for others to assess the quality of the information being presented, systematized through peer review before publication. Confidence in the results is expressed through both p-values, the probability one would expect to get the result that was actually observed (akin to declaring your confidence on a scale of zero to ten), and confidence intervals (akin to declaring ranges of plausible alternatives). Scientists, by institutionalizing the expression of uncertainty, invite their community to share relevant information and to test and challenge the results and explanations. The information that gets shared back might confirm, disconfirm, or refine published hypotheses. The goal is to advance knowledge rather than affirm what we already believe. This is why science advances at a fast clip.*

---

*Legendary physicist Richard Feynman encapsulated this way that scientists communicate uncertainty and how they strive to avoid the extremes of right and

By communicating our own uncertainty when sharing beliefs with others, we are inviting the people in our lives to act like scientists with us. This advances our beliefs at a faster clip because we miss out on fewer opportunities to get new information, information that would help us to calibrate the beliefs we have.

Acknowledging that decisions are bets based on our beliefs, getting comfortable with uncertainty, and redefining right and wrong are integral to a good overall approach to decision-making. But I don't expect that, having dumped all these concepts in your lap, you should somehow know the best way to use them. These patterns are so engrained in our thinking that it takes more than knowing the problem or even having the right outlook to overcome the irrationalities that hold us back. What I've done so far, really, is identify the target; now that we are facing the right direction, thinking in bets is a tool to be *somewhat* better at hitting it.

---

wrong when he said, "Statements of science are not of what is true and what is not true, but statements of what is known to different degrees of certainty. . . . Every one of the concepts of science is on a scale graduated somewhere between, but at neither end of, absolute falsity or absolute truth." (This appears in a collection of his short works, *The Pleasure of Finding Things Out*.)

CHAPTER 3

Bet to Learn:
Fielding the Unfolding Future

Nick the Greek, and other lessons from the Crystal Lounge

When I first started playing poker, I lived in Columbus, Montana, population 1,200. The nearest poker game was forty miles away in downtown Billings, in the basement of a bar called the Crystal Lounge. Every day, I drove those forty miles, arriving by early afternoon. I would play until the evening, and drive home.

The game was filled with characters out of a clichéd vision of Montana: ranchers and farmers killing time in the off-season, filling the basement room with smoke wafting over the brims of their cowboy hats. It was 1992 but it could have just as easily been 1952 from the décor and the grizzled countenances of the locals. The only thing suggesting that John Wayne wasn't going to mosey on in was a handful of misfits, including me (a woman and the youngest player by a few decades, on the lam from defending my dissertation at the University of Pennsylvania) and a player named "Nick the Greek."

If your name is Nick, you come from Greece, and you gamble,

they're going to call you Nick the Greek, as sure as they'll call you Tiny if you weigh more than 350 pounds. (And, yes, there was a guy named Tiny, real name Elwood, who regularly played in the game.) This Nick the Greek was of the small-time Billings variety. He was the general manager of the hotel across the street, having gotten transferred from Greece by the hotel chain. He left work for a couple of hours every afternoon like clockwork to play in the game.

Nick the Greek had formed an unusual set of beliefs that guided his poker decisions. I knew this because he described them to me and the other players, at length, using the results of particular hands to punctuate his points. He fixated on the relatively common belief that the element of surprise was important in poker. (Don't be predictable, mix up your play—that sort of stuff.) Then he jacked it up on steroids. To him, a starting pair of aces, the mathematically best two cards you can get dealt, was the worst hand because everyone predictably played it.

"They always expect you to have aces. You get killed with that hand."

By that logic, he explained, the very best two starting cards to play were the *mathematically weakest* two cards you could receive, a seven and a deuce of different suits—a hand almost any player avoids.

"I bet you never saw it coming," he would say when he turned over that hand and won a pot. And because he played seven-deuce all the time, occasionally the stars would line up and he'd win. I also remember times when he threw away a pair of aces, faceup, at the first sign of a bet. (Never mind that he was compromising a vital element of his strategy of subterfuge by constantly *showing and telling* us he was doing this. Given that he had such an entrenched set of beliefs, it's not surprising that he didn't see the incongruity.)

Nick the Greek, needless to say, rarely came out ahead. Yet he never changed his strategy, often complaining about his bad luck when he lost, though never in a bitter way. He was a friendly guy, pleasant to play with—the perfect poker opponent. I tried to time my daily arrivals so I'd be in the game when he made his afternoon appearance.

One day, Nick the Greek didn't show up to the game. When I asked where he was, another player muttered, confidentially (though it seemed everyone in the game already knew about this), "Oh, he got sent back."

"Sent back?"

"Yeah, to Greece. They deported him."

I can't say that Nick the Greek's deportation was the result of his wacky poker beliefs, but I have my suspicions. Other players speculated that he went broke, or dipped into the till at the hotel, or lost his work visa because he was playing poker every day on company time.

I can say that Nick the Greek lost a lot of money based on his beliefs—or, more accurately, because he ignored lots of feedback that his strategy was a losing one. He eventually went broke because he didn't recognize learning opportunities as they arose.

If Nick the Greek were unique in his resistance to learning from the outcomes he was having at the poker table, I suppose he would just be a footnote for me, a funny story of a guy unique in his ability to hold tight to his strategy despite that strategy resulting in a lot of losing. But, while an extreme case to be sure, Nick the Greek wasn't all that unique. And that was a puzzle for me. I was taught, as all psychology students are, that learning

occurs when you get lots of feedback tied closely in time to decisions and actions. If we took that at face value, poker would be
an ideal learning environment. You make a bet, get an immediate
response from opponents, and win or lose the hand (with real-
money consequences), all within minutes.

So why was Nick the Greek, who had been playing for years,
unable to learn from his mistakes? Why was a novice like me
cleaning up in the game? The answer is that while experience is
necessary to becoming an expert, it's not sufficient.

Experience can be an effective teacher. But, clearly, only some
students listen to their teachers. The people who learn from experience improve, advance, and (with a little bit of luck) become
experts and leaders in their fields. I benefited from adopting the
learning habits of some of the phenomenal poker players I was
exposed to along the way. We can all benefit from those practical
strategies to become better decision-makers. Thinking in bets
can help us get there.

But before getting to the solutions, we must first understand
the problem. What are the obstacles in our way that make learning from experience so difficult? We all clearly have a desire to
reach our long-term goals. Listening to what our outcomes have
to teach us is necessary to do that. So what is systematically getting in the way?

Outcomes are feedback

We can't just "absorb" experiences and expect to learn. As novelist and philosopher Aldous Huxley recognized, "Experience is not
what happens to a man; it is what a man does with what happens

to him." There is a big difference between getting experience and becoming an expert. That difference lies in the ability to identify when the outcomes of our decisions have something to teach us and what that lesson might be.

Any decision, whether it's putting $2 on Count de Change at the racetrack or telling your kids they can eat whatever they want, is a bet on what will likely create the most favorable future for us. The future we have bet on unfolds as a series of outcomes. We bet on staying up late to watch the end of a football game and we sleep through our alarm, wake up tired, get to work late, and get reprimanded by the boss. Or we stay up late and any of the myriad other outcomes follows, including waking up perfectly on time and making it to work early. Whichever future actually unfolds, when we decide to stay up late to see the end of the game, we are making a bet that we will be happier in the future for having seen the final play. We bet on moving to Des Moines and we find our dream job, meet the love of our life, and take up yoga. Or, like John Hennigan, we move there, hate it within two days, and have to buy our way home for $15,000. We bet on firing a division president or calling a pass play, and the future unfolds as it does. We can represent this like so:

BETTING ON A FUTURE

BELIEF $\longrightarrow$ BET $\longrightarrow$ (SET OF OUTCOMES)

As the future unfolds into a set of outcomes, we are faced with another decision: Why did something happen the way it did?

How we figure out what—if anything—we should learn from an outcome becomes another bet. As outcomes come our way, figuring out whether those outcomes were caused mainly by luck or whether they were the predictable result of particular decisions we made is a bet of great consequence. If we determine our decisions drove the outcome, we can feed the data we get following those decisions back into belief formation and updating, creating a learning loop:

LEARNING LOOP 1

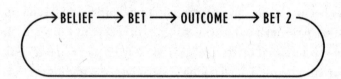

BELIEF ⟶ BET ⟶ OUTCOME ⟶ BET 2

We have the opportunity to learn from the way the future unfolds to improve our beliefs and decisions going forward. The more evidence we get from experience, the less uncertainty we have about our beliefs and choices. Actively using outcomes to examine our beliefs and bets closes the feedback loop, reducing uncertainty. This is the heavy lifting of how we learn.

Ideally, our beliefs and our bets improve with time as we learn from experience. Ideally, the more information we have, the better we get at making decisions about which possible future to bet on. Ideally, as we learn from experience we get better at assessing the likelihood of a particular outcome given any decision, making our predictions about the future more accurate. As you may have guessed, when it comes to how we process experience, "ideally" doesn't always apply.

Learning might proceed in a more ideal way if life were more like chess than poker. The connection between outcome quality and decision quality would be clearer because there would be less uncertainty. The challenge is that any single outcome can happen for multiple reasons. The unfolding future is a big data dump that we have to sort and interpret. And the world doesn't connect the dots for us between outcomes and causes.

If a patient comes into a doctor's office with a cough, the doctor must work backward from that one symptom, that one outcome of a possible disease process, to decide among the multiple reasons the patient might have that cough. Is it because of a virus? Bacteria? Cancer? A neurological disorder? Because a cough looks roughly the same whether it is from cancer or a virus, working backward from the symptom to the cause is difficult. The stakes are high. Misdiagnose the cause, and the patient might die. That is why doctors require years of training to properly diagnose patients.

When the future coughs on us, it is hard to tell why.

Imagine calls to a customer by two salespeople from the same company. In January, Joe pitches the company's products and gets $1,000 in orders. In August, Jane calls on the same customer and gets $10,000 in orders. What gives? Was it because Jane is a better salesperson than Joe? Or was it because the company updated its product line in February? Did a low-cost competitor go out of business in April? Or is the difference in their success due to any of a variety of other unconsidered reasons? It's hard to know why because we can't go back in time and run the controlled experiment where Joe and Jane switch places. And the way the company sorts this outcome can affect decisions on training, pricing, and product development.

This problem is top of mind for poker players. Most poker hands end in a cloud of incomplete information: one player bets, no one calls the bet, the bettor is awarded the pot, and no one is required to reveal their hidden cards. After those hands, the players are left guessing why they won or lost the hand. Did the winner have a superior hand? Did the loser fold the best hand? Could the player who won the hand have made more money if they chose a different line of play? Could the player who lost have made the winner forfeit if they chose to play the hand differently? In answering these questions, none of the players knows what cards their opponents actually held, or how the players would have reacted to a different sequence of betting decisions. How poker players adjust their play from experience determines their future results. How they fill in all those blanks is a vitally important bet on whether they get better at the game.

We are good at identifying the "-ER" goals we want to pursue (better, smarter, richer, healthier, whatever). But we fall short in achieving our "-ER" because of the difficulty in executing all the little decisions along the way to our goals. The bets we make on when and how to close the feedback loop are part of the execution, all those in-the-moment decisions about whether something is a learning opportunity. To reach our long-term goals, we have to improve at sorting out when the unfolding future has something to teach us, when to close the feedback loop.

And the first step to doing this well is in recognizing that things sometimes happen because of the other form of uncertainty: luck.

Luck vs. skill: fielding outcomes

The way our lives turn out is the result of two things: the influence of skill and the influence of luck. For the purposes of this discussion, any outcome that is the result of our decision-making is in the skill category. If making the same decision again would predictably result in the same outcome, or if changing the decision would predictably result in a different outcome, then the outcome following that decision was due to skill. The quality of our decision-making was the main influence over how things turned out. If, however, an outcome occurs because of things that we can't control (like the actions of others, the weather, or our genes), the result would be due to luck. If our decisions didn't have much impact on the way things turned out, then luck would be the main influence.*

When a golfer hits a tee shot, where the ball lands is the result of the influence of skill and luck, whether it is a first-time golfer or Rory McIlroy. The elements of skill, those things directly in the golfer's control that influence the outcome, include club choice, setup, and all the detailed mechanics of the golf swing. Elements of luck include a sudden gust of wind, somebody yelling their name as they swing, the ball landing in a divot or hitting a sprinkler head, the age of the golfer, the golfer's genes, and the opportunities they received (or didn't receive) up to the moment of the shot.

An outcome like losing weight could be the direct result of a change in diet or increased exercise (skill), or a sudden change in our metabolism or a famine (luck). We could get in a car crash because we didn't stop at a red light (skill) or because another driver ran a red light (luck). A student could do poorly on a test because they didn't study (skill) or because the teacher is mean

---

*It's impossible to have a detailed discussion about outcomes and learning without going into detail on what's luck and what's skill (and what's a combination), which I do when necessary. For a treatment that more fully explores the differences between skill and luck, I recommend Michael Mauboussin's *The Success Equation: Untangling Skill and Luck in Business, Sports, and Investing*, along with other sources cited in the Selected Bibliography and Recommendations for Further Reading.

(luck). I can lose a hand of poker because I made poor decisions, applying the skill elements of the game poorly, or because the other player got lucky.

Chalk up an outcome to skill, and we take credit for the result. Chalk up an outcome to luck, and it wasn't in our control. For any outcome, we are faced with this initial sorting decision. That decision is a bet on whether the outcome belongs in the "luck" bucket or the "skill" bucket. This is where Nick the Greek went wrong.

We can update the learning loop to represent this like so:

LEARNING LOOP 2

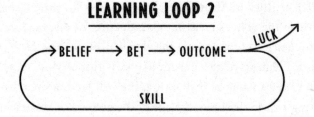

Think about this like we are an outfielder catching a fly ball with runners on base. Fielders have to make in-the-moment game decisions about where to throw the ball: hit the cutoff man, throw behind a base runner, throw out an advancing base runner. Where the outfielder throws after fielding the ball is a bet.

We make similar bets about where to "throw" an outcome: into the "skill bucket" (in our control) or the "luck bucket" (outside of our control). This initial fielding of outcomes, if done well, allows us to focus on experiences that have something to teach us (skill) and ignore those that don't (luck). Get this right and, with experience, we get closer to whatever "-ER" we are striving for: better, smarter, healthier, happier, wealthier, etc.

It is hard to get this right. Absent omniscience, it is difficult to tell why anything happened the way it did. The bet on whether to field outcomes into the luck or skill bucket is difficult to execute because of ambiguity.

Working backward is hard: the SnackWell's Phenomenon

In the nineties, millions of people jumped on the SnackWell's bandwagon. Nabisco developed these devil's food cookies as a leading product to take advantage of the now-discredited belief that fat, not sugar, makes you fat. Foods made with less fat were, at the time, considered healthier. With the blessing of the U.S. government, companies swapped in sugar for fat as a flavoring ingredient. SnackWell's came in a green package, the color associated with "low fat" and, therefore, "healthy"—like spinach!

For all those people trying to lose weight or make healthier snacking choices, SnackWell's were a delicious godsend. Snack-Well's eaters bet their health on substituting these cookies for other types of snacks like, say, cashews, which are high in fat. You could ingest sugar-laden SnackWell's by the box, because sugar wasn't the enemy. Fat was the enemy, and the packaging screamed "LOW FAT!"

Of course, we know now that obesity rose significantly during the low-fat craze. (Michael Pollan used the phrase "Snack-Well's Phenomenon" in describing people increasing their consumption of something that has less of a bad ingredient.) As those SnackWell's eaters gained weight, it wasn't easy for them to figure out why. Should the weight gain be fielded into the skill bucket, used as feedback that their belief about the health value of SnackWell's was inaccurate? Or was the weight gain due to bad luck, like a slow metabolism or something else that wasn't their fault or at least didn't have to do with their choice to eat Snack-Well's? If the weight gain got fielded into the luck bucket, it wouldn't be a signal to alter the choice to eat SnackWell's.

Looking back *now*, it seems obvious how the weight gain should have been fielded. But it is only obvious once you *know* that SnackWell's are an unhealthy choice. We have the benefit of twenty years of new research, more and better-quality information about what causes weight gain. The folks on the low-fat bandwagon had only their weight gain to learn from. The cards remained concealed.

Working backward from the way things turn out isn't easy. We can get to the same health outcome (weight gain) by different routes. One person might choose SnackWell's; another might choose Oreos (also a Nabisco product, developed by the same person who invented SnackWell's); a third might choose lentils and kale. If all three people gain weight, how can any of them figure it out for sure?

Outcomes don't tell us what's our fault and what isn't, what we should take credit for and what we shouldn't. Unlike in chess, we can't simply work backward from the quality of the outcome to determine the quality of our beliefs or decisions. This makes learning from outcomes a pretty haphazard process. A negative outcome could be a signal to go in and examine our decision-making. That outcome could also be due to bad luck, unrelated to our decision, in which case treating that outcome as a signal to change future decisions would be a mistake. A good outcome could signal that we made a good decision. It could also mean that we got lucky, in which case we would be making a mistake to use that outcome as a signal to repeat that decision in the future.

When Nick the Greek won with a seven and a deuce, he fielded that outcome into the skill bucket, taking credit for his brilliant strategy. When he lost with that hand—a much more common occurrence—he wrote it off as bad luck. His fielding error meant he never questioned his beliefs, no matter how much he lost. We're all like Nick the Greek sometimes. Uncertainty—luck and hidden information—gave him the leeway to make fielding errors about why he was losing. We all face uncertainty. And we all make fielding errors.

Rats get tripped up by uncertainty in a way that should appear very familiar to us. Classical stimulus-response experiments have shown that the introduction of uncertainty drastically slows learning. When rats are trained on a *fixed* reward schedule (for example, a pellet for every tenth press of a lever), they learn pretty fast to press that lever for food. If you withdraw the reward, the lever-pressing behavior is quickly extinguished. The rats figure out that no more food is on its way.

But when you reward the rats on a variable or intermittent reinforcement schedule (a pellet that comes *on average* every tenth lever press), that introduces uncertainty. The average number of lever presses for the reward is the same, but the rat could get a reward on the next press or not for thirty presses. In other words, the rats are rewarded the way humans usually are: having no way to know with certainty what will happen on the next try. When you withdraw the reward from those rats, the lever-pressing behavior extinguishes only after a very long time of fruitless lever pushing, sometimes thousands of tries.

We might imagine the rats thinking, "I bet the next lever press will get me a pellet. . . . I've just been getting unlucky . . . I'm due." Actually, we don't even have to imagine this. We can hear it if we listen to what people say while they play slot machines. Slot machines operate on a variable-payoff system. It's no wonder that, despite those machines being among the worst bets in the casino, the banks of slots in a casino are packed. In the end, our rat brains dominate.

If this all doesn't seem difficult enough, outcomes are rarely all skill or all luck. Even when we make the most egregious mistakes and get appropriately negative outcomes, luck plays a role. For every drunk driver who swerves into a ditch and flips his car, there are several who swerve harmlessly across multilane highways. It might feel like the drunk driver in the ditch deserved that outcome, but the luck of the road conditions and presence or absence of other drivers also played a role. When we do everything right, like drive through a green light perfectly sober and live to tell the tale, there is also an element of luck. No one else simultaneously ran a red light and hit us. There *wasn't* a patch of ice on the road to make us lose control of our vehicle. We *didn't* run over a piece of debris and blow a tire.

When we field our outcomes as the future unfolds, we always run into this problem: the way things turn out could be the result of our decisions, luck, or some combination of the two. Just as we are almost never 100% wrong or right, outcomes are almost never 100% due to luck or skill. Learning from experience doesn't offer us the orderliness of chess or, for that matter, folding and sorting laundry. Getting insight into the way uncertainty trips us up, whether the errors we make are patterned (hint: they are) and what motivates those errors, should give us clues for figuring out achievable strategies to calibrate the bets we make on our outcomes.

"If it weren't for luck, I'd win every one"

Just as with motivated reasoning, our fielding errors aren't random. They are, borrowing from psychologist and behavioral economist Dan Ariely,* "predictably irrational." The way we field outcomes is predictably patterned: we take credit for the good stuff and blame the bad stuff on luck so it won't be our fault. The result is that we don't learn from experience well.

"Self-serving bias" is the term for this pattern of fielding outcomes. Psychologist Fritz Heider was a pioneer in studying how people make luck and skill attributions about the results of their behavior. He said we study our outcomes like scientists, but like "naïve scientists." When we figure out why something happened, we look for a plausible reason, but one that also fits our wishes. Heider said, "It is usually a reason that flatters us, puts us in a good light, and it is imbued with an added potency by the attribution."

Our capacity for self-deception has few boundaries. Look at the reasons people give for their accidents on actual auto insurance forms: "I collided with a stationary truck coming the other way." "A pedestrian hit me and went under my car." "The guy was all over the road. I had to swerve a number of times before I hit him." "An invisible car came out of nowhere, struck my car, and vanished." "The pedestrian had no idea which direction to run,

---

*Ariely, a professor of psychology and behavioral economics at Duke University, is simultaneously a leading researcher in the discipline of behavioral economics and responsible for introducing millions of people to the practical aspects of behavioral economics through popular TED Talks, best-selling books, a blog, a card game, and even an app. His most popular book is titled *Predictably Irrational*.

so I ran over him." "The telephone pole was approaching. I was attempting to swerve out of its way when it struck my car."*

Stanford law professor and social psychologist Robert Mac-Coun studied accounts of auto accidents and found that in 75% of accounts, the victims blamed someone else for their injuries. In multiple-vehicle accidents, 91% of drivers blamed someone else. Most remarkably, MacCoun found that in *single*-vehicle accidents, 37% of drivers still found a way to pin the blame on someone else.

We can't write this off to lack of self-knowledge by a few bad drivers. John von Neumann, considered a terror on the roads of Princeton, New Jersey, once offered this explanation after smashing his car: "I was proceeding down the road. The trees on the right were passing me in orderly fashion at 60 MPH. Suddenly, one of them stepped out in my path. Boom!" Et tu, JvN? Et tu?

This predictable fielding error is probably the single most significant problem for poker players. I watched it firsthand with Nick the Greek at the Crystal Lounge. When he lost with seven-deuce, it was because he got unlucky that time. When he won playing those cards, it was because his plan of "surprise attack" was so brilliant. Off-loading the losses to luck and onboarding the wins to skill meant he persisted in overestimating the likelihood of winning with seven-deuce. He kept betting on a losing future.

And this is not confined to Nick the Greeks of the small-time Billings variety. Phil Hellmuth, the biggest winner in

---

*I lifted these from an article by Robert MacCoun (described in the following paragraph) and repeat them without guilt. First, they are incredibly amusing and informative; the greater crime would be not sharing them. Second, MacCoun acknowledged that he got them from the book *Anguished English*, written by my father, Richard Lederer.

World Series of Poker history (fifteen championship bracelets and counting), famously fell prey to this fielding error. After getting eliminated from a televised poker tournament, Hellmuth said on camera to ESPN, "If it weren't for luck, I'd win every one." This line has become legend in the poker world. (It was even the basis for a song, "I'd Win Everytime [If It Wasn't for Luck]" in *All In: The Poker Musical*, a show based on Phil's life.) When the ESPN episode aired, there was a collective gasp in the poker community. After all, Phil is saying that if the luck element were eliminated from poker—if he were playing chess—his poker skills are so superior that he would win every tournament he entered. So, clearly, any negative outcomes are due to luck, and any positive outcomes are the result of his superior skill.

Poker players may have gasped, but the only difference between Phil and everyone else is that he said this *out loud and on television*. Most of us just have the sense to keep the sentiment to ourselves, especially when the cameras and mics are on. But, trust me, we are all vulnerable to the exact same thinking.

I, certainly, am not exempt. When I was playing poker, I did my share of taking credit for winning and complaining about bad luck when I lost. It's a fundamental urge. I've been conscious of that tendency in all areas of my life. Remember, we can know it's a visual illusion, but that doesn't keep us from still seeing it.

Self-serving bias has immediate and obvious consequences for our ability to learn from experience.* Blaming the bulk of our

---

* Because self-serving bias promotes an inaccurate view of the world, it raises the question of how self-serving bias has survived natural selection. There may be an evolutionary basis for this potentially costly self-deception. People who are self-confident attract better mates, improving the chances their genes get passed on. Because we are good at detecting deception, to deceive others about our self-confidence, we had to first deceive ourselves. As evolutionary biologist Robert

bad outcomes on luck means we miss opportunities to examine our decisions to see where we can do better. Taking credit for the good stuff means we will often reinforce decisions that shouldn't be reinforced and miss opportunities to see where we could have done better. To be sure, some of the bad stuff that happens is mainly due to luck. And some of the good stuff that happens is mainly due to skill. I just know that's not true all the time. 100% of our bad outcomes aren't because we got unlucky and 100% of our good outcomes aren't because we are so awesome. Yet that is how we process the future as it unfolds.

The predictable pattern of blaming the bad stuff on the world and taking credit for the good stuff is by no means limited to poker or car accidents. It's everywhere.

When Chris Christie participated in a debate before the Republican presidential primary in Iowa in early 2016, he played the part of behavioral psychologist in his attack on Hillary Clinton's response to the tragic outcome in Benghazi: "She refuses to be held accountable for anything that goes wrong. If it had gone right, believe me, she would have been running around to be able to take credit for it." Whether or not the accusation is correct, Christie certainly got the human tendency right: we take credit for good things and deflect blame for bad things. Ironically, only minutes earlier, he offered a pretty competitive example of the bias in himself. When asked by the moderator if the GOP should

---

Trivers noted in his foreword to the original 1976 edition of Richard Dawkins's *The Selfish Gene*, the evolution of self-deception is much more complicated than previously imagined. "Thus, the conventional view that natural selection favors nervous systems which produce ever more accurate images of the world must be a very naïve view of mental evolution." Dawkins, in turn, considered Trivers, for his work, one of the heroes of his groundbreaking book, devoting four chapters of *The Selfish Gene* to developing Trivers's ideas.

take a chance on nominating him in light of Bridgegate, he answered, "Sure, because there's been three different investigations that have proven that I knew nothing." Then he added, "And let me tell you something else. I inherited a state in New Jersey that was downtrodden and beaten by liberal Democratic policies, high taxes, high regulation. And this year, in 2015, New Jersey had the best year of job growth that our state has ever had in the last fifteen years. That's because we've put conservative policies in place."

That's a pretty fast pivot from "that bad outcome isn't my fault" to "and let me tell you the good outcome I can take credit for."

I described this pattern during an address at a meeting of the International Academy of Trial Lawyers (IATL). One lawyer in the audience rushed to tell me after the speech about a senior partner he trained under when he was first out of law school. "You won't believe how on-point this is, Annie. I assisted this partner at several trials and at the end of each day, he would analyze the witness testimony the same way. If the witness helped our case, he would say, 'You see how well I prepared that witness? When you know how to prepare a witness, you get the results you want.' If the witness hurt our case, he would tell me, 'That guy refused to listen to me.' It never varied."

I'm betting any parent of a school-aged child knows this. On occasions when my kids have done poorly on a test, it seems to have never been because they didn't study. "The teacher doesn't like me. Everybody did poorly. The teacher put material on the test we didn't cover in class. You can ask anyone!"

Self-serving bias is a deeply embedded and robust thinking pattern. Understanding why this pattern emerges is the first step to developing practical strategies to improve our ability to learn from experience. These strategies encourage us to be more ratio-nal in the way we field outcomes, fostering open-mindedness in considering all the possible causes of an outcome, not just the ones that flatter us.

All-or-nothing thinking rears its head again

Black-and-white thinking, uncolored by the reality of uncer-tainty, is a driver of both motivated reasoning and self-serving bias. If our only options are being 100% right or 100% wrong, with nothing in between, then information that potentially con-tradicts a belief requires a total downgrade, from right all the way to wrong. There is no "somewhat less sure" option in an all-or-nothing world, so we ignore or discredit the information to hold steadfast in our belief.

Both of these biases cause us to see our outcomes through the equivalent of a funhouse mirror. The reflection distorts real-ity, maximizing the appearance of our skill in good outcomes. For bad outcomes, it makes skill all but disappear, while luck looms giant.

Just as with motivated reasoning, self-serving bias arises from our drive to create a positive self-narrative. In that narra-tive, taking credit for something good is the same as saying we made the right decision. And being right feels good. Likewise, thinking that something bad was our fault means we made a wrong decision, and being wrong feels bad. When our self-image is at stake, we treat our fielding decisions as 100% or 0%: right versus wrong, skill versus luck, our responsibility versus outside our control. There are no shades of grey.

Fielding outcomes with the goal of promoting our self-narrative and doing it in an all-or-nothing fashion alters our ability to make smart bets about why the future unfolded in a particular way. Learning from experience is difficult—and sometimes impossible—with this kind of biased, broad-brush thinking. Outcomes are rarely the result of our decision quality alone or chance alone, and outcome quality is not a perfect indicator of the influence of luck or skill. When it comes to self-serving bias, we act as if our good outcomes are perfectly correlated to good skill and our bad outcomes are perfectly correlated to bad luck.* Whether it is a poker hand, an auto accident, a football call, a trial outcome, or a business success, there are elements of luck and skill in virtually any outcome.

That the motivation to update our self-image in a positive way underlies self-serving bias gives us an idea of where we might look for solutions to overcome the bias. Maybe we could stop clinging to ego, giving up on that need to have a positive narrative of our lives. Maybe we could still drive a positive narrative

---

*This is a systematic bias, not a guarantee that we *always* grab credit or *always* deflect blame. There are some people, to be sure, who exhibit the opposite of self-serving bias, treating everything bad that happens as their fault and attributing anything good in their lives to luck. That pattern is much rarer (and more likely in women). Several sources in the Selected Bibliography and Recommendations for Further Reading describe these aspects of self-serving bias. James Shepperd and colleagues, in particular, surveyed the literature in *Social and Personality Psychology Compass* for the motivations and explanations behind self-serving bias. Their survey includes research on self-serving bias in women. In addition to being a potential symptom of depression, that pattern isn't any better because it is equally inaccurate. All bad things can't be your fault and all good things can't be due to luck, just as the reverse can't be true. If we can't find a way to value accuracy in fielding outcomes, we are going to throw away a lot of learning opportunities regardless of which kind of error we make.

but, instead of updating through credit and blame, we could get off on striving to be more objective and open-minded in assessing the influence of luck and skill on our outcomes. Maybe we could put in the time and hard work to retrain the way we process results, moving toward getting our positive self-image updates from accurate fielding, from truthseeking.

Or maybe we could detour around the obstacles altogether by finding a work-around that doesn't require us to address self-serving bias at all.

People watching

One could conceivably argue that maybe self-serving bias isn't such a big deal because we can learn from other people's experience. Maybe the solution that has evolved is to compensate for the obstacles in learning from our own experience by watching other people do stuff. There are more than seven billion other people on the planet who do stuff all the time. As Yogi Berra said, "You can observe a lot by watching."

Watching is an established learning method. There is an entire industry devoted to collecting other people's outcomes. When you read the *Harvard Business Review* or any kind of business or management case study, you're trying to learn from others. An important element of medical education is watching doctors perform medical procedures or other caregivers do their jobs up close. They watch, then they assist . . . and then, hopefully, they've learned. Who would want a surgeon who says, "This will be the first time I've seen inside a live human body"?

It's possible we could follow that example, going to school on the experiences of the people around us.

In poker, the bulk of what goes on is watching. An experienced player will choose to play only about 20% of the hands they are dealt, forfeiting the other 80% of the hands before even getting past the first round of betting. That means about 80% of the time is spent just watching other people play. Even if a poker player doesn't learn all that efficiently from the outcomes of the hands they play themselves, there is still a whole lot to be learned from watching what happens to the other players in the game. After all, there is four times as much watching everyone else as there is playing a hand yourself.

Not only are all those other people's outcomes plentiful, they are also *free* (aside from any ante). When a poker player chooses to play a hand, they are putting their own money at risk. When a poker player is just watching the game, they get to sit back while other people put money at risk. That's an opportunity to learn at no extra cost.

When any of us makes decisions in life away from the poker table, we always have something at risk: money, time, health, happiness, etc. When it's someone else's decision, we don't have to pay to learn. They do. There's a lot of free information out there.

Unfortunately, learning from watching others is just as fraught with bias. Just as there is a pattern in the way we field our own outcomes, we field the outcomes of our peers predictably. We use the same black-and-white thinking as with our own outcomes, but now we flip the script. Where we blame our own bad outcomes on bad luck, when it comes to our peers, bad outcomes are clearly their fault. While our own good outcomes are due to our awesome decision-making, when it comes to other people, good outcomes are because they got lucky. As artist and writer Jean Cocteau said, "We must believe in luck. For how else can we explain the success of those we don't like?"

When it comes to watching the bad outcomes of other people, we load the blame on them, quickly and heavily. One of the most famous moments in baseball history, in which 40,000 people at a baseball stadium and tens of millions around the world instantly blamed an otherwise typical fan for keeping the Chicago Cubs out of the World Series, demonstrates this. The incident is known as the Bartman play.

In 2003, the Chicago Cubs were one game from reaching their first World Series since 1945. They led three games to two in the series against the Florida Marlins, and led Game Six with one out in the top of the eighth inning. A Marlins hitter lifted a foul fly toward the left-field stands. At the base of the sloping wall separating spectators from the field, Cubs left fielder Moises Alou reached his glove over his head for the ball as several spectators on the other side of the wall also reached for it. One of the 40,000 spectators at Wrigley Field, Steve Bartman, deflected the ball, which then bounced off the railing, landing at the feet of another spectator. Alou stormed away, expressing anger at the fan who kept him from attempting to catch the ball.

The Cubs had a 3–0 lead at the time Bartman, those folks near him, and Moises Alou reached for the foul ball. Had Alou caught it, the Cubs would have been four outs from reaching the World Series. Here's how the future unfolded after Bartman touched the ball: The Cubs lost the game, and Game Seven too, failing again to reach the World Series. Bartman got the blame, first from the 40,000 people present (who pointed and chanted "A**hole!," threw beer and garbage at him, and yelled death threats), then from the

millions of Cubs fans, not just on sports and news shows replay-
ing the incident at the time but for more than a decade. One person who actually assaulted Bartman while he was surrounded by
stadium security said, "I wanted to expose him for ruining what
could have been a once-in-a-lifetime experience."

Steve Bartman had a bad outcome. He reached for the ball,
and the Cubs eventually lost. Was that due to his bad decision-
making or bad luck? To be sure, he made the decision to reach
for the ball, so there was some skill in that. He also, however, had
an overwhelming amount of bad luck. Almost uniformly, people
discounted that bad luck, blaming Bartman for the loss of that
game and the series itself.

Alex Gibney's ESPN documentary on the Bartman play,
Catching Hell, displays the double standard, showing the replay
from numerous angles and interviewing spectators and members
of the media from the scene. Gibney noted (and the footage
clearly showed), "There are a lot of people who went for that ball."
One fan, who lunged right next to Bartman for the ball, couldn't
deny that he had reached for the ball, the same as Bartman. "I
went for the ball. There's no way . . . I obviously went for the ball."
Yet, he tried to claim that, unlike Bartman, he never would have
interfered with the play: "Once I saw [Moises Alou's] glove, I had
no interest in the ball." That fan, at once, took credit for his good
outcome in not having touched the ball and placed blame squarely
on Bartman's decision-making rather than bad luck.

While everybody in the vicinity behaved the same way,
Bartman was the unlucky one who touched the baseball. But the
fans didn't see it as bad luck. They saw it as his fault. Worse yet,
none of the subsequent things that happened in the game—all
clearly outside Bartman's control—mitigated his responsibility.
Remember that after that ball landed in the stands, the Cubs

were in the same position they were in before the Bartman play. They still had the Marlins down to their last five outs, with a 3–0 lead in the game, their ace pitcher hurling a shutout, and a 3–2 lead in a best-of-seven series. That batter who hit the foul ball was still at the plate, with a 3–2 count. The Marlins went on to score *eight runs* in the inning, seven of them after (two batters later) the Cubs shortstop, Alex Gonzalez, bobbled an inning-ending double-play ball for an error.

Bartman had a lot of bad luck to end up with that result, much of which had to do with the play of the team, over which Bartman clearly had no control. The fans, nevertheless, laid all the blame on Bartman rather than on, say, Gonzalez. Nearby fans yelled, "Rot in hell! Everyone in Chicago hates you! You suck!" As he walked through the concourse, people yelled, "We're gonna kill you! Go to prison!" "Put a twelve-gauge in his mouth and pull the trigger!"

It would be nice if a story line developed that gave Steve Bartman credit for the Cubs winning the World Series in 2016. After all, Steve Bartman was a key player in the chain of events responsible for a moribund franchise hiring baseball-turnaround specialist Theo Epstein as president of baseball operations and Joe Maddon as manager. Not surprisingly, that narrative hasn't gotten any traction.*

---

*The Cubs had an outstanding season in 2015 and won the World Series in 2016. Since the day after the 2003 incident, Bartman had refused all opportunities to comment or become part of the subsequent story—that is until August 2017, when the Cubs offered and Bartman accepted a World Series ring. Bartman used the opportunity to issue a statement about how we treat each other. NPR.org quoted part of his statement: "'Although I do not consider myself worthy of such an honor,' Steve Bartman said in a statement, 'I am deeply moved and sincerely grateful . . . I humbly receive the ring not only as a symbol of one of the most

We see this pattern of blaming others for bad outcomes and failing to give them credit for good ones all over the place. When someone else at work gets a promotion instead of us, do we admit they worked harder than and deserved it more than we did? No, it was because they schmoozed the boss. If someone does better on a test at school, it was because the teacher likes them more. If someone explains the circumstances of a car accident and how it wasn't their fault, we roll our eyes. We assume the cause was their bad driving.

When I started in poker, I followed the same pattern (and still fight the urge in every area of my life to this day). Even though I was quick to take credit for my own successes and blame bad luck for my losses, I flipped this when evaluating other players. I didn't give other players enough credit for winning (or, viewed another way, give other players credit for my losing) and I was quick to blame their losses on their poor play.

When I first started, my brother gave me a list of cards that were good to play, written on a napkin while we were eating in a coffee shop at Binion's Horseshoe Casino. I clutched this napkin like I was Moses clutching the Ten Commandments. When I saw people win with hands that were not on my brother's list, I dismissed it as good luck since they clearly did not know how to play. I was so closed-minded to the thought that they might deserve credit for winning that I didn't even bother to describe these hands to my brother to ask him if there might be a good reason they would play a hand off the list.

As my understanding of the game grew over time, I realized the hands on that list weren't the only hands you could ever play.

historic achievements in sports, but as an important reminder for how we should treat each other in today's society.'"

For one thing, only playing hands on the list meant you would never bluff. My brother gave me that list to keep me, a total novice, out of trouble. He gave me that list because the hands he was telling me to play would limit the mistakes a total beginner might make. I didn't know that, depending on all sorts of factors, sometimes there are hands that wouldn't be on the list that would be perfectly okay to play.

Even though I had access to the list writer, I never asked my brother why these guys were playing these off-list cards. My biased assessment of why they were winning slowed my learning down considerably. I missed out on a lot of opportunities to make money because I dismissed other players as lucky when I might have been learning from watching them. To be sure, some of those people shouldn't have been playing those hands and were actually playing poorly. But, as I figured out almost a year into playing, not all of them.

The systematic errors in the way we field the outcomes of our peers comes at a real cost. It doesn't just come at the cost of reaching our goals but also at the cost of compassion for others.

Other people's outcomes reflect on us

We all want to feel good about ourselves in the moment, even if it's at the expense of our long-term goals. Just as with motivated reasoning and self-serving bias, blaming others for their bad results and failing to give them credit for their good ones is under the influence of ego. Taking credit for a win lifts our personal narrative. So too does knocking down a peer by finding them at fault for a loss. That's schadenfreude: deriving pleasure from someone else's misfortune. Schadenfreude is basically the opposite of compassion.

Ideally, our happiness would depend on how things turn out for us regardless of how things turn out for anyone else. Yet, on a fundamental level, fielding someone's bad outcome as their fault feels good to us. On a fundamental level, fielding someone's good outcome as luck helps our narrative along.

This outcome fielding follows a logical pattern in zero-sum games like poker. When I am competing head-to-head in a poker hand, I *must* follow this fielding pattern to square my self-serving interpretation of my own outcomes with the outcomes of my opponent. If I win a hand in poker, my opponent loses. If I lose a hand in poker, my opponent wins. Wins and losses are symmetrical. If I field my win as having to do with my skillful play, then my opponent in the hand must have lost because of their less skillful play. Likewise, if I field my loss as having to do with luck, then my opponent must have won due to luck as well. Any other interpretation would create cognitive dissonance.

Thinking about it this way, we see that the way we field other people's outcomes is just part of self-serving bias. Viewed through this lens, the pattern begins to make sense.

But this comparison of our results to others isn't confined to zero-sum games where one player directly loses to the other (or where one lawyer loses to opposing counsel, or where one salesperson loses a sale to a competitor, etc.). We are really in competition for resources with everyone. Our genes are competitive. As Richard Dawkins points out, natural selection proceeds by competition among the phenotypes of genes so we literally evolved to compete, a drive that allowed our species to survive. Engaging the world through the lens of competition is deeply embedded in our animal brains. It's not enough to boost our self-image solely by our own successes. If someone we view as a peer is winning, we feel like we're losing by comparison. We benchmark ourselves to them. If their kids are doing better in school than ours, what are we doing wrong with our kids? If their company is in the news because it is about to go public, what's wrong with us that we're just inching forward in our work?

We think we know the ingredients for happiness. Sonja Lyubomirsky, a psychology professor at the University of California, Riverside, and popular author on the subject of happiness, summarized several reviews of the literature on the elements we commonly consider: "a comfortable income, robust health, a supportive marriage, and lack of tragedy or trauma." Lyubomirsky noted, however, that "the general conclusion from almost a century of research on the determinants of well-being is that objective circumstances, demographic variables, and life events are correlated with happiness less strongly than intuition and everyday experience tell us they ought to be. By several estimates, all of these variables put together account for no more than 8% to 15% of the variance in happiness." What accounts for most of the variance in happiness is how we're doing *comparatively*. (The breadth and depth of all that research on happiness and its implications is important, but it's beyond what we need to understand our issue with sorting others' outcomes. I encourage you to read Lyubomirsky's work on the subject, Daniel Gilbert's *Stumbling on Happiness*, and Jonathan Haidt's *The Happiness Hypothesis*, cited in the Selected Bibliography and Recommendations for Further Reading.)

A consistent example of how we price our own happiness relative to others comes from a version of the party game "Would You Rather . . . ?" When you ask people if they would rather earn $70,000 in 1900 or $70,000 now, a significant number choose

1900. True, the average yearly income in 1900 was about $450. So we'd be doing phenomenally well compared to our peers from 1900. But no amount of money in 1900 could buy Novocain or antibiotics or a refrigerator or air-conditioning or a powerful computer we could hold in one hand. About the only thing $70,000 bought in 1900 that it couldn't buy today was the opportunity to soar above most everyone else. We'd rather lap the field in 1900 with an average life expectancy of only forty-seven years than sit in the middle of the pack now with an average life expectancy of over seventy-six years (and a computer in our palm).

A lot of the way we feel about ourselves comes from how we think we compare with others. This robust and pervasive habit of mind impedes learning. Luckily, habits can be changed, whether the habit is biting your nails or decrying your terrible luck when you lose. By shifting what it is that makes us feel good about ourselves, we can move toward a more rational fielding of outcomes and a more compassionate view of others. We can learn better and be more open-minded if we work toward a positive narrative driven by engagement in truthseeking and striving toward accuracy and objectivity: giving others credit when it's due, admitting when our decisions could have been better, and acknowledging that almost nothing is black and white.

Reshaping habit

Phil Ivey is one of those guys who can easily admit when he could have done better. Ivey is one of the world's best poker players, a player almost universally admired by other professional poker players for his exceptional skill and confidence in his game. Starting in his early twenties, he built a reputation as a top cash-game player, a top tournament player, a top heads-up player, a top mixed-game player—a top player in every form and format of poker. In a profession where, as I've explained, most people are awash in self-serving bias, Phil Ivey is an exception.

In 2004, my brother provided televised final-table commentary for a tournament in which Phil Ivey smoked a star-studded final table. After his win, the two of them went to a restaurant for dinner, during which Ivey deconstructed every potential playing error he thought he might have made on the way to victory, asking my brother's opinion about each strategic decision. A more run-of-the-mill player might have spent the time talking about how great they played, relishing the victory. Not Ivey. For him, the opportunity to learn from his mistakes was much more important than treating that dinner as a self-satisfying celebration. He earned a half-million dollars and won a lengthy poker tournament over world-class competition, but all he wanted to do was discuss with a fellow pro where he might have made better decisions.

I heard an identical story secondhand about Ivey at another otherwise celebratory dinner following one of his now ten World Series of Poker victories. Again, from what I understand, he spent the evening discussing in intricate detail with some other pros the points in hands where he could have made better decisions. Phil Ivey, clearly, has different habits than most poker players—and most people in any endeavor—in how he fields his outcomes.

Habits operate in a neurological loop consisting of three parts: the cue, the routine, and the reward. A habit could involve eating cookies: the cue might be hunger, the routine going to the pantry and grabbing a cookie, and the reward a sugar high. Or, in poker, the cue might be winning a hand, the routine taking credit for it, the reward a boost to our ego. Charles Duhigg, in *The Power of*

Habit, offers the golden rule of habit change—that the best way to deal with a habit is to respect the habit loop: "To change a habit, you must keep the old cue, and deliver the old reward, but insert a new routine."

When we have a good outcome, it cues the routine of crediting the result to our awesome decision-making, delivering the reward of a positive update to our self-narrative. A bad outcome cues the routine of off-loading responsibility for the result, delivering the reward of avoiding a negative self-narrative update. With the same cues, we flip the routine for the outcomes of peers, but the reward is the same—feeling good about ourselves.

The good news is that we can work to change this habit of mind by substituting what makes us feel good. The golden rule of habit change says we don't have to give up the reward of a positive update to our narrative, nor should we. Duhigg recognizes that respecting the habit loop means respecting the way our brain is built.

Our brain is built to seek positive self-image updates. It is also built to view ourselves in competition with our peers. We can't install new hardware. Working with the way our brains are built in reshaping habit has a higher chance of success than working against it. Better to change the part that is more plastic: the routine of what gives us the good feeling in our narrative and the features by which we compare ourselves to others.

At least as far back as Pavlov, behavioral researchers* have recognized the power of substitution in physiological loops. In his famous experiments, his colleague noticed that dogs salivated

---

*Ivan Pavlov's work was so revolutionary that "behavioral research" as we commonly understand it didn't even exist. Pavlov was a physician and physiologist, researching the canine digestive system.

when they were about to be fed. Because they associated a particular technician with food, the presence of the technician triggered the dogs' salivation response. Pavlov discovered the dogs could learn to associate just about any stimulus with food, including his famous bell, triggering the salivary response.

We can work to change the bell we ring, substituting what makes us salivate. We can work to get the reward of feeling good about ourselves from being a good credit-giver, a good mistake-admitter, a good finder-of-mistakes-in-good-outcomes, a good learner, and (as a result) a good decision-maker. Instead of feeling bad when we have to admit a mistake, what if the bad feeling came from the thought that we might be missing a learning opportunity just to avoid blame? Or that we might be basking in the credit of a good result instead of, like Phil Ivey, recognizing where we could have done better? If we work toward that, we can transform the unproductive habits of mind of self-serving bias and motivated reasoning into productive ones. If we put in the work to practice this routine, we can field more of our outcomes in an open-minded, more objective way, motivated by accuracy and truthseeking to drive learning. The habit of mind will change, and our decision-making will better align with executing on our long-term goals.

There are people who, like Phil Ivey, have substituted the routine of truthseeking for the outcome-oriented instinct to focus on seeking credit and avoiding blame. When we look at the people performing at the highest level of their chosen field, we find that the self-serving bias that interferes with learning often recedes and even disappears. The people with the most legitimate claim to a bulletproof self-narrative have developed habits around accurate self-critique.

In sports, the athletes at the top of the game look at outcomes to spur further improvement. American soccer great Mia Hamm said, "Many people say I'm the best women's soccer player in the world. I don't think so. And because of that, someday I just might be." Such quotes can be discounted as a polite way of dealing with the media. There are plenty of contrary examples burned in our consciousness, like John McEnroe arguing line calls or golf pros who have turned missed putts into a ritual of staring at the offending line of the putt and tapping down phantom spike marks. Those aren't anything more than performance tics. It's practically a ritual on the PGA Tour that if a player misses a makeable putt, he has to stare at the green like it was somehow at fault. What you don't see are practice rituals like Phil Mickelson's, in which he places ten balls in a circle, three feet from the hole. He has to sink all ten, and then repeat the process *nine more times.* Players of Phil Mickelson's caliber couldn't engage in such a demanding regimen if they actually assigned much blame to spike marks.

Changing the routine is hard and takes work. But we can leverage our natural tendency to derive some of our self-esteem by how we compare to our peers. Just as Duhigg recommends respecting the habit loop, we can also respect that we are built for competition, and that our self-narrative doesn't exist in a vacuum. Keep the reward of feeling like we are doing well compared to our peers, but change the features by which we compare ourselves: be a better credit-giver than your peers, more willing than others to admit mistakes, more willing to explore possible reasons for an outcome with an open mind, even, and especially, if that might cast you in a bad light or shine a good light on someone else. In this way we can feel that we are doing well by comparison because we are doing something unusual and hard that most people don't do. That makes us feel exceptional.

Once we start listening for it, we hear a chorus out in the

world like I heard during breaks in poker tournaments: "things are going great because I'm making such good decisions"; "things went poorly because I got so unlucky." That's what the lawyer heard from his senior partner in each evening's postmortem of the trial. That's what we heard from Chris Christie in the 2016 Republican presidential debate. That's what I heard in every poker room I was ever in. There were times, and there still are, when I'm part of that chorus. Increasingly, though, I've learned to use that chorus to avoid self-serving bias rather than giving in to it. When I admitted mistakes, when I recognized the luck element in my successes, when I gave other players credit for making some good decisions, when I was eager to share a hand that I thought I played poorly because I might learn something from it, that chorus reminded me that what I was doing was hard, and that others weren't often doing it. Identifying learning opportunities that other players were missing made me feel good about myself, reinforcing my routine change.

Ideally, we wouldn't compare ourselves with others or get a good feeling when the comparison favors us. We might adopt the mindful practices of Buddhist monks, observing the flow of inner thoughts, emotions, and bodily sensations without judging them as good or bad at all. That's a great goal, and I'm all for a regular mindful practice. It will, the research indicates, help improve quality of life and is worth pursuing. But getting all the way there is a tall order if we don't want to quit our day jobs and move to Tibet. It works against the way our brains evolved, against our competitive drive. As a parallel practice, the more practical and immediate solution is to work with what we've got, using that comparison to strengthen our focus on accuracy and truthseeking. Plus, we won't have to give up our lives and find a remote mountaintop to live on.

We need a mindset shift. We need a plan to develop a more productive habit of mind. That starts in deliberative mind and requires foresight and practice, but if it takes hold, it can become an established habit, running automatically and changing the way we reflexively think.

We can get to this mindset shift by behaving as if we have something at risk when we sort outcomes into the luck and skill buckets, because we do *have a lot at risk* on that fielding decision. Thinking in bets is a smart way to start building habits that achieve our long-term goals.

"Wanna bet?" redux

Treating outcome fielding as a bet can accomplish the mindset shift necessary to reshape habit. If someone challenged us to a meaningful bet on how we fielded an outcome, we would find ourselves quickly moving beyond self-serving bias. If we wanted to win that bet, we wouldn't reflexively field bad outcomes as all luck or good ones as all skill. (If you walked into a poker room and threw around words like "always" and "never," you'd soon find yourself challenged to a bunch of bets. It's easy to win a bet against someone who takes extreme positions.)

Imagine getting into an accident at an intersection after losing control of your car on a patch of ice you couldn't see. Your first thought would likely be that you got unlucky. But what if you had to bet on that? Depending on the details, there would be a lot of alternatives to just plain bad luck you would now consider. Based on the weather, maybe you could have anticipated some ice on the road. Maybe you were driving too fast for the weather conditions. Once the car started sliding, maybe you could have steered differently or maybe you pumped the brakes when you shouldn't have. Maybe you could have taken a safer route, choosing a main road that would have been salted. Maybe you should have kept the Mustang in the garage and taken the Suburban.

Some of the reasons we come up with may be easy to discount. And some may not. The key is that in explicitly recognizing that the way we field an outcome is a bet, we consider a greater number of alternative causes more seriously than we otherwise would have. That is truthseeking. This is what Phil Ivey does.

The prospect of a bet makes us examine and refine our beliefs, in this case the belief about whether luck or skill was the main influence in the way things turned out. Betting on what we believe makes us take a closer look by making explicit what is already implicit: we have a great deal at risk in assessing why anything turned out the way it did. That sure sounds like a bet worth taking seriously.

When we treat outcome fielding as a bet, it pushes us to field outcomes more objectively into the appropriate buckets because that is how bets are won. Winning feels good. Winning is a positive update to our personal narrative. Winning is a reward. With enough practice, reinforced by the reward of feeling good about ourselves, thinking of fielding outcomes as bets will become a habit of mind.

Thinking in bets triggers a more open-minded exploration of alternative hypotheses, of reasons supporting conclusions *opposite* to the routine of self-serving bias. We are more likely to explore the opposite side of an argument more often and more seriously—and that will move us closer to the truth of the matter.

Thinking in bets also triggers perspective taking, leveraging the difference between how we field our own outcomes versus others' outcomes to get closer to the objective truth. We know we tend to discount the success of our peers and place responsibility firmly on their shoulders for their failures. A good strategy for figuring out which way to bet would be to imagine if that outcome had happened to us. If a competitor closes a big sale, we know about our tendency to discount their skill. But if we imagine that we had been the one who closed the sale, we are more likely to find the things to give them credit for, that they did well and that we can learn from. Likewise, when we close the big sale, let's spare a little of the self-congratulations and, instead, examine that great result the way we'd examine it if it happened to someone else. We'll be more likely to find the things we could have done even better and identify those factors that we had no control over. Perspective taking gets us closer to the truth because that truth generally lies in the middle of the way we field outcomes for ourselves and the way we field them for others. By taking someone else's perspective, we are more likely to land in that middle ground.

Once we start actively training ourselves in testing alternative hypotheses and perspective taking, it becomes clear that outcomes are rarely 100% luck or 100% skill. This means that when new information comes in, we have options beyond unquestioned confirmation or reversal. We can modify our beliefs along a spectrum because we know it *is* a spectrum, not a choice between opposites without middle ground.

This makes us more compassionate, both toward ourselves and others. Treating outcome fielding as bets constantly reminds us outcomes are rarely attributable to a single cause and there is almost always uncertainty in figuring out the various causes. Identifying a negative outcome doesn't have the same personal sting if you turn it into a positive by finding things to learn from it. You don't have to be on the defensive side of every negative outcome because you can recognize, in addition to things you can improve, things you did well and things outside your control. You realize that not knowing is okay.

Certainly, in exchange for losing the fear of taking blame for bad outcomes, you also lose the unadulterated high of claiming good outcomes were 100% skill. That's a trade you should take. Remember, losing feels about twice as bad as winning feels good; being wrong feels about twice as bad as being right feels good. We are in a better place when we don't have to live at the edges. Euphoria or misery, with no choices in between, is not a very self-compassionate way to live.

You also become more compassionate toward other people when you treat fielding outcomes as bets. When you look at the outcomes of others from their perspective, you have to ask yourself, "What if that had happened to me?" You come up with more compassionate assessments of other people where bad things aren't always their fault and good things aren't always luck. You are more likely to walk in their shoes. Imagine how Bartman's life would have changed if more people worked to think this way.

The hard way

Thinking in bets is hard, especially initially. It has to start as a deliberative process, and will feel clunky, weird, and slow. Certainly, there will be times it doesn't make sense. Like if you don't get a promotion at work, you're probably going to wonder how you're supposed to feel better acknowledging that so-and-so was more deserving and that you could learn a lot from them. It takes work to avoid the temptation to blame it on the boss being a jerk who doesn't know how to evaluate talent.

That feeling is natural. I built my poker career out of these principles of learning and truthseeking, yet I still catch myself falling into the self-serving bias and motivated reasoning traps. Duhigg tells us that reshaping a habit requires time, preparation, practice, and repetition.

Look at other kinds of habit changes. If I had a habit of getting out of bed at midnight to eat a cookie, it takes work as well as will to change that habit. I have to identify the habit I want to change, figure out the routine to substitute, and practice that routine in deliberative mind until the habit is reshaped. I would need to stock apples in the house, and keep them more readily available than cookies. Then I need to actually eat the apple at midnight instead of reaching for the cookie, repeating this routine until it becomes a new habit. That takes work and willpower and time.

Despite the difficulties, striving for accuracy through probabilistic thinking is a worthwhile routine to pursue. For one thing, it won't always be so difficult. We have to start doing this with deliberation and effort, but it eventually becomes a habit of mind. Just like declaring uncertainty in your beliefs, it eventually goes from a somewhat goofy and awkward extra step to a habit integral to how you view the world around you.

To be sure, thinking in bets is not a miracle cure. Thinking in bets won't make self-serving bias disappear or motivated reasoning vanish into thin air. But it will make those things better. And a little bit better is all we need to transform our lives. If we field just a few extra outcomes more accurately, if we catch just a few extra learning opportunities, it will make a huge difference in what we learn, when we learn, and how much we learn.

Poker's compressed version of real-world decision-making showed me how being a little better at decision-making could make a big difference. A poker game can consist of a few hundred hands. Every hand can require up to twenty decisions. If, over the course of a game, there were a hundred outcomes that provided learning opportunities and we caught ten of them, we would still be missing 90% of our chances to learn. We wouldn't have transcended the way our brains function and built ourselves a different brain, but we don't need to. If our opponents are people like Nick the Greek, they are missing almost every learning opportunity. We're obviously going to do better than they do just catching 10%. If another of our opponents is someone just like us, but who isn't working to transform their outcome-processing routines, maybe they (this prior version of ourselves) will pick up five opportunities. Again, we are missing 90%, and we are still going to clean up on an opponent who is trying to learn but doesn't know how.*

The benefits of recognizing just a few extra learning opportunities compound over time. The cumulative effect of being a little better at decision-making, like compounding interest, can have huge effects in the long run on everything that we do. When we catch that extra occasional learning opportunity, it puts us in a better position for future opportunities of the same type. Any improvement in our decision quality puts us in a better position in the future. Think of it like a ship sailing from New

---

*These numbers are obviously made up but are at least a decent approximation in reality. If the worst poker player in the world finds 0 of 100 learning opportunities, the best poker player in the world is nowhere near 100 for 100. Remember, Phil Ivey (who has earned over $26 million in tournament poker and potentially a much higher figure in high-stakes cash games) still obsesses over mistakes he made in some of his biggest triumphs.

York to London. If the ship's navigator introduces a one-degree navigation error, it would start off as barely noticeable. Unchecked, however, the ship would veer farther and farther off course and would miss London by miles, as that one-degree miscalculation compounds mile over mile. Thinking in bets corrects your course. And even a small correction will get you more safely to your destination.

The first step is identifying the habit of mind that we want to reshape and how to reshape it. That first step is hard and takes time and effort and a lot of missteps along the way. So the second step is recognizing that it is easier to make these changes if we aren't alone in the process. Recruiting help is key to creating faster and more robust change, strengthening and training our new truthseeking routines.

CHAPTER 4

The Buddy System

"Maybe you're the problem, do you think!"

When Lauren Conrad, star of MTV's *The Hills*, appeared on the *Late Show with David Letterman* in October 2008, her interview took an unexpected turn. The first minute was standard talk-show banter for a twenty-two-year-old star of a successful reality series: the amount of drama in her life. Less than a minute later, Conrad asked Letterman if he was calling her an idiot.

She started off the interview by discussing her ongoing feud with her by-then-former roommate Heidi Montag and Heidi's boyfriend Spencer Pratt. In case you're not familiar, here is the backstory: Lauren and Heidi's friendship ended when they came to blows at a birthday party after Lauren accused Heidi and Spencer of starting rumors that she had made a sex tape. In addition, Lauren developed friendships with Stephanie (Spencer's sister) and Holly (Heidi's sister), complicating the social and family encounters of everyone involved. Lauren tried without success to strengthen the relationship between her roommates, Audrina and Lo. This strained Lauren's friendship with Audrina, who reestablished her friendship with Heidi. Brody Jenner was also in the mix, dating Lauren, questioning her date with a *Teen Vogue* model, dating someone else himself, arguing with Spencer about his friendship with Lauren, getting accused of starting the rumors about Lauren's sex tape, etc.

All of that drama happening in Conrad's life is what David Letterman was referring to when he interjected, "That raises the question, maybe you're the problem, do you think?" That quip sent an interview that was supposed to be a puffy, promotional chat into an uncomfortable tailspin.

Letterman immediately realized that he had taken the conversation into much deeper, more serious territory than either of them could have anticipated. He tried to soften the blow in a self-deprecating way, adding that he had done the same thing, for years refusing to close the learning loop by assuming everybody around him was an idiot.

"Let me give you an example from my own life. . . . For a long time . . . I thought, 'Geez, people are idiots.' Then it occurred to me, 'Is it possible that everybody's an idiot? Maybe I'm the idiot,' and it turns out I am."

Conrad clearly didn't want to hear it, replying, "Does that make me an idiot, then?" Websites devoted to reality TV, gossip, media, and popular culture immortalized the moment, and that's how they saw it: Letterman "basically calls Conrad an idiot" (Gawker.com), "ripped into" Conrad (Trendhunter.com), "makes fun of Lauren Conrad" (Starpulse.com).

Letterman's comment was actually quite perceptive. His mistake was offering up the insight in an inappropriate forum to someone who hadn't agreed to that kind of truthseeking exchange.

Conrad certainly had a lot of drama in her life: enough that

MTV created *two* successive shows to document it. But, like most people do, she characterized the drama as a series of things happening *to* her. In other words, the drama was outside her control (luck). Letterman suggested some of it could be fielded into the skill bucket, a suggestion that might have been helpful to Conrad in the future if she had been receptive to it. Not surprisingly, she wasn't.

Letterman had offered the helpful alternative hypothesis, unexpectedly, on a late-night talk show where the norm is fluff and PR. Perhaps Letterman's approach would have been more appropriate in an Oprah Winfrey–style prime-time interview. Or on one of those reality therapy shows where reality stars agree to such an exchange. As it was, he violated the assumed social contract by challenging Conrad to bet on her outcome fielding when she hadn't agreed to truthseek with him.

That exchange was similar to my interaction at the poker tournament with the six-seven of diamonds guy. I thought he was asking for my advice, so I responded by asking for more information to get an idea of whether he accurately fielded his losing outcome as luck. He was expecting me to adhere to the norm of being a sympathetic ear for a hard-luck story. When I attempted to delve into the details, I violated this implied contract. I Lettermanned him.

Such interactions are reminders that not all situations are appropriate for truthseeking, nor are all people interested in the pursuit. That being said, any of us who wants to get better at thinking in bets would benefit from having more David Lettermans in our lives. As the "original" Letterman learned from the awkward exchange with Lauren Conrad, Lettermanning needs agreement by both parties to be effective.

The red pill or the blue pill?

In the classic science-fiction film *The Matrix*, when Neo (played by Keanu Reeves) meets Morpheus (the hero-hacker played by Laurence Fishburne), Neo asks Morpheus to tell him what "the matrix" is. Morpheus offers to show Neo, giving him the choice between taking a blue pill and a red pill.

"You take the blue pill, the story ends. You wake up in your bed and believe whatever you want to believe. You take the red pill, you stay in Wonderland and I show you how deep the rabbit hole goes."

As Neo reaches toward a pill, Morpheus reminds him, "Remember, all I am offering is the truth. Nothing more."

Neo chooses to see the world as it really is. He takes the red pill and is pounded with a series of devastating truths. His comfortable world is a dream created by machines to enslave him as an energy source. His job and lifestyle, his clothes, his appearance, and the entire fabric of his life are an illusion implanted in his brain. In the actual world, taking the red pill causes his body to be unplugged from his feeding pod, flushed into a sewer, and picked up by Morpheus's pirate ship, the *Nebuchadnezzar*. As rebels against the machines, Morpheus and his crew (and now Neo, due to his choice) live in cramped quarters, sleep in uncomfortable cells, eat gruel, and wear rags. Machines are out to destroy them.

The trade-off is that Neo sees the world as it actually is and, in the end, gets to defeat the machines that have enslaved humanity.

In the movie, the matrix was built to be a more comfortable version of the world. Our brains, likewise, have evolved to make our version of the world more comfortable: our beliefs are nearly always correct; favorable outcomes are the result of our skill;

there are plausible reasons why unfavorable outcomes are beyond our control; and we compare favorably with our peers. We deny or at least dilute the most painful parts of the message.

Giving that up is not the easiest choice. Living in the matrix is comfortable. So is the natural way we process information to protect our self-image in the moment. By choosing to exit the matrix, we are asserting that striving for a more objective representation of the world, even if it is uncomfortable at times, will make us happier and more successful in the long run.

But it's a trade-off that isn't for everyone; it must be freely chosen to be productive and sustainable. Morpheus (unlike Letterman) didn't just go around ripping people out of the matrix against their will. He asked Neo to make the choice and exit the matrix with him.

If you have gotten this far in this book, I'm guessing that you are choosing the red pill over the blue pill.

When I started playing poker, I chose truthseeking. Like Neo, I did it reluctantly and wasn't sure what I was getting into. My brother took a blunt approach with me. My instinct was to complain about my bad luck and to marvel at how poorly others played, decrying the injustice of any hand I might have lost. He wanted to talk about where I had questions about my strategic decisions, where I felt I might have made mistakes, and where I was confused on what to do in a hand. I recognized he was passing along the approach he learned with his friends, a group of smart, analytical East Coast players, many of whom, like Erik Seidel,* were on their way to establishing themselves as legends

---

*Erik is one of the best and most respected poker players of all time. He has won (at this writing) eight World Series of Poker championship bracelets and over $34.5 million in tournament poker winnings. When I started playing in the World

at the game. In addition to introducing me to this approach, he also encouraged these phenomenal professionals to treat me as a peer when discussing poker.

I was lucky to have access at such an early stage in my career to this group of world-class players who became my learning pod in poker. And I was also lucky that if I wanted to engage that group about poker, I had to ask about my strategic decisions. I had to resist my urge to moan about my bad luck and focus instead on where I felt I might have made mistakes and where I was confused on what to do in a hand. Because I agreed to the group's rules of engagement, I had to learn to focus on the things I could control (my own decisions), let go of the things I couldn't (luck), and work to be able to accurately tell the difference between the two.

I learned from this experience that thinking in bets was easier if I had other people to help me. (Even Neo needed help to defeat the machines.) Remember the buddy system from school field trips or camp? Teachers or counselors would pair everybody up with a buddy. Our buddy was supposed to keep us from wandering off or getting into water too deep, and we did the same for our buddy. A good decision group is a grown-up version of the buddy system. To be sure, even with help, none of us will ever be able to perfectly overcome our natural biases in the way we process information; I certainly never have. But if we can find a few people to choose to form a truthseeking pod with us and help us do the hard work connected with it, it will move the needle—just a little bit, but with improvements that accumulate and compound over time. We will be more successful in fighting bias, seeing

---

Series at Binion's Horseshoe in the early nineties, he had already won events there three years running.

the world more objectively, and, as a result, we will make better decisions. Doing it on our own is just harder.

Members of our decision pod could be our friends, or members of our family, or an informal pod of coworkers, or an enterprise strategy group, or a professional organization where members can talk about their decision-making. Forming or joining a group where the focus is on thinking in bets means modifying the usual social contract. It means agreeing to be open-minded to those who disagree with us, giving credit where it's due, and taking responsibility where it's appropriate, even (and especially) when it makes us uncomfortable. That's why, when we do it with others, we need to make it clear the social contract is being modified, or feelings will get hurt, defensiveness will rear its ugly head, and, just like Lauren Conrad, your audience won't want to hear what you have to say. So, while we find some people to think in bets with us, with the rest of the world, it is generally better to observe the prevailing social contract and not go around saying, "Wanna bet?" willy-nilly. (That doesn't mean we can't ever engage in truthseeking outside of our group. Our approach just needs to be less head-on, less Letterman-like. More on that later, after we explore communications *within* the group.)

Out in the world, groups form all over the place because people recognize how others can help us; the concept of working together on our individual challenges is a familiar one. Having the help of others provides many decision-making benefits, but one of the most obvious is that other people can spot our errors better than we can. We can help others in our pod overcome their blind-spot bias and they can help us overcome the same.

Whatever the obstacles to recruiting people into a decision group (and this chapter points out several, along with strategies for overcoming them), it is worth it to get a buddy to watch your back—or your blind spot. The fortunate thing is that we need to find only a handful of people willing to do the exploratory thinking necessary for truthseeking. In fact, as long as there are three people in the group (two to disagree and one to referee*), the truthseeking group can be stable and productive.

It's also helpful to recognize that people serve different purposes in our lives. Even if we place a high value on truthseeking, that doesn't mean everyone in our lives has to adopt that or communicate with us in that way. Truthseeking isn't a cult; we don't have to cut off people who don't share that commitment. Our Pilates friends or our football friends or any of our friends shouldn't have to take the red pill to remain our friends. Different friends fill different needs and not all of them need to be cut from the same cloth. Those different groups can also provide much-needed balance in our lives. After all, it takes effort to acknowledge and explore our mistakes without feeling bad about ourselves, to forgo credit for a great result, and to realize, with an open mind, that not all our beliefs are true. Truthseeking flies in the face of a lot of comfortable behaviors; it's hard work and we need breaks to replenish our willpower.

In fact, in my poker strategy group, we understood the need to occasionally opt out and off-load intense emotions before engaging in the work of accurately fielding an outcome. If, for example, one of us just got eliminated from a tournament, it was acceptable, every once in a while, to say, "For right now, I just need to moan about my bad luck." The key was that when we did that, we recognized it was a temporary exception from the hard

---

*Thanks to Phil Tetlock for giving me that great turn of phrase.

work we were doing together and to which we would return when the emotional rawness of the moment passed.

We know our decision-making can improve if we find other people to join us in truthseeking. And we know we need an agreement. What's in that agreement? What are the features of a productive decision-making pod? The remainder of this chapter is devoted to offering answers to those questions. Chapter 5 builds on that by providing a blueprint for rules of engagement within truthseeking groups, how to keep the group from drifting off course, and the productive habits of mind the group can reinforce in each of us.

Not all groups are created equal

A well-chartered group can be particularly useful for habits that are difficult to break or change. This is not a crazy or even novel idea. We are all familiar with how the group approach can help with reshaping habits involving eating, consuming alcohol, and physical activity. The most well-known example of a productive group approach is Alcoholics Anonymous (AA).

The first of AA's founders, Bill W., initially refrained from drinking through a difficult process that included years of failure, hopelessness, hospitalization, drugs, and a transformative religious experience. To *maintain* sobriety, however, he realized that he needed to talk to another alcoholic. Bill W. recruited Dr. Bob, the second founder of AA, on a trip to Akron, Ohio. Dr. Bob, considered by family and doctors to be a hopeless and incurable alcoholic, kept Bill W. from drinking on the trip. In turn, Bill W.

eventually helped Dr. Bob give up drinking. AA has subsequently helped millions of people get and stay sober, and led to organizations trying the same approach with other difficult-to-tackle habits like narcotics abuse, smoking, unhealthy eating, and abusive relationships. That all sprang from the concept that we can do better with the help of others.

But, while a group *can* function to be better than the sum of the individuals, it doesn't automatically turn out that way. Being in a group can improve our decision quality by exploring alternatives and recognizing where our thinking might be biased, but a group can also exacerbate our tendency to confirm what we already believe. Philip Tetlock and Jennifer Lerner, leaders in the science of group interaction, described the two kinds of group reasoning styles in an influential 2002 paper: "Whereas confirmatory thought involves a one-sided attempt to rationalize a particular point of view, exploratory thought involves even-handed consideration of alternative points of view." In other words, confirmatory thought amplifies bias, promoting and encouraging motivated reasoning because its main purpose is justification. Confirmatory thought promotes a love and celebration of one's own beliefs, distorting how the group processes information and works through decisions, the result of which can be groupthink. Exploratory thought, on the other hand, encourages an open-minded and objective consideration of alternative hypotheses and a tolerance of dissent to combat bias. Exploratory thought helps the members of a group reason toward a more accurate representation of the world.

Without an explicit charter for exploratory thought and accountability to that charter, our tendency when we interact with others follows our individual tendency, which is toward confirmation. The expression "echo chamber" instantly conjures up the image of what results from our natural drift toward confirmatory thought. That was the chorus I heard among some groups of players during breaks of poker tournaments. When one player brought up how unlucky they had gotten, another would nod in assent as a prelude to telling their own hard-luck story, which, in turn, would be nodded at and assented to by the group.

Lerner and Tetlock offer insight into what should be included in the group agreement to avoid confirmatory thought and promote exploratory thought. "Complex and open-minded thought is most likely to be activated when decision makers learn prior to forming any opinions that they will be accountable to an audience (a) whose views are unknown, (b) who is interested in accuracy, (c) who is reasonably well-informed, and (d) who has a legitimate reason for inquiring into the reasons behind participants' judgments/choices." Their 2002 paper was one of several they coauthored supporting the conclusion that groups can improve the thinking of individual decision-makers when the individuals are *accountable* to a group whose interest is in *accuracy*.

In addition to accountability and an interest in accuracy, the charter should also encourage and celebrate a *diversity of perspectives* to challenge biased thinking by individual members. Jonathan Haidt, a professor at New York University's Stern School of Business, is a leading expert in exploring group thought in politics. Haidt, in his book *The Righteous Mind: Why Good People Are Divided by Politics and Religion*, built on Tetlock's work, connecting it with the need for diversity. "If you put individuals together in the right way, such that some individuals can use their reasoning powers to disconfirm the claims of others, and all individuals feel some common bond or shared fate that allows them to interact civilly, you can create a group that ends up producing good reasoning as an emergent property of the social system. This is why it's so important to have intellectual and ideological diversity within any group or institution whose goal is to find truth."

In combination, the advice of these experts in group interaction adds up to a pretty good blueprint for a truthseeking charter:

(1) A focus on accuracy (over confirmation), which includes rewarding truthseeking, objectivity, and open-mindedness within the group;

(2) Accountability, for which members have advance notice; and

(3) Openness to a diversity of ideas.

An agreement along these lines creates a common bond and shared fate among members, allowing the group to produce sound reasoning.

None of this should be surprising to anyone who recognizes the benefits of thinking in bets. We don't win bets by being in love with our own ideas. We win bets by relentlessly striving to calibrate our beliefs and predictions about the future to more accurately represent the world. In the long run, the more objective person will win against the more biased person. In that way, betting is a form of accountability to accuracy. Calibration requires an open-minded consideration of diverse points of view and alternative hypotheses. Wrapping all that into your group's charter makes a lot of sense.

The charter of the group must be communicated unambiguously, as Erik Seidel made clear to me. I had met Erik when I was a teenager, but when I started running into him at poker tournaments, it was the first time we were interacting in a business setting. Early on in my career, I saw Erik during a break in

THE BUDDY SYSTEM | 131

a tournament, and started moaning to him about my bad luck in losing a big hand. In three sentences, he laid out all the elements of a productive group charter. "I don't want to hear it. I'm not trying to hurt your feelings, but if you have a question about a hand, you can ask me about strategy all day long. I just don't think there's much purpose in a poker story if the point is about something you had no control over, like bad luck."

When you think about a charter for truthseeking interactions, Erik Seidel pretty much nailed it. He told me the rules of being in a pod with him. He discouraged me from confirmatory or biased thought like "I got unlucky." He encouraged me to find things I might have control over and how to improve decisions about those. I knew he would hold me accountable to these things in future interactions. We would explore diverse ideas because he insisted that be the focus of our interactions.

Because I was lucky enough to be part of a group with a truthseeking charter, there was no question that my poker decision-making improved. When I could consult them on in-progress decisions, like whether to move up in stakes or bankroll management or game selection, their advice reduced the number of errors I was making. Likewise, access to their range of strategies and experiences improved the quality of my thinking and decisions on a continuing basis. When I had questions or didn't understand why something happened, they would see things I didn't. When they had questions or needed advice on a hand, I wasn't just helping them work through a decision they made but would often get insights into my own game. Those interactions led to improvements in my game I would have overlooked or, at best, figured out on my own only after making a lot of costly errors.

Even better, interacting with similarly motivated people improves the ability to combat bias not just during direct interactions but when we are making and analyzing decisions on our own. The group gets into our head—in a good way—reshaping our decision habits.

The group rewards focus on accuracy

We all want to be thought well of, especially by people we respect. Lerner and Tetlock recognized that our craving for approval is incredibly strong and incentivizing. In most laboratory situations, they noted, study participants expected to explain their actions to someone they'd never met and never expected to meet again. "What is remarkable about this literature is that—despite the prevalence of these minimalist manipulations—participants still reliably respond as if audience approval matters." It's great to get approval from people we respect, but we crave approval so badly, we'll still work to get it from a stranger. A productive decision group can harness this desire by rewarding accuracy and intellectual honesty with social approval.

Motivated reasoning and self-serving bias are two habits of mind that are deeply rooted in how our brains work. We have a huge investment in confirmatory thought, and we fall into these biases all the time without even knowing it. Confirmatory thought is hard to spot, hard to change, and, if we do try changing it, hard to self-reinforce. It is one thing to commit to rewarding ourselves for thinking in bets, but it is a lot easier if we get others to do the work of rewarding us.

Groups like AA demonstrate how a supportive group can provide the reward for doing the hard work of changing a habit routine, just by its approval. For engaging in the difficult work involved in sobriety, local AA groups give tokens or chips celebrating the length of individual members' sobriety. The tokens (which members often carry or customize as jewelry) are a tangible reminder that others acknowledge you are accomplishing something difficult. There are chips for marking one to sixty-five years of sobriety. There are also chips given for every month of sobriety in the first year. There is even a chip given for being sober for twenty-four hours.

I experienced firsthand the power of a group's approval to reshape individual thinking habits. I got my fix by *trying* to be the best credit-giver, the best mistake-admitter, and the best finder-of-mistakes-in-good-outcomes. The reward was their enthusiastic engagement and deep dives introducing me to the nuances of poker strategy. It was also rewarding to have these intelligent, successful players take my questions seriously and increasingly ask for *my* opinions. In contrast, I felt disapproval from them when I acted against the charter and complained about my bad luck, or expected them to confirm how great I played simply because I was winning.

While I never got close to attaining the goal of a pure focus on accuracy, my group helped me to give a little more credit than I otherwise would have, to spot a few more mistakes than I would have spotted on my own, to be more open-minded to strategic choices that I disagreed with. That moved me, even if just a little bit at a time, toward my goal of getting closer to the objective truth. And that little bit had a huge long-run impact on my success.

When I started playing poker, "discussing hands" consisted mostly of my complaining about bad luck when I lost. My brother quickly got sick of my moaning. He laid down the law and said I was only allowed to ask him about hands that I had won. If I wanted him to engage with me, I had to identify some point in those hands where I might have made a mistake.

Talking about winning (even if we are identifying mistakes along the way to a win) is less painful than talking about losing, allowing new habits to be more easily trained. Identifying mistakes in hands I won reinforced the separation between outcomes and decision quality. These discussions also made me feel good about analyzing and questioning my decisions because of the approval I got from Howard and the players I looked up to. I used that approval as evidence that I understood the game and had promise as a player. When they complimented me for finding alternative approaches in my winning hands or understanding the contribution of luck, that felt terrific. In time, I could expand this approach to identifying learning opportunities in any hand I played, not just the winning ones.

Once we are in a group that regularly reinforces exploratory thought, the routine becomes reflexive, running on its own. Exploratory thought becomes a new habit of mind, the new routine, and one that is self-reinforced. In a Pavlovian way, after enough approval from the group for doing the hard work of thinking in bets, we get the same good feeling from focusing on accuracy on our own. We internalize the group's approval, and, as a matter of habit, we begin to do the kind of things that would earn it when we are away from the group (which is, after all, most of the time).

"One Hundred White Castles . . . and a large chocolate shake": how accountability improves decision-making

David Grey is a high-stakes poker player and professional gambler, and a good friend. After a night at a racetrack and a bowling alley in New Jersey, David and a bunch of other bettors were hungry. It was late. Someone suggested White Castle. A discussion broke out about how many burgers the biggest eater in the group, Ira the Whale, could eat.

When they got Ira the Whale to say he could eat 100 burgers (remember, White Castle burgers are small), most of the group, not surprisingly, wanted to bet against him. David was an exception. "I was a young guy, just getting started. Fifty dollars was a big win or loss for me. There was about $2,000 out against Ira the Whale. I bet $200 on him because I thought he could do it."

When they got to White Castle, Ira the Whale decided to order the burgers twenty at a time. David knew he was a lock to win as soon as Ira the Whale ordered the first twenty, because Ira the Whale also ordered a milkshake and fries.

After finishing the 100 burgers and after he and David collected their bets, Ira the Whale ordered another twenty burgers to go, "for Mrs. Whale."

Accountability is a willingness or obligation to answer for our actions or beliefs to others. A bet is a form of accountability. If we're in love with our own opinions, it can cost us in a bet. Ira the Whale held the other gamblers accountable for their beliefs about whether he could eat 100 White Castle burgers. Accountability is why John Hennigan (briefly) moved to Des Moines. After spending time in that kind of environment, you become hypervigilant about your level of confidence in your beliefs. No one is forced to make or take such bets, but the prospect is a reminder that you can always be held accountable for the accuracy of what you believe and say. It is truly putting your money where your mouth is.

Being in an environment where the challenge of a bet is always looming works to reduce motivated reasoning. Such an environment changes the frame through which we view disconfirming information, reinforcing the frame change that our truthseeking group rewards. Evidence that might contradict a belief we hold is no longer viewed through as hurtful a frame. Rather, it is viewed as helpful because it can improve our chances of making a better bet. And winning a bet triggers a reinforcing positive update.

Accountability, like reinforcement of accuracy, also improves our decision-making and information processing when we are away from the group because we *know in advance* that we will have to answer to the group for our decisions. Early in my poker career, my poker group recommended that a way to avoid the effects of self-serving bias when I was losing was to have a preset "loss limit"—if I lost $600 at the stakes I was playing, I would leave the game. The smart, experienced players advising me knew that in the moment of losing, I might not be my most rational self in assessing whether I was losing because I was getting unlucky or losing because I was playing poorly. A predetermined loss limit acts as a check against irrationally chasing losses, but self-enforcement is a problem. If you have more money in your pocket, you might still take it out. If you're out of money, casinos have ATMs and machines that let you get cash advances on your credit cards. Poker players are also pretty liberal about lending money to losing players.

I was much less likely to break a loss limit because I knew I was accountable to my pod. If I reached my loss limit and my inner voice said, "This game is so good that I should put up more money and keep playing," it also reminded me I'd have to answer for the decision to a group of players I respected. Accountability made me run that conversation in my head, in which I started explaining how I was just getting unlucky and they would expose why I was likely biased in my assessment, helping me resist the urge to buy more chips. And, after leaving a losing game and going home, I could offset some of the sting of losing by running the conversation where my pod would approve of my decision to quit the game when I told them about it.

Imagining how the discussion will go helps us to spot more errors on our own and catch them more quickly.

The group ideally exposes us to a diversity of viewpoints

John Stuart Mill is one of the heroes of thinking in bets. More than one hundred and fifty years after writing *On Liberty*, his thinking on social and political philosophy remains startlingly current. One of the frequent themes in *On Liberty* is the importance of diversity of opinion. Diversity and dissent are not only checks on fallibility, but the only means of testing the ultimate truth of an opinion: "The only way in which a human being can make some approach to knowing the whole of a subject, is by hearing what can be said about it by persons of every variety of opinion, and studying all modes in which it can be looked at by every character of mind. No wise man ever acquired his wisdom in any mode but this; nor is it in the nature of human intellect to become wise in any other manner."

There is a simple beauty in Mill's insight. On our own, we

have just one viewpoint. That's our limitation as humans. But if we take a bunch of people with that limitation and put them together in a group, we get exposed to diverse opinions, can test alternative hypotheses, and move toward accuracy. It is almost impossible for us, on our own, to get the diversity of viewpoints provided by the combined manpower of a well-formed decision pod. To get a more objective view of the world, we need an environment that exposes us to alternate hypotheses and different perspectives. That doesn't apply only to the world around us: to view *ourselves* in a more realistic way, we need other people to fill in our blind spots.

We already know why we're right. What we need help with is why we are wrong.

A group with diverse viewpoints can help us by sharing the work suggested in the previous two chapters to combat motivated reasoning about beliefs and biased outcome fielding. When we think in bets, we run through a series of questions to examine the accuracy of our beliefs. For example:

- Why might my belief not be true?
- What other evidence might be out there bearing on my belief?
- Are there similar areas I can look toward to gauge whether similar beliefs to mine are true?
- What sources of information could I have missed or minimized on the way to reaching my belief?
- What are the reasons someone else could have a different belief, what's their support, and why might they be right instead of me?
- What other perspectives are there as to why things turned out the way they did?

Just by asking ourselves these questions, we are taking a big step toward calibration. But there is only so much we can do to answer these questions on our own. We only get exposed to the information we have been exposed to, only live the experiences we have experienced, only think of the hypotheses that we can conceive of. It's hard to know what reasons someone else could have for believing something different. We aren't them. We haven't had their experiences. We don't know what different information they have. But they do.

Much of our biased information processing stems from the amount of rope that uncertainty affords us. Well-deployed diversity of viewpoints in a group can reduce uncertainty due to incomplete information by filling in the gaps in what we know, making life start to fit more neatly on a chessboard.

Others aren't wrapped up in preserving our narrative, anchored by our biases. It is a lot easier to have someone else offer their perspective than for you to imagine you're another person and think about what their perspective might be. A diverse group can do some of the heavy lifting of de-biasing for us. A poker table is a naturally diverse setting because we generally don't select who we play with for their opinions. Even better, when there is disagreement stemming from the diverse opinions represented at a poker table, the discussion may naturally progress toward betting on it. These are ideal circumstances for promoting accuracy.

Numerous groups have recognized the need to engineer the kind of diversity and encouragement of dissent that naturally occurs at a poker table. The State Department, since the Vietnam War, has had a formal Dissent Channel, where employees can have their dissenting views heard and addressed without fear of penalty. The American Foreign Service Association, the professional organization of foreign-service employees, has *four* separate awards it gives annually to members "to recognize and encourage constructive dissent and risk-taking in the Foreign Service." The Dissent Channel has been credited with a policy change that helped end the genocidal war in Bosnia. In June 2016, fifty-one State Department employees signed a memo calling for President Obama to strengthen American military efforts in Syria. In late January 2017, approximately one thousand employees signed a dissent cable in response to President Trump's executive order suspending immigration from seven Muslim-majority countries. The Dissent Channel represents something hopeful in our nation's decision-making process. In an environment of increased polarization, foreign-service employees can make their voices heard about policies with which they disagree, and do it regardless of whether the administration is Democrat or Republican. Allowing dissent has a value that transcends party politics.

After September 11, the CIA created "red teams" that, according to Georgetown law professor Neal Katyal in a *New York Times* op-ed, "are dedicated to arguing against the intelligence community's conventional wisdom and spotting flaws in logic and analysis." Senior Obama administration officials, following the raid that killed Osama bin Laden, mentioned red-team analysis among the methods used to measure the degree of confidence that bin Laden, in the absence of visual or auditory confirmation, was in the compound subject to the raid.

Dissent channels and red teams are a beautiful implementation of Mill's bedrock principle that we can't know the truth of a matter without hearing the other side. This commitment to diversity of opinion is something that we would be wise to apply to our own decision groups. For example, if a corporate strategy group is figuring out how to integrate operations following a merger, someone who initially opposed the merger would be good to have as part of the group. Perhaps they have reasons why the two sales departments won't mesh—whatever their reasons, they could help the majority move forward with a wiser approach by taking those reasons into account.

Diversity is the foundation of productive group decision-making, but we can't underestimate how hard it is to maintain. We all tend to gravitate toward people who are near clones of us. After all, it feels good to hear our ideas echoed back to us. If there is any doubt about how easy it can be to fall into this confirmatory drift, we can even see this tendency in groups we consider some of the most dedicated to truthseeking: judges and scientists.

Federal judges: drift happens

Cass Sunstein, now a Harvard law professor, conducted a massive study with colleagues when he was on the faculty at the University of Chicago Law School, on ideological diversity in federal judicial panels. Sunstein recognized at the outset that the U.S. Courts of Appeals are "an extraordinary and longstanding natural experiment" in diversity. Appellate court panels are composed of three judges randomly drawn from that circuit's pool. Each circuit's pool includes life-tenured judges chosen (when an opening occurs or Congress recognizes the need for additional judges) by the sitting president. In any particular appeal, you could get a panel of three Democrat appointees, three Republican appointees, or a two-to-one mix in either direction.

The study, encompassing over 6,000 federal appeals and nearly 20,000 individual votes, found, not surprisingly, that judicial voting generally followed political lines. Pure, unaided open-mindedness, even by life-tenured judges sworn to uphold the law, is hard.

When there was political diversity on the panels, the researchers found several areas where that diversity improved the panel's work. Even though, in most cases, two politically similar judges could dictate the panel's outcome, there were significant differences between heterogeneous and homogeneous panels. A single panelist from the other party had "a large disciplining effect."

They found, for example, "strong evidence of ideological dampening" in environmental cases. Democrat appointees, who overall voted for plaintiffs 43% of the time, voted for plaintiffs just 10% of the time when sitting with two Republican appointees. Republican appointees, who overall voted for plaintiffs 20% of the time, voted for plaintiffs 42% of the time when seated with two Democrat appointees. This held up across most of the twenty-five categories of cases in which they had a sufficiently large sample to reach a conclusion.

The authors concluded that the result endorsed the importance of exposure to diverse viewpoints: "What is necessary is reasonable diversity, or diversity of reasonable views . . . and that it is important to ensure that judges, no less than anyone else, are exposed to it, and not merely through the arguments of advocates."

Sunstein's group found that federal appellate judges *need* the diverse viewpoint of an opposing-party appointee. Judges, they found, followed the human instinct of succumbing to groupthink. "Our data provide strong evidence that like-minded judges also go to extremes: the probability that a judge will vote in one or another direction is greatly increased by the presence of judges appointed by the president of the same political party. In short, we claim to show both strong conformity effects and group polarization within federal courts of appeals."

The growing polarization of the Supreme Court is a case in point. Each justice now has four clerks, all of whom have similar credentials: top-of-the-class graduates of top law schools, law review editors, and clerkships with federal appeals court judges. The clerks, over the years, have played an increasingly important role in helping the justices with their intellectual workload, discussing details of cases and drafting initial versions of opinions.

Prior to the appointment of Chief Justice Roberts in 2005, it was an informal badge of honor, especially among some of the conservative members of the court, that they hired clerks with ideological backgrounds that differed from theirs. Bob Woodward and Scott Armstrong, in *The Brethren*, described how Justice Powell "prided himself on hiring liberal clerks. He would tell his clerks that the conservative side of the issues came to him naturally. Their job was to present the other side, to challenge him. He would rather encounter a compelling argument for another position in the privacy of his own chambers, than to meet it unexpectedly at conference or in a dissent."

Chief Justice Burger hired equally from the ranks of former clerks of Democrat- and Republican-appointed judges. Chief Justice Rehnquist, who served on the court with Burger and succeeded him, arrived at the court suspicious of the role liberal clerks could have in influencing his opinion. According to *The Brethren*, however, that attitude disappeared almost immediately. Rehnquist believed "the legal and moral interchanges that liberal clerks thrived on were good for the Justices and for the Court."

Justice Scalia, when he served on the D.C. circuit and in his early years on the Supreme Court, was known for seeking out clerks with liberal ideologies.

As the Supreme Court has become more divided, this practice has all but ceased. According to a *New York Times* article in 2010, only Justice Breyer regularly employed clerks who had worked for circuit judges appointed by presidents of both parties. Since 2005, Scalia had hired no clerks with experience working for Democrat-appointed judges. In light of the shift in hiring practices, it should not be so surprising that the court has become more polarized. The justices are in the process of creating their own echo chambers.

Justice Thomas, from 1986 to the time the article was written, was 84-for-84 in hiring clerks who had worked for Republican-appointed judges. Not surprisingly, according to data compiled from the *Journal of Law, Economics, and Organization*, he is the justice furthest from the ideological center of the court, much further right than the most liberal-leaning justice (Sotomayor) is left.

Thomas once said, "I won't hire clerks who have profound disagreements with me. It's like trying to train a pig. It wastes your time, and it aggravates the pig."* That makes sense only if you believe the goal of a decision group is to train people to agree with you. But if your goal is to develop the best decision process, that is an odd sentiment indeed.

This polarization warns against forming a decision group that is a collection of clones who share the same opinions and knowledge sources we do. The more homogeneous we get, the

---

*Thomas was paraphrasing a quote often attributed to Mark Twain: "Never try to teach a pig to sing. It wastes your time and annoys the pig."

more the group will promote and amplify confirmatory thought. Sadly, that's exactly what we drift toward. Even Supreme Court justices do that. We are all familiar with this tendency in politics; it's the complaint on both sides of the political aisle. Conservatives complain that liberals live in an echo chamber where they just repeat and confirm their point of view. They aren't open to new information or ideas that don't fit what they already believe. That's the exact same criticism liberals have of conservatives.

Although the Internet and the breadth of multimedia news outlets provide us with limitless access to diverse opinions, they also give us an unprecedented opportunity to descend into a bubble, getting our information from sources we know will share our view of the world. We often don't even realize when we are in the echo chamber ourselves, because we're so in love with our own ideas that it all just sounds sensible and right. In political discourse, virtually everyone, even those familiar with groupthink, will assert, "I'm in the rational group exchanging ideas and thinking these things through. The people on the other side, though, are in an echo chamber."

We must be vigilant about this drift in our groups and be prepared to fight it. Whether it is the forming of a group of friends or a pod at work—or hiring for diversity of viewpoint and tolerance for dissent when you are able to guide an enterprise's culture toward accuracy—we should guard against gravitating toward clones of ourselves. We should also recognize that it's really hard: the norm is toward homogeneity; we're all guilty of it; and we don't even notice that we're doing it.

Social psychologists: confirmatory drift and Heterodox Academy

In 2011, Jon Haidt, speaking to an audience of 1,000 social psychologists, noted the lack of viewpoint diversity in their field. He reported that he could identify only one conservative social psychologist with any degree of field-wide recognition.

Surveys of sociologists' professional organizations have found that 85%–96% of members responding self-identified as left of center, voted for Obama in 2012, or scored left of center on a questionnaire of political views. (Most of the remaining 4%–15% identified as centrist or moderate rather than conservative.) The trend has a long tail, but it has been accelerating. In the 1990s, liberals among social psychologists outnumbered conservatives 4-to-1. More recent surveys show that the ratio has grown to greater than 10-to-1, sometimes far greater. A tendency to hire for a conforming worldview combined with the discouraging aspects of being so decisively outnumbered ideologically suggests that, unchecked, this situation won't get better. According to the surveys establishing this trend toward homogeneity, about 10% of faculty respondents identified as conservative, compared with just 2% of grad students and postdoctoral candidates.

Haidt, along with Philip Tetlock and four others (social psychologists José Duarte, Jarret Crawford, and Lee Jussim, and sociologist Charlotta Stern) founded an organization called Heterodox Academy, to fight this drift toward homogeneity of thought in science and academics as a whole. In 2015, they published their findings in the journal *Behavioral and Brain Sciences* (*BBS*), along with thirty-three pieces of open peer commentary. The *BBS* paper explained and documented the political imbalance in social psychology, how it reduces the quality of science, and what can be done to improve the situation.

Social psychology is particularly vulnerable to the effects of political imbalance. Social psychologists are researching many of the hot-button issues dividing the political Left and Right: racism, sexism, stereotypes, and responses to power and authority. Coming from a community composed almost entirely of liberal-leaning scientists, the quality and impact of research can suffer.

The authors identified instances in which political values became "embedded into research questions in ways that make some constructs unobservable and unmeasurable, thereby invalidating attempts at hypothesis testing." This occurred in several experiments involving attitudes on environmental issues and attempts to link ideology to unethical behavior. They also identified the risk of researchers concentrating on topics that validated their shared narrative and avoiding topics that contested that narrative, such as stereotype accuracy and the scope and direction of prejudice. Finally, they pointed to the obvious problem inherent in the legitimacy of research characterizing conservatives as dogmatic and intolerant done by a discipline that is over 10-to-1 liberal leaning.

First, the Heterodox Academy effort shows that there is a natural drift toward homogeneity and confirmatory thought. We all experience this gravitation toward people who think like we do. Scientists, overwhelmingly trained and chartered toward truthseeking, aren't immune. As the authors of the *BBS* paper recognized, "Even research communities of highly intelligent and well-meaning individuals can fall prey to confirmation bias, as IQ is *positively* correlated with the number of reasons people find to support their own side in an argument." That's how robust these biases are. We see that even judges and scientists succumb to these biases. We shouldn't feel bad, whatever our situation, about admitting that we also need help.

Second, groups with diverse viewpoints are the best protection against confirmatory thought. Peer review, the gold standard that epitomizes the open-mindedness and hypothesis testing of the scientific method, "offers much less protection against error when the community of peers is politically homogeneous." In other words, the opinions of group members aren't much help if it is a group of clones. Experimental studies cited in the *BBS* paper found that confirmation bias led reviewers "to work extra hard to find flaws with papers whose conclusions they dislike, and to be more permissive about methodological issues when they endorse the conclusions." The authors of the *BBS* paper concluded that "[n]obody has found a way to eradicate confirmation bias in individuals, but we can diversify the field to the point to where individual viewpoint biases begin to cancel out each other."

The *BBS* paper, and the continuing work of Heterodox Academy, includes specific recommendations geared toward encouraging diversity and dissenting opinions. I encourage you to read the specific recommendations, which include things like a stated antidiscrimination policy (against opposing viewpoints), developing ways to encourage people with contrary viewpoints to join the group and engage in the process, and surveying to gauge the actual heterogeneity or homogeneity of opinion in the group. These are exactly the kinds of things we would do well to adopt (and, where necessary, adapt) for groups in our personal lives and in the workplace.

Even among those who are committed to truthseeking, judges and academics, we can see how strong the tendency is to seek out confirmation of our beliefs. If you have any doubt this is true for all of us, put this book down for a moment and check your Twitter feed for whom you follow. It's a pretty safe bet that the bulk of them are ideologically aligned with you. If that's the case, start following some people from the other side of the aisle.

Wanna bet (on science)?

If thinking in bets helps us de-bias, couldn't we apply it to help solve the Heterodox Academy problem? One might guess that scientists would be more accurate if they had to bet on the likelihood that results would replicate as compared to traditional peer review, which can be vulnerable to viewpoint bias. Especially in an anonymous betting market, confirming the strength of your pre-existing ideology or betting solely on the basis that replication of a study confirms your own work or beliefs counts for nothing. The way a scientist would be "right" in such a betting market is by using their skill in a superior way to make the most objective bets on whether results would or would not replicate. Researchers who knew in advance their work would be subject to a market test would also face an additional form of accountability that would likely modulate their reporting of results.

At least one study has found that, yes, a betting market where scientists wager on the likelihood of experimental results replicating was more accurate than expert opinion alone. In psychology, there has been a controversy over the last decade about a potentially large number of published studies with results subsequent researchers could not replicate. The Reproducibility Project: Psychology has been working on replicating studies from top psychology journals. Anna Dreber, a behavioral economist at the Stockholm School of Economics, with several colleagues set up a betting market based on these replication attempts. They recruited a bunch of experts in the relevant fields and asked their opinions on the likelihood the Reproducibility Project would replicate the results of forty-four studies. They then gave those experts money to bet on each study's replication in a prediction market.

Experts engaging in traditional peer review, providing their opinion on whether an experimental result would replicate, were right 58% of the time. A betting market in which the traders were the exact same experts and those experts had money on the line predicted correctly 71% of the time.

A lot of people were surprised to learn that the expert opinion expressed as a bet was more accurate than expert opinion expressed through peer review, since peer review is considered a rock-solid foundation of the scientific method. Of course, this result shouldn't be surprising to readers of this book. We know that scientists are dedicated to truthseeking and take peer review seriously. Arguably, there is already an implied betting element in the scientific process, in that researchers and peer reviewers have a reputational stake in the quality of their review. But we know that scientists, like judges—and like *us*—are human and subject to these patterns of confirmatory thought. Making the risk explicit rather than implicit refocuses us all to be more objective.

A growing number of businesses are, in fact, implementing betting markets to solve for the difficulties in getting and encouraging contrary opinions. Companies implementing prediction markets to test decisions include Google, Microsoft, General Electric, Eli Lilly, Pfizer, and Siemens. People are more willing to offer their opinion when the goal is to win a bet rather than get along with people in a room.

Accuracy, accountability, and diversity wrapped into a group's charter all contribute to better decision-making, especially if the group promotes thinking in bets. Now that we understand the elements of a good charter, we move on to the rules of engagement for a productive decision group, how to most effectively communicate with one another. A pioneering sociologist actually designed a set of truthseeking norms for a group (scientists) that form a pretty good blueprint for engagement. I don't know if he was a bettor, but he was influenced by something very relevant to thinking about bias, rationality, and the potential gulf between perception and reality: he was a magician.

CHAPTER 5

Dissent to Win

CUDOS to a magician

Meyer R. Schkolnick was born on the Fourth of July, 1910, in South Philadelphia. He performed magic at birthday parties as a teenager and considered a career as a performer. He adopted the performing name "Robert Merlin." Then a friend convinced him that a teen magician naming himself after Merlin was too on the nose, so he performed as Robert Merton. When Robert K. Merton (to distinguish him from his son, economist and Nobel laureate Robert C. Merton) died in 2003, the *New York Times* called him "one of the most influential sociologists of the 20th century."

The founders of Heterodox Academy, in the *BBS* paper, specifically recognized Merton's 1942 and 1973 papers, in which he established norms for the scientific community known by the acronym CUDOS: "An ideologically balanced science that routinely resorted to adversarial collaborations to resolve empirical disputes would bear a striking resemblance to Robert Merton's ideal-type model of a self-correcting epistemic community, one organized around the norms of CUDOS." Per the *BBS* paper, CUDOS stands for

Communism (data belong to the group),

Universalism (apply uniform standards to claims and evidence, regardless of where they came from),

Disinterestedness (vigilance against potential conflicts that can influence the group's evaluation), and

Organized Skepticism (discussion among the group to encourage engagement and dissent).

If you want to pick a role model for designing a group's practical rules of engagement, you can't do better than Merton. To start, he coined the phrase "role model," along with "self-fulfilling prophecy," "reference group," "unintended consequences," and "focus group." He founded the science of sociology and was the first sociologist awarded the National Medal of Science.

Merton began his academic career in the 1930s, studying the history of institutional influences on the scientific community. To him, it was a story of many periods of scientific advancement spurred on by geopolitical influences, but also periods of struggle to maintain independence from those influences. His life spanned both world wars and the Cold War, in which he studied and witnessed nationalist movements in which people "arrayed their political selves in the garb of scientists," explicitly evaluating scientific knowledge based on political and national affiliations.

In 1942, Merton wrote about the normative structure of science. He tinkered with the paper over the next thirty-one years, publishing the final version as part of a book in 1973. This twelve-page paper is an excellent manual for developing rules of engagement for any truthseeking group. I recognized its application to my poker group and professional and workplace groups I've encountered in speaking and consulting. Each element of CUDOS—communism, universalism, disinterestedness, and organized skepticism—can be broadly applied and adapted to push a group toward objectivity. When there is a drift toward confirmation and away from exploring accuracy, it's likely the result of the failure to nurture one of Merton's norms. Not surprisingly, Merton's paper would make an excellent career guide for anyone seeking to be a profitable bettor, or a profitable decision-maker period.

Mertonian communism: more is more

The Mertonian norm of communism (obviously, not the political system) refers to the communal ownership of data within groups. Merton argued that, in academics, an individual researcher's data must eventually be shared with the scientific community at large for knowledge to advance. "Secrecy is the antithesis of this norm; full and open communication its enactment." In science, this means that the community has an agreement that research results cannot properly be reviewed without access to the data and a detailed description of the experimental design and methods. Researchers are entitled to keep data private until published but once they accomplish that, they should throw the doors open to give the community every opportunity to make a proper assessment. Any attempt at accuracy is bound to fall short if the truthseeking group has only limited access to potentially pertinent information. Without all the facts, accuracy suffers.

This ideal of scientific sharing was similarly described by physicist Richard Feynman in a 1974 lecture as "a kind of utter honesty—a kind of leaning over backwards. For example, if you're doing an experiment, you should report everything that you think might make it invalid—not only what you think is right about it: other causes that could possibly explain your results . . ."

It is unrealistic to think we can perfectly achieve Feynman's ideal; even scientists struggle with it. Within our own decision pod, we should strive to abide by the rule that "more is more." Get all the information out there. Indulge the broadest definition of what could conceivably be relevant. Reward the process of pulling the skeletons of our own reasoning out of the closet. As a rule of thumb, if we have an urge to leave out a detail because it makes us uncomfortable or requires even more clarification to explain away, those are exactly the details we must share. The mere fact of our hesitation and discomfort is a signal that such information may be critical to providing a complete and balanced account. Likewise, as members of a group evaluating a decision, we should take such hesitation as a signal to explore further.

To the extent we regard self-governance in the United States as a truthseeking experiment, we have established that openness in the sharing of information is a cornerstone of making and accounting for decisions by the government. The free-press and free-speech guarantees of the Constitution recognize the importance of *self*-expression, but they also exist because we need mechanisms to assure that information makes it to the public. The government serves the people, so the people own the data and have a right to have the data shared with them. Statutes like the Freedom of Information Act have the same purpose. Without free access to information, it is impossible to make reasoned assessments of our government.

Sharing data and information, like the other elements of a truthseeking charter, is done by agreement. Academics agree to share results. The government shares information by agreement with the people. Without an agreement, we can't and shouldn't compel others to share information they don't want to share. We all have a right of privacy. Companies and other entities have rights to trade secrets and to protect their intellectual property. But within our group, an agreement to share details pertinent to assessing the quality of a decision is part of a productive truthseeking charter.

If the group is discussing a decision and it doesn't have all the details, it might be because the person providing them doesn't realize the relevance of some of the data. Or it could mean the person telling the story has a bias toward encouraging a certain narrative that they likely aren't even aware of. After all, as Jonathan Haidt points out, we are all our own best PR agents, spinning a narrative that shines the most flattering light on us.

We have all experienced situations where we get two accounts of the same event, but the versions are dramatically different because they are informed by different facts and perspectives. This is known as the Rashomon Effect, named for the 1950 cinematic classic *Rashomon*, directed by Akira Kurosawa. The central element of the otherwise simple plot was how incompleteness is a tool for bias. In the film, four people give separate, drastically different accounts of a scene they all observed, the seduction (or rape) of a woman by a bandit, the bandit's duel with her husband (if there was a duel), and the husband's death (from losing the duel, murder, or suicide).

Even without conflicting versions, the Rashomon Effect reminds us that we can't assume one version of a story is accurate or complete. We can't count on someone else to provide the other side of the story, or any individual's version to provide a full and objective accounting of all the relevant information. That's why, within a decision group, it is helpful to commit to this Mertonian norm on both sides of the discussion. When presenting a decision for discussion, we should be mindful of details we might be omitting and be extra-safe by adding anything that could possibly be relevant. On the evaluation side, we must query each other to extract those details when necessary.

My consultation with the CEO who traced his company's problems to firing the president demonstrated the value of a commitment to data sharing. After he described what happened, I requested a lot more information. As he got into details of the hiring process for that executive and approaches to dealing with the president's deficiencies on the job, that led to further questions about those decisions, which, in turn, led to more details being shared. He was identifying what he thought was a bad decision, justified by his initial description of the situation. After we got every detail out of all the dimensions of the decision, we reached a different conclusion: the decision to fire the president had been quite reasonable strategically. It just happened to turn out badly.

Be a data sharer. That's what experts do. In fact, that's one of the reasons experts become experts. They understand that sharing data is the best way to move toward accuracy because it extracts insight from your listeners of the highest fidelity.

You should hear the amount of detail a top poker player puts into the description of a hand when they are workshopping that hand with another player. A layperson would think, "That seems like a lot of irrelevant, nitpicky detail. Why are they saying all that stuff?" When two expert poker players get together to trade views and opinions about hands, the detail is extraordinary: the positions of everyone acting in the hand; the size of the bets and the size of the pot after each action; what they know about how their opponent(s) has played when they have encountered them in the past; how they were playing in the particular game they were in; how they were playing in the most recent hands in that game (particularly whether they were winning or losing recently); how many chips each person had throughout the hand; what their opponents know about them, etc., etc. What the experts recognize is that the more detail you provide, the better the assessment of decision quality you get. And because the same types of details are always expected, expert players essentially work from a template, so there is less opportunity to convey only the information that might lead the listener down a garden path to a desired conclusion.

Hall of Fame football coach John Madden, in a documentary about Vince Lombardi, told a story about how, as a young assistant coach, he attended a coaching clinic where Lombardi spoke about one play: the power sweep, a running play that he made famous with the Green Bay Packers in the 1960s. Lombardi held the audience spellbound as he described that one play for eight hours. Madden said, "I went in there cocky, thinking I knew everything there was to know about football, and he spent eight hours talking about this one play. . . . I realized then that I actually knew nothing about football."

We are naturally reluctant to share information that could encourage others to find fault in our decision-making. My group made this easier by making me feel good about committing myself to improvement. When I shared details that cast me in what

I perceived to be a bad light, I got a positive self-image update from the approval of players I respected. In my consulting, I've encouraged companies to make sure they don't define "winning" solely by results or providing a self-enhancing narrative. If part of corporate success consists of providing the most accurate, objective, and detailed evaluation of what's going on, employees will compete to win on those terms. That will reward better habits of mind.

Agree to be a data sharer and reward others in your decision group for telling more of the story.

Universalism: don't shoot the message

The well-known advice "don't shoot the messenger" is actually good shorthand for the reasons why we want to protect and encourage dissenting ideas. Plutarch's *Life of Lucullus* provided an early, literal example: the king of Armenia got advance notice that Lucullus's troops were approaching. He killed the messenger for delivering that message and, henceforth, messengers stopped reporting such intelligence. Obviously, if you don't like the message, you shouldn't take it out on the messenger.

The Mertonian norm of universalism is the converse. "Truth-claims, whatever their source, are to be subjected to preestablished impersonal criteria." It means acceptance or rejection of an idea must not "depend on the personal or social attributes of their protagonist." "Don't shoot the message," for some reason, hasn't gotten the same historical or literary attention, but it addresses an equally important decision-making issue: don't disparage or ignore an idea just because you don't like who or where it came from.

When we have a negative opinion about the person delivering the message, we close our minds to what they are saying and miss a lot of learning opportunities because of it. Likewise, when we have a positive opinion of the messenger, we tend to accept the message without much vetting. Both are bad.

Whether the situation involves facts, ideas, beliefs, opinions, or predictions, the substance of the information has merit (or lack of merit) separate from where it came from. If you're deciding the truth of whether the earth is round, it doesn't matter if the idea came from your best friend or George Washington or Benito Mussolini. The accuracy of the statement should be evaluated independent of its source.

If we're going to improve our beliefs, we'll be better off if we include people and information sources we're likely to disagree with. Who better to raise the possibility that we're wrong, and the reasons?

I learned an early lesson in my poker career about universalism. I started playing poker using that list of hands my brother Howard wrote on a napkin. I treated this initial advice like a holy document. Therefore, when I saw someone playing hands off-list, I immediately labeled them as a bad player. When I saw such a player subsequently execute a strategy I didn't have as part of my game, I dismissed it. Doing that across the board (especially when I was labeling these players as "bad" based on one view of a sound beginner's strategy) was an expensive lesson in universalism. For so many things going on at the table in the first years of my poker career, I shot the message.

I was guilty of the same thing David Letterman admitted

in his explanation to Lauren Conrad. He spent a long time assuming people around him were idiots before considering the alternative hypothesis, "Maybe I'm the idiot." In poker, I was the idiot.

As I learned that Howard's list was just a safe way to get me started and not the Magna Carta scrawled in crayon on a napkin, I developed an exercise to practice and reinforce universalism. When I had the impulse to dismiss someone as a bad player, I made myself find something that they did well. It was an exercise I could do for myself, and I could get help from my group in analyzing the strategies I thought those players might be executing well. That commitment led to many benefits.

Of course, I learned some new and profitable strategies and tactics. I also developed a more complete picture of other players' strategies. Even when I determined that the strategic choices of that player weren't, in the end, profitable, I had a deeper understanding of my opponent's game, which helped me devise counterstrategies. I had started thinking more deeply about the way my opponents thought. And in some instances, I recognized that I had underestimated the skills of certain players who I initially thought were profitable for me to play against. That led me to make more objective decisions about game selection. And my poker group benefited from this exercise as well because, in workshopping the strategies with each other, we multiplied the number of playing techniques we could observe and discuss. Admitting that the people I played against had things to teach me was hard, and my group helped me feel proud of myself when I resisted the urge to just complain about how lucky my opponents were.

Nearly any group can create an exercise to develop and reinforce the open-mindedness universalism requires. As an example, with politics so polarized, we forget the obvious truth that no one has only good ideas or only bad ideas. Liberals would do well to take some time to read and watch more conservative news sources, and conservatives would do well to take some time to read and watch more liberal news sources—not with the goal of confirming that the other side is a collection of idiots who have nothing of value to say but to specifically and purposely find things they *agree* with. When we do this, we learn things we wouldn't otherwise have learned. Our views will likely become moderated in the same way judges from opposite sides of the political aisle moderate each other. Even if, in the end, we don't find much to agree with, we will understand the opposing position better—and ours as well. We'll be practicing what John Stuart Mill preached.

Another way to disentangle the message from the messenger is to imagine the message coming from a source we value much more or much less. If we hear an account from someone we like, imagine if someone we didn't like told us the same story, and vice versa. This can be incorporated into an exploratory group's work, asking each other, "How would we feel about this if we heard it from a much different source?" We can take this process of vetting information in the group further, initially and intentionally omitting where or whom we heard the idea from. Leading off our story by identifying the messenger could interfere with the group's commitment to universalism, biasing them to agree with or discredit the message depending on their opinion of the messenger. So leave the source out to start, giving the group the maximum opportunity to form an impression without shooting (or celebrating) the message based on their opinion of the messenger (separate from the expertise and credibility of the messenger).

John Stuart Mill made it clear that the *only* way to gain knowledge and approach truth is by examining every variety of opinion. We learn things we didn't know. We calibrate better. Even when the result of that examination confirms our initial position, we understand that position better if we open ourselves to every side of the issue. That requires open-mindedness to the messages that come from places we don't like.

Disinterestedness: we all have a conflict of interest, and it's contagious

Back in the 1960s, the scientific community was at odds about whether sugar or fat was the culprit in the increasing rates of heart disease. In 1967, three Harvard scientists conducted a comprehensive review of the research to date, published in the *New England Journal of Medicine*, that firmly pointed the finger at fat as the culprit. The paper was, not surprisingly, influential in the debate on diet and heart disease. After all, the *NEJM* is and was a prestigious publication and the researchers were, all three, from Harvard. Blaming fat and exonerating sugar affected the diets of hundreds of millions of people for decades, a belief that caused a shift in eating habits that has been linked to the massive increase in obesity rates and diabetes.

The influence of this paper and its negative effects on America's eating habits and health provides a stunning demonstration of the imperative of disinterestedness. It was recently discovered that a trade group representing the sugar industry had paid the three Harvard scientists to write the paper, according to an article published in *JAMA Internal Medicine* in November 2016. Not surprisingly, consistent with the agenda of the sugar industry that had paid them, the researchers attacked the methodology of studies finding a link between sugar and heart disease and defended studies finding no link. The scientists' attacks on and defenses of the methodology of studies on fat and heart disease followed the same pro-sugar pattern.

The scientists involved are all dead. Were they alive, it's possible, if we could ask them, that they may not have even consciously known they were being influenced. Given human nature, they likely, at least, would have defended the truth of what they wrote and denied that the sugar industry dictated or influenced their thinking on the subject. Regardless, had the conflict of interest been disclosed, the scientific community would have viewed their conclusions with much more skepticism, taking into account the possibility of bias due to the researchers' financial interest. At the time, the *NEJM* did not require such disclosures. (That policy changed in 1984.) That omission prevented an accurate assessment of the findings, resulting in serious harm to the health of the nation.

We tend to think about conflicts of interest in the financial sense, like the researchers getting paid by the sugar industry. But conflicts of interest come in many flavors. Our brains have built-in conflicts of interest, interpreting the world around us to confirm our beliefs, to avoid having to admit ignorance or error, to take credit for good results following our decisions, to find reasons bad results following our decisions were due to factors outside our control, to compare well with our peers, and to live in a world where the way things turn out makes sense. We are not naturally disinterested. We don't process information independent of the way we wish the world to be.

Remember the thought experiment I suggested at the beginning of the book about what the headlines would have looked like if Pete Carroll's pass call had won the 2015 Super Bowl? Those headlines would have been about his brilliance. People would have analyzed Carroll's decision differently. Knowing how something turned out creates a conflict of interest that expresses itself as resulting.

Richard Feynman recognized that in physics—a branch of science that most of us consider as objective as 2 + 2 = 4—there is still demonstrable outcome bias. He found that if those analyzing data knew, or could even just intuit, the hypothesis being tested, the analysis would be more likely to support the hypothesis being tested. The measurements might be objective, but slicing and dicing the data is vulnerable to bias, even unconsciously. According to Robert MacCoun and physics Nobel laureate Saul Perlmutter in a 2015 *Nature* article, outcome-blind analysis has spread to several areas of particle physics and cosmology, where it "is often considered the only way to trust many results." Because the idea—introducing a random variable so that those analyzing the data could not surmise the outcome the researcher might be hoping for—is hardly known in biological, psychological, and social sciences, the authors concluded these methods "might improve trust and integrity in many sciences, including those with high-stakes analyses that are easily plagued by bias." Outcome blindness enforces disinterestedness.

We can apply this idea of outcome blindness to the way we communicate information as we workshop decisions about our far more ambiguous pursuits—like describing a poker hand, or a family argument, or the results of a market test for a new product. If the group is going to help us make and evaluate decisions in an unbiased way, we don't want to infect them in the way the data analysts were infected if they could surmise the hypothesis being tested. Telling someone how a story ends encourages them to be resulters, to interpret the details to fit that outcome. If I won a hand, it was more likely my group would assess my strategy as good. If I lost, the reverse would be true. Win a case at trial, the strategy is brilliant. Lose, and mistakes were made. We treat outcomes as good signals for decision quality, as if we were playing chess. If the outcome is known, it will bias the assessment of the decision quality to align with the outcome quality.

If the group is blind to the outcome, it produces higher fidelity evaluation of decision quality. The best way to do this is to deconstruct decisions before an outcome is known. Attorneys can evaluate trial strategy before the verdict comes in. Sales teams can evaluate strategy before learning whether they've closed the sale. Traders can vet process prior to positions being established or prior to options expiring. After the outcome, make it a habit when seeking advice to give the details without revealing the outcome. In poker, it isn't practical to analyze hands before knowing how they turn out since the results come within seconds of the decisions. To address this, many expert poker players often omit the outcome when seeking advice about their play.

This became such a natural habit that I didn't realize, until I started conducting poker seminars for players newer to the game, that this was not the norm for everyone. When I used hands I had played as illustrations, I would describe the hand up to the decision point I was discussing and no further, leaving off how the hand ended. This was, after all, how I had been trained by my poker group. When we finished the discussion, it was jarring to watch a roomful of people look at me like I had left them teetering on the edge of a cliff.

"Wait! How did the hand turn out?"

I gave them the red pill: "It doesn't matter."

Of course, we don't have to be describing a poker hand to use this strategy to promote disinterestedness. Anyone can provide the narrative only up to the point of the decision under consideration, leaving off the outcome so as not to infect their listeners with bias. And outcomes aren't the only problem. Beliefs are also contagious. If our listeners know what we believe to be true, they will likely work pretty hard to justify our beliefs, often without even knowing they are doing it. They will develop an ideological conflict of interest created by our informing our listeners of our beliefs. So when trying to vet some piece of information, some fact or opinion, we would do well to shield our listeners from what our opinion is as we seek the group's opinion.

Simply put, the group is less likely to succumb to ideological conflicts of interest when they don't know what the interest is. That's MacCoun and Perlmutter's point.

Another way a group can de-bias members is to reward them for skill in debating opposing points of view and finding merit in opposing positions. When members of the group disagree, a debate may be of only marginal value because the people debating are biased toward confirming their position, often creating stalemate. If two people disagree, a referee can get them to each argue the other's position with the goal of being the best debater. This acts to shift the interest to open-mindedness to the opposing opinion rather than confirmation of their original position. They can't win the debate if they can't forcefully and credibly argue the other side. The key is for the group to have a charter that rewards objective consideration of alternative hypotheses so that winning the debate feels better than supporting the pre-existing position. The group's reinforcement ought to discourage us from creating a straw-man argument when we're arguing against our beliefs, and encourage us to feel good about winning the debate. This is one of the reasons it's good for a group to have at least three members, two to disagree and one to referee.

What I've generally found is that two people whose positions on an issue are far apart will move toward the middle after a debate or skilled explanation of the opposing position. Engaging in this type of exchange creates an understanding of and appreciation for other points of view much deeper and more powerful than just listening to the other perspective. Ultimately, it gives us a deeper understanding of our own position. Once again, we are reminded of John Stuart Mill's assertion that this kind of open-mindedness is the *only* way to learn.

Organized skepticism: real skeptics make arguments and friends

Skepticism gets a bum rap because it tends to be associated with negative character traits. Someone who disagrees could be considered "disagreeable." Someone who dissents may be creating "dissention." Maybe part of it is that "skeptical" sounds like "cynical." Yet true skepticism is consistent with good manners, civil discourse, and friendly communications.

Skepticism is about approaching the world by asking why things might not be true rather than why they are true. It's a recognition that, while there is an objective truth, everything we believe about the world is not true. Thinking in bets embodies skepticism by encouraging us to examine what we do and don't know and what our level of confidence is in our beliefs and predictions. This moves us closer to what is objectively true.

A productive decision group would do well to organize around skepticism. That should also be its communications guide, because true skepticism isn't confrontational. Thinking in bets demands the imperative of skepticism. Without embracing uncertainty, we can't rationally bet on our beliefs. And we need to be particularly skeptical of information that agrees with us because we know that we are biased to just accept and applaud confirming evidence. If we don't "lean over backwards" (as Richard Feynman famously said) to figure out where we could be wrong, we are going to make some pretty bad bets.

If we embrace uncertainty and wrap that into the way we communicate with the group, confrontational dissent evaporates because we start from a place of not being sure. Just as we can wrap our uncertainty into the way we express our beliefs ("I'm 60% sure the waiter is going to mess up my order"), when we implement the norm of skepticism, we naturally modulate expression of dissent with others. Expression of disagreement is, after all, just another way to express our own beliefs, which we acknowledge are probabilistic in nature. Therefore, overtly expressing the uncertainty in a dissenting belief follows. No longer do we dissent with declarations of "You're wrong!" Rather, we engage by saying, "I'm not sure about that." Or even just ask, "Are *you* sure about that?" or "Have you considered this other way of thinking about it?" We engage this way simply because that is faithful to uncertainty. Organized skepticism invites people into a cooperative exploration. People are more open to hearing differing perspectives expressed this way.

Skepticism should be encouraged and, where possible, operationalized. The term "devil's advocate" developed centuries ago from the Catholic Church's practice, during the canonization process, of hiring someone to present arguments *against* sainthood. Just as the CIA has red teams and the State Department has its Dissent Channel, we can incorporate dissent into our business and personal lives. We can create a pod whose job (literally, in business, or figuratively, in our personal life) is to present the other side, to argue why a strategy might be ill-advised, why a prediction might be off, or why an idea might be ill informed. In so doing, the red team naturally raises alternate hypotheses. Likewise, companies can implement an anonymous dissent channel, giving any employee, from the mail room to the boardroom, a venue to express dissenting opinions, alternative strategies, novel ideas, and points of view that may disagree with the prevailing viewpoint of the company without fear of repercussions. The company should do its best to reward this constructive dissent by taking the suggestions seriously or the expression of diverse viewpoints won't be reinforced.

Less formally, look for opportunities to recruit a devil's advocate on an ad hoc basis. When seeking advice, we can ask specific questions to encourage the other person to figure out reasons why we might be wrong. That way, they won't be as reticent to challenge the action we want to pursue; we're *asking* for it, so it's not oppositional for them to disagree or give us advice contrary to what they think we want to hear.

Make no mistake: the process of seeing ourselves and the world more accurately and objectively is hard and makes us think about things we generally avoid. The group needs rules of engagement that don't make this harder by letting members get away with being nasty or dismissive. And we need to be aware that even a softer serve of dissent to those who have not agreed to the truthseeking charter can be perceived as confrontational. See David Letterman for details.

Communicating with the world beyond our group

This chapter has focused primarily on forming truthseeking groups on our own initiative or being part of such groups. Unless we have control over the culture around us,* those of us more actively seeking dissent will generally be in the minority when we are away from our group. That doesn't mean that truthseeking is off-limits in those settings. It just means we have to take the most constructive, civil elements of truthseeking communication and introduce them carefully. There are several ways to communicate to maximize our ability to engage in a truthseeking way with anyone.

First, express uncertainty. Uncertainty not only improves truthseeking within groups but also invites everyone around us to share helpful information and dissenting opinions. Fear of being wrong (or of having to suggest someone else is wrong) countervails the social contract of confirmation, often causing people to withhold valuable insights and opinions from us. If we start by making clear our own uncertainty, our audience is more likely to understand that any discussion that follows will not involve right

---

*When we are in a position of influence over an enterprise's hiring and culture, the same ideas apply. Hiring to a truthseeking charter and shaping a culture that rewards people for exploratory thought and expression of diverse viewpoints will serve an enterprise well. In fact, if we don't actively promote such a policy, we risk *discouraging* truthseeking due to people with diverse viewpoints feeling isolated or selecting out. One of the chief concerns of Heterodox Academy is figuring out how to get more conservatives to become social scientists or engage in exploratory thought with social scientists. That's a tough sell: no one likes the idea of being the lone holdout in a real-life version of *12 Angry Men*, especially with their reputation and livelihood at stake.

versus wrong, maximizing our truthseeking exchanges with those outside our chartered group.

Second, lead with assent. For example, listen for the things you agree with, state those and be specific, and then follow with "and" instead of "but." If there is one thing we have learned thus far it is that we like having our ideas affirmed. If we want to engage someone with whom we have some disagreement (inside or outside our group), they will be more open and less defensive if we start with those areas of agreement, which there surely will be. It is rare that we disagree with everything that someone has to say. By putting into practice the strategies that promote universalism, actively looking for the ideas that we agree with, we will more naturally engage people in the process of learning with us. We will also be more open-minded to what others have to say as well, enhancing our ability to calibrate our own beliefs.

When we lead with assent, our listeners will be more open to any dissent that might follow. In addition, when the new information is presented as *supplementing* rather than *negating* what has come before, our listeners will be much more open to what we have to say. The simplest rhetorical touches can make a difference. If someone expresses a belief or prediction that doesn't sound well calibrated and we have relevant information, try to say *and*, as in, "I agree with you that [insert specific concepts and ideas we agree with], AND . . ." After "and," add the additional information. In the same exchange, if we said, "I agree with you that [insert specific concepts and ideas you agree with], BUT . . . ," that challenge puts people on the defensive. "And" is an offer to contribute. "But" is a denial and repudiation of what came before.

We can think of this broadly as an attempt to avoid the language of "no." In the performance art of improvisation, the first advice is that when someone starts a scene, you should respond with "yes, and . . ." "Yes" means you are accepting the construct of the situation. "And" means you are adding to it. That's an excellent guideline in any situation in which you want to encourage exploratory thought. The important thing is to try to find areas of agreement to maintain the spirit of partnership in seeking the truth. In expressing potentially contradictory or dissenting information, our language ideally minimizes the element of disagreement.

Third, ask for a temporary agreement to engage in truth-seeking. If someone is off-loading emotion to us, we can ask them if they are just looking to vent or if they are looking for advice. If they aren't looking for advice, that's fine. The rules of engagement have been made clear. Sometimes, people just want to vent. I certainly do. It's in our nature. We want to be supportive of the people around us, and that includes comforting them when they just need some understanding and sympathy. But sometimes they'll say they are looking for advice, and that is potentially an agreement to opt in to some truthseeking. (Even then, tread lightly because people may say they want advice when what they really want is to be affirmed.)

This type of temporary agreement is really just a reverse version of the kind of temporary opting out that we did in my poker group when someone just had to vent about an especially intense, still-raw loss. Flipping that on its head, it doesn't have to be offensive to ask, "Do you want to just let it all out, or are you thinking of what to do about it next?"

Finally, focus on the future. As I said at the beginning of this book, we are generally pretty good at identifying the positive goals we are striving for; our problem is in the execution of the decisions along the way to reaching those goals. People dislike engaging with their poor execution. That requires taking responsibility for what is often a bad outcome, which, as David Letterman found out, will shut down the conversation. Rather than rehashing what has already happened, try instead to engage about what the person might do so that things will turn out better going forward. Whether it's our kids, other family members, friends, relationship partners, coworkers, or even ourselves, we share the common trait of generally being more rational about the future than the past. It's harder to get defensive about something that hasn't happened yet.

Imagine if David Letterman had said, "It's too bad you have all these kooky people creating all that drama in your life. Have you thought about how you might get rid of all this drama in the future?" If Lauren Conrad had said something "dramatic," like "I've got so many problems I can't even think about the future," or "I'm stuck with these people so there's nothing I can do about it," that obviously would be a good time to end the discussion. But the more likely result is that she would have engaged. And that focus on the future could get her to circle back to figure out why all the drama occurred; she wouldn't be able to sensibly answer the question about the future without examining the past. When we validate the other person's experience of the past and refocus on exploration of the future, they can get to their past decisions on their own.

This is a good approach to communicating with our children, who, with their developing egos, don't necessarily need a red pill shoved down their throats. A child isn't equipped to consent to the challenges of truthseeking exchanges. But they can be nudged. I know, in *The Matrix*, Morpheus took Neo to visit the Oracle and, while waiting in the lobby, he saw children bending spoons with their minds and engaging in other precocious red-pill behavior. But real-life kids are sensitive to feeling judged. And no real-life parent wants a kid with the ability to mentally send cutlery flying across the room.

My son was expert at fielding bad test scores as the teacher's fault. I had to be careful not to Letterman him. Instead, I would tell him, "It must be hard to have a teacher like that. Do you think there's anything you can do to improve your grade in the future?" That at once provided validation and led to productive discussions about subjects like developing strategies for preparing for future tests and setting up meetings with the teacher to figure out what the teacher was looking for in assignments. Meeting with the teacher also created a good impression that would likely be reflected in future grades. Ultimately, even with our own kids' decisions, rehashing outcomes can create defensiveness. The future, on the other hand, can always be better if we can get them to focus on things in their control.

These methods of communicating with people outside our truthseeking group focus on future goals and future actions. When it works, they take a short trip into the future, beyond the frustrations of the present and toward ways to improve things they can control. Accountability to a truthseeking group is also, in some ways, a time-travel portal. Because we know we will have to answer to the group, we start thinking in advance of how that will go. Anticipating and rehearsing those rational discussions can improve our initial decision-making and analysis, at a time when we might not otherwise be so rational.

That leads to the final decision strategy of this book: ways to use time-travel techniques for better decision-making. By recruiting past and future versions of yourself, you can become your own buddy.

CHAPTER 6

Adventures in Mental Time Travel

Let Marty McFly run into Marty McFly

Thanks to the success of the three Back to the Future movies, our go-to source on the rules of time travel is more likely to be Doc Brown than Dr. Stephen Hawking. The first rule, emphasized by the trilogy and repeated by nearly every time-travel movie since, is "Whatever you do, don't meet up with yourself!" Doc Brown (Christopher Lloyd) explains to Marty McFly (Michael J. Fox) in *Back to the Future: Part II* (1989) that "the encounter could create a time paradox, the results of which could cause a chain reaction that would unravel the very fabric of the space-time continuum and destroy the entire universe. Granted, that's the worst-case scenario. The destruction might, in fact, be very localized, limited to merely our own galaxy."

"Don't meet up with yourself" has become an unquestioned element of the "science" of time travel. In *Timecop* (1994), because "the same matter can't occupy the same space at the same time,"

Jean-Claude Van Damme's character destroys the villain by pushing his past and future versions together. The villain turns into a liquefied blob and disappears from existence.

In real-life decision-making, when we bring our past- or future-self into the equation, the space-time continuum doesn't unravel. Far from turning us into a liquefied blob, a visit from past or future versions of us helps present-us make better bets. When making decisions, isolating ourselves from thinking about similar decisions in the past and possible future consequences is frequently the very thing that turns us into a blob, mired by in-the-moment thinking where the scope of time is distorted. As decision-makers, we *want* to collide with past and future versions of ourselves. Our capacity for mental time travel makes this possible. As is the case with accountability, such meetings can lead to better decisions: at the moment of the decision, accountability to our group can pop us briefly into the future to imagine the conversation about the decision we will have with that group. Running that conversation will often remind us to stay on a more rational path.

Just as we can recruit other people to be our decision buddies, we can recruit other versions of ourselves to act as our own decision buddies. We can harness the power of mental time traveling, operationalizing it, encouraging it, and figuring out ways to cause that collision of past, present, and future as much as possible. Present-us needs that help, and past-us and future-us can be the best decision buddies for the job.*

---

*There is an entire field of study on mental time travel and its benefits to decision-making. Neuroscientist Endel Tulving, a psychology professor at the University of Toronto, pioneered analysis and research into chronesthesia, the term for

Poker players have unique decision challenges that get them thinking a lot about how to get this collision of past-, present- and future-self to occur at the moment of making a decision and executing on it. Because decisions in poker are made so quickly, players don't have the luxury of time in coordinating their rational, long-term, strategic plans with their decisions at the poker table. And all those decisions made under severe time constraints have immediate consequences expressed as an exchange of poker chips. The constant exchange of chips reminds players that there is risk in every decision. Of course, the direction in which the chips flow in the short term only loosely correlates with decision quality. You can win a hand after making bad decisions and lose a hand after making good ones. But the mere fact that chips are changing hands is a reminder that every decision has consequences—that all those execution decisions you make along the way really matter.

Away from the poker table, we don't feel or experience the consequences of most of the decisions we make right away. If we are winning or losing to a particular decision, the consequences may take time to reveal themselves. If we make a losing eating decision, like substituting SnackWell's for apples, there's no immediate outcome that lets us know there might have been a cost to that choice. If we repeat that kind of decision enough, there will be consequences, but they take time to play out. In business, if a leader ignores the ideas of an intern because "What does an intern possibly know?" it could take years for that intern to

---

mental time travel through the ability to be aware of our past or future. For further material on the neuroscience of time travel and its decision-making benefits, see the Selected Bibliography and Recommendations for Further Reading.

become a successful competitor before that mistake becomes obvious. If the trajectory of that business suffers because of the poverty of new ideas, the owner of the business might never realize the effect of that attitude.

The best poker players develop practical ways to incorporate their long-term strategic goals into their in-the-moment decisions. The rest of this chapter is devoted to many of these strategies designed to recruit past- and future-us to help with all the execution decisions we have to make to reach our long-term goals. As with all the strategies in this book, we must recognize that no strategy can turn us into perfectly rational actors. In addition, we can make the best possible decisions and still not get the result we want. Improving decision quality is about *increasing* our chances of good outcomes, not *guaranteeing* them. Even when that effort makes a small difference—more rational thinking and fewer emotional decisions, translated into an increased probability of better outcomes—it can have a significant impact on how our lives turn out. Good results compound. Good processes become habits, and make possible future calibration and improvement.

Those methods involve a lot of mental time travel, and those poker players could teach Marty McFly and Doc Brown a thing or two.

Night Jerry

For all the scientific research on the battle between our immediate desires and long-term goals, a particularly succinct explanation comes from Jerry Seinfeld, on why he doesn't get enough sleep: "I stay up late at night because I'm Night Guy. Night Guy wants to stay up late. 'What about getting up after five hours of sleep?' 'That's Morning Guy's problem. That's not my problem. I'm Night Guy. I stay up as late as I want.' So you get up in the morning: you're exhausted, you're groggy. 'Oooh, I hate that Night Guy.' See, Night Guy always screws Morning Guy."

That's a good example of how we struggle in the present to take care of our future-self. Night Jerry is always going to want to stay up late and, if Morning Jerry has no say in the decision, Night Jerry will get his way regardless of what's in Jerry's longer-term best interest. When we make in-the-moment decisions (and don't ponder the past or future), we are more likely to be irrational and impulsive.*

This tendency we all have to favor our present-self at the expense of our future-self is called temporal discounting.† We

---

* Of course, being in deliberative mind is no guarantee of rationality. As I've noted regarding Dan Kahan's work on motivated reasoning, people performing complicated tasks with statistics—clearly a deliberative- or System 2–type task—were susceptible to reasoning to make the math come out consistent with their prior beliefs. And the people with the most math skill had the strongest tendency to do that. Daniel Kahneman has also recognized that System 2 should not be considered immune to bias.

We are capable of all kinds of irrationality in deliberative mind. If we get out of reflexive mind, however, we can reduce the likelihood of emotionally driven decisions and decrease the influence of bias through self-reflection and vigilance. One way to do this is to take advantage of mental time-travel strategies.

† From four-year-olds to adults, temporal discounting is a universal issue. The most famous experiment about the difficulty (and importance) of being patient, known as the Marshmallow Test, was performed by professor Walter Mischel and colleagues at Stanford starting in the early 1960s. At Stanford's Bing Nursery School, they offered children a choice between a smaller reward (like one marshmallow) that they could have immediately, or a larger reward (like two marshmallows) if they were willing to wait, alone, for up to twenty minutes. The children

are willing to take an irrationally large discount to get a reward now instead of waiting for a bigger reward later. An example of temporal discounting among adults includes a study from the military drawdown in the 1990s that led tens of thousands of military employees to choose lump-sum retirement payments at drastically discounted rates instead of guaranteed annuity payments. The men and women of the U.S. military took lump-sum payments worth $2.5 billion, a 40% discount compared to the present value of the annuity payments they would have received. (For additional sources on temporal discounting, see the Selected Bibliography and Recommendations for Further Reading.)

When Night Jerry stays up late, it's because it benefits him *now*; he discounts the benefits that come later from going to bed. Saving for retirement is a temporal discounting problem: the gratification of spending discretionary income is immediate. Putting it away for retirement means we have to wait decades to get enjoyment from that money. We are built for temporal discounting, for using the resources that are available to us now as

---

used every imaginable trick to wait for the larger reward. They made faces, covered their eyes, turned their chairs around, cupped their hands around the marshmallow without touching it, covered their mouths, smelled the marshmallow, and carried on wordless conversations (from nearly imperceptible admonitions to animated arguments). Mischel and his colleagues saw struggles that "could bring tears to your eyes, have you applauding their creativeness and cheering them on, and give you fresh hope" for the potential of young children.

Subsequent studies following up on the marshmallow kids have shown that the ability to delay gratification is correlated with markers of success throughout adolescence and into adulthood: higher SAT scores, better social and cognitive functioning ratings, lower body mass index, lower likelihood of addiction, better sense of self-worth, and higher ability to pursue goals and adapt to frustration and stress.

opposed to saving them for a future version of us that we aren't particularly in touch with in the moment of the decision. Time traveling can get us in touch with that future version of us. It can get future-us to remind present-us, "Hey, don't discount!" Or at least, "Don't discount so much!"

When we think about the past and the future, we engage deliberative mind, improving our ability to make a more rational decision. When we imagine the future, we don't just make it up out of whole cloth, inventing a future based on nothing that we have ever seen or experienced. Our vision of the future, rather, is rooted in our memories of the past. The future we imagine is a novel reassembling of our past experiences. Given that, it shouldn't be surprising that the same neural network is engaged when we imagine the future as when we remember the past. Thinking about the future is *remembering* the future, putting memories together in a creative way to imagine a possible way things might turn out. Those brain pathways include the hippocampus (a key structure for memory) and the prefrontal cortex, which controls System 2, deliberative decision-making. It is our cognitive control center.* By engaging those pathways, Night Jerry can access memories like oversleeping and missing appointments or dozing off during morning meetings that he can use to imagine how tired Morning Jerry will be or what's going to happen to Morning Jerry's schedule when he doesn't want to get up or how his day will go when he can't pay attention.

Wouldn't it be great if Morning Jerry could travel back in

---

*For a good overview on the research in this area, see "The Future of Memory: Remembering, Imagining, and the Brain," by Daniel Schacter and colleagues, cited in the Selected Bibliography and Recommendations for Further Reading.

time and tap Night Jerry on the shoulder to tell him to go to bed? As it turns out, there's an app for that.

From advancements in photo techniques and virtual reality, there is software that can show you a prediction of what you will look like decades into the future. If you feel, like most adults, bad about seeing your parents age, these images of future-you can be unsettling, like looking into a sadist-designed funhouse mirror. Fortunately, they've found ways to put this age-progression technology to more productive uses than just making us stare into the void of our own mortality.

Saving for retirement is a Night Jerry–versus–Morning Jerry problem. If Night Jerry isn't even thinking ahead to tomorrow morning, he's certainly not thinking ahead several decades to retirement. Retirement planning involves a series of decisions in which our present-self can act to the detriment or benefit of our future-self. When we set retirement goals, we are necessarily thinking about our future-self's goals—how much we need to save for that older version of us to live comfortably. Our spending decisions, however, don't seem to be particularly focused on what's best for our seventy-year-old-self. In fact, a quick Google search on the topic quickly reveals that our retirement savings are dangerously low. According to one study by the Center for Retirement Research at Boston College, "roughly half of today's working households will not be able to maintain their standard of living in retirement." Depending on which estimate you read, the shortfall could be $6.8 to $14 *trillion*.

Several organizations and companies with an interest in encouraging retirement planning have resources that allow clients to "meet" their future-selves as they make retirement decisions. In the simplest versions of these tools, clients plug in their age, income, savings practices, and retirement goals. The apps then show the client the financial situation and lifestyle their future-self can expect, compared with the present.

Prudential Retirement, AARP, and others have versions of these apps that emphasize the consequences of retirement planning by *visually* introducing us to our future-self. Bank of America Merrill Lynch in 2012 (for web-access computing) and 2014 (for mobile devices) introduced Merrill Edge, which includes a tool called "Face Retirement." Customers upload a picture of themselves and get to see, according to the press release, "a life-like 3D animation of their future self, enabling them to envision every wrinkle they could encounter at retirement age—and beyond." Night Jerry gets a glimpse of what Morning Jerry looks like without enough sleep to function.

This idea that seeing our aged future-self could help us make better allocation decisions is based, in part, on research by Jeremy Bailenson and Laura Carstensen of Stanford University's Freeman Spogli Institute for International Studies. They used immersive virtual-reality technology in a lab setting to demonstrate how a visit from Morning Jerry will help Night Jerry make better decisions. Subjects entered a virtual-reality environment, after which they were asked to allocate $1,000 among accounts for various purposes, one of which was a hypothetical retirement account. Subjects seeing a digital representation of their present-self in the mirror allocated on average $73.90 to the retirement account. Other subjects looking in that mirror saw an age-progressed version of themselves. This latter group of subjects, on average, allocated $178.10 to the retirement account. This is a startling example of how future-us can act as an effective decision buddy for present-us.

Bringing our future-self into the decision gets us started thinking about the future consequences of those in-the-moment decisions. Fundamentally, Morning Jerry and Night Jerry are living the same life, and getting Morning Jerry into Night Jerry's face will remind him of that. Seeing our aged-self in the mirror, along with a spreadsheet showing us how future-us has to struggle to get by, is a persuasive reminder to put aside some discretionary spending money for retirement. It's that tap on the shoulder from our future-self. "Hey, don't forget about me. I'm going to exist and I'd like you to please take that into account."

We're not perfectly rational when we ponder the past or the future and engage deliberative mind, but we are more likely to make choices consistent with our long-term goals when we can get out of the moment and engage our past- and future-selves. We want Night Jerry and Morning Jerry colliding on the decision of when to get some sleep. We want all those Marty McFlys to get the additional perspective of all the other Marty McFlys. And we want our aged, wrinkly self colliding with us when we decide between spending more money now on something like a nicer car versus saving more money for retirement.

Moving regret in front of our decisions

Philosophers agree that regret is one of the most intense emotions we feel, but they have argued about whether it is productive or useful. Nietzsche said that remorse was "adding to the first act of stupidity a second." Thoreau, on the other hand, praised the power of regret: "Make the most of your regrets; never smother your sorrow, but tend and cherish it till it comes to have a separate and integral interest. To regret deeply is to live afresh."

The problem isn't so much whether regret is an unproductive emotion. It's that regret occurs after the fact, instead of before. As Nietzsche points out, regret can do nothing to change what has already happened. We just wallow in remorse about something over which we no longer have any control. But if regret occurred before a decision instead of after, the experience of regret might get us to change a choice likely to result in a bad outcome. Then we could embrace Thoreau's view and harness the power of regret because it would serve a valuable purpose. It would be helpful, then, if we could get regret to do some time traveling of its own, moving before our decisions instead of after them. That way, regret might be able to keep us from making a bad bet. In addition, it wouldn't, as Nietzsche implied, rear its head later by causing us to make a remorse-fueled second mistake.

Morning Jerry regretted Night Jerry's decision to stay up late, but it was too late for him to do anything about it. When we see the retirement-savings shortfall in this country, there is no doubt that many of the future, retired versions of us are going to regret the financial allocation decisions that younger-us made, after it is too late to fix it. The age-progression imaging works to address this issue of regret occurring when it's already too late. By giving us a look at the retirement-aged version of ourselves, it gives us a chance to experience some regret that we didn't plan adequately for retirement *before* we've made inadequate plans. That was one of the purposes of my loss limit in poker. Because of the loss-limit agreement I had made with myself and my group, I ran the conversation in my head that I'd be forced to have when I explained why I kept playing beyond my limit. It gave me a chance to regret the decision before I bought more chips.

One of our time-travel goals is to create moments like that, where we can interrupt an in-the-moment decision and take some time to consider the decision from the perspective of our past and future. We can then create a habit routine around these decision interrupts to encourage this perspective taking, asking ourselves a set of simple questions at the moment of the decision designed to get future-us and past-us involved. We can do this by imagining how future-us is likely to feel about the decision or by imagining how we might feel about the decision today if past-us had made it. The approaches are complementary; whether you choose to travel to the past or travel to the future depends solely on what approach you find most effective.

Business journalist and author Suzy Welch developed a popular tool known as 10-10-10 that has the effect of bringing future-us into more of our in-the-moment decisions. "Every 10-10-10 process starts with a question. . . . [W]hat are the consequences of each of my options in ten minutes? In ten months? In ten years?" This set of questions triggers mental time travel that cues that accountability conversation (also encouraged by a truthseeking decision group). We can build on Welch's tool by asking the questions through the frame of the past: "How would I feel today if I had made this decision ten minutes ago? Ten months ago? Ten years ago?" Whichever frame we choose, we draw on our past experiences (including similar decisions we may have regretted) in answering the questions, recruiting into the decision those less-reactive brain pathways that control executive functioning.

In poker, because the decisions are all made in the moment and the consequences are big and immediate, routines like 10-10-10 are a survival skill. I recognized in poker that in the same way that I was not the best judge of how I was playing after losing a certain amount of money, I was also not the best judge of the quality of my poker after about six to eight hours of play. Just as we can convince ourselves we are sober enough to drive, it is easy for poker players to convince themselves that they are alert enough to keep playing after many hours of intense, intellectually taxing work. In my more rational moments, away from the tables, I knew I would be better off if I played just six to eight hours per session. When I reached that point in a session and considered continuing past that time limit, I could use a 10-10-10-like strategy to recruit my past- and future-self: How have I felt when I kept playing in the past? How has it generally worked out? When I look back, do I feel I was playing my best? This routine of asking myself these questions helped mitigate the in-the-moment risk that, as I was losing my mental edge, I might try to convince myself that the game was so great that I had to keep playing.

Moving regret in front of a decision has numerous benefits. First, obviously, it can influence us to make a better decision. Second, it helps us treat ourselves (regardless of the actual decision) more compassionately after the fact. We can anticipate and prepare for negative outcomes. By planning ahead, we can devise a plan to respond to a negative outcome instead of just reacting to it. We can also familiarize ourselves with the likelihood of a negative outcome and how it will feel. Coming to peace with a bad outcome in advance will feel better than refusing to acknowledge it, facing it only after it has happened.

After-the-fact regret can consume us. Like all emotions, regret initially feels intense but gets better with time. Time-travel strategies can help us remember that the intensity of what we feel now will subside over time. And that helps reduce the emotion we feel in the moment, making it less likely that we will prove Nietzsche right and add a second act of stupidity to the first.

A flat tire, the ticker, and a zoom lens

Imagine you are standing on a narrow strip of concrete on the shoulder of the highway. Behind you is your car, hazard lights flashing. The rear tire on the driver's side is shredded. It is fully dark and the drizzle has turned into a cold, heavy downpour. You've called roadside assistance, twice, and both times (after long hold times) spoken with operators who've told you someone will arrive "as soon as they get there after responding to your call." You decide to change the tire yourself, only to discover you have no jack. You're soaked to the skin and cold.

How does it feel? It likely feels like the worst moment of your life. You are likely bemoaning how unlucky you are, wondering why these things always happen to you. You are miserable and you can't imagine feeling any other way.*

That's how it feels in the moment. But if the flat tire had happened a year ago, do you think it would have an effect on your happiness today, or your overall happiness over the past year? Not likely. It likely wouldn't cause your overall happiness to tick

---

*Professor Ronald Howard, director of the Decisions and Ethics Center at Stanford and the founder of decision analysis, uses countless entertaining variations of how decision bias gets exposed in the common but bothersome flat-tire situation. My favorite is his version where a guy gets a flat tire in front of a mental hospital. A patient from the hospital watches through the fence as the guy, affected by having an audience, steps on the hub cap holding the four nuts from the tire he removed, and they roll down a sewer. The guy feels angry, flustered, helpless. The patient calls through the fence, "Why don't you remove one nut from each of the other three tires and put those three on the spare?" The guy says, "That's a brilliant idea. What are you doing in a place like this?" The patient tells him, "I may be crazy, but I'm not stupid."

up or down. It would probably have faded to a funny story (or a story you try to make sound funny) told at cocktail parties.

In our decision-making lives, we aren't that good at taking this kind of perspective—at accessing the past and future to get a better view of how any given moment might fit into the scope of time. It just feels how it feels in the moment and we react to it. We want to create opportunities to take the broader perspective prior to making decisions driven by the magnified feelings we have in the moment. A 10-10-10 strategy does that, getting us to imagine the decision or outcome in the perspective of the past and the future.

The flat tire isn't as awful as it seems in the moment. This kind of time-travel strategy calms down the in-the-moment emotions we have about an event, so we can get back to using the more rational part of our brain. Recruiting past-us and future-us in this way activates the neural pathways that engage the prefrontal cortex, inhibiting emotional mind and keeping events in more rational perspective. This discourages us from magnifying the present moment, blowing it out of proportion and overreacting to it.

This overestimation of the impact of any individual moment on our overall happiness is the emotional equivalent of watching the ticker in the financial world. We make a long-term stock investment because we want it to appreciate over years or decades. Yet there we are, watching a downward tick over a few minutes, consumed by imagining the worst. What's the volume? Is it heavier than usual? Better check the news stories. Better check the message boards to find out what rumors are circulating.

A stock like Berkshire Hathaway reveals why ticker watching isn't a particularly productive endeavor when you are investing for the long run. Look at this chart of Berkshire's performance since 1964:

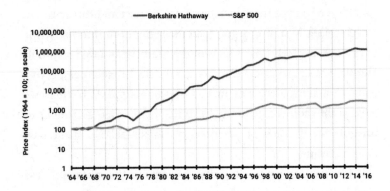

Now zoom in on a random day in late January 2017. The upticks and downticks look large and potentially frightening. You can imagine sitting at the low point around 11:30, feeling like your losses are spiraling.

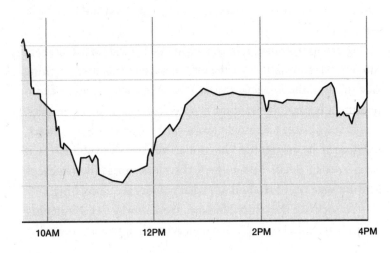

If you zoomed in on the performance of Berkshire Hathaway stock during the banking crisis, September 2008 to March 2009, you would feel terrible most *days*:

BERKSHIRE HATHAWAY (SEPT. 2008–MARCH 2009)

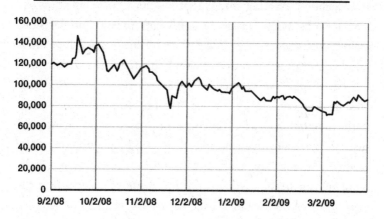

Yet we know from the first chart, the big picture, that all those minute-to-minute and even day-to-day changes had little effect on the investment's general upward trajectory.

Our problem is that we're ticker watchers of our own lives. Happiness (however we individually define it) is not best measured by looking at the ticker, zooming in and magnifying moment-by-moment or day-by-day movements. We would be better off thinking about our happiness as a long-term stock holding. We would do well to view our happiness through a wide-angle lens, striving for a long, sustaining upward trend in our happiness stock, so it resembles the first Berkshire Hathaway chart.

Mental time travel makes that kind of perspective possible. We can use our past- and future-selves to pull us out of the moment and remind us when we're watching the ticker, looking at our lives through that lens on extreme zoom.

When we view these upticks and downticks under the magnification of that in-the-moment zoom lens, our emotional responses are, similarly, amplified. Like the flat tire in the rain, we are capable of treating things that will have little effect on our long-term happiness as having significant impact. Our decision-making becomes reactive, focused on off-loading negative emotions or sustaining positive emotions from the latest change in the status quo. We can see how this can result in self-serving bias: fielding outcomes to off-load the negative emotions we feel in the moment from a bad outcome by blaming them on luck and sustaining the positive emotions from good outcomes by taking credit for them. The decisions driven by the emotions of the moment can become a self-fulfilling prophecy, degrading the quality of the bets we make, increasing the chances of bad outcomes, and making things worse.

"Yeah, but what have you done for me lately?"

Watching the ticker doesn't just magnify what has happened in the very recent past. It distorts our view of it as well. To understand the additional element of distortion, the casino is a great place to look.

Imagine that you go to a casino for an evening of blackjack with your friends. In the first half hour, you go on a winning streak and are ahead $1,000. You keep playing because you and your friends are having such a good time. For the next hour and a half, it seems like you never win a hand. You lose back the

$1,000 and break even for the night. How are you feeling about that?

Now imagine that you lose $1,000 in the first half hour and stick around playing with your friends because they are having a great time. In the next hour and a half you go on a winning streak that erases the early loss, and you end up breaking even for the night. How are you feeling about that?

I'm guessing you are pretty sad and morose about starting off with the big win, only to break even. In the second example, you're probably so happy that the drinks are on you. While you took a different path to get there, in both cases you didn't win or lose a dime at the end of the two hours. But in one case you are really sad about the result and the other really happy.

As they say in the infomercial world, "But, wait! There's more!"

Imagine you go up that same $1,000 in the first half hour but now, over the next hour and a half, you can't seem to win a hand and lose $900 back, ending the night with a $100 win. How does that feel? Now imagine that you lost that same $1,000 in the first half hour but then went on a winning streak to end the night down only $100. How does that feel? Most likely, you're pretty glum about the $100 win but still buying drinks for everyone after recovering from that terrible start to only lose $100. So you're sad that you won $100 and happy that you lost $100.

The way we field outcomes is path dependent. It doesn't so much matter where we end up as how we got there. What has happened in the recent past drives our emotional response much more than how we are doing overall. That's how we can win $100 and be sad, and lose $100 and be happy. The zoom lens doesn't just magnify, it distorts. This is true whether we are in a casino, making investment decisions, in a relationship, or on the side of the road with a flat tire. If we got a big promotion last week and have a flat tire right now, we are cursing our lives, complaining about how unlucky we are. Our feelings are not a reaction to the average of how things are going. We feel sad if we are breaking even (or winning) on an investment that used to be valued much higher. In relationships, even small disagreements seem big in the midst of the disagreement. The problem in all these situations (and countless others) is that our in-the-moment emotions affect the quality of the decisions we make in those moments, and we are very willing to make decisions when we are not emotionally fit to do so.

Now imagine if you had gone for that night of blackjack a year ago. When you think about the outcomes as having happened in the distant past, it is likely your preference for the results reverses, landing in a more rational place. You are now happier about the $100 win than about the $100 loss. Once we pull ourselves out of the moment through time-traveling exercises, we can see these things in proportion to their size, free of the distortion caused by whether the ticker just moved up or down.

This is a constant challenge in poker. While the moving scoreboard has the upside of reminding players that all their decisions have consequences, there is also a downside. The scoreboard, like a stock ticker, reflects the most recent changes, creating a risk that players get caught up in ticker watching, responding emotionally and disproportionately to momentary fluctuations. Poker players think about this problem a lot.

Tilt

Surfers have more than twenty terms to describe different kinds of waves. The reason is that the type of wave, the way it breaks, the direction it's coming from, the bottom depth, etc., create differing challenges for surfers. There are *closeouts* (waves that break all at once) and *double-ups* (a type of wave created when two waves meet to form one wave) and *reforms* (a wave that will break, then die down, then break again). Non-surfers just call all of these "waves." On rare occasions when we non-surfers need to be more specific, we just add a lot of extra words. Those extra words don't cost us much because it doesn't come up very often—maybe never. But for people involved in specialized activities, it's worth it to be able to communicate a complex concept in a single word that laypeople would need lengthy phrases to convey. Having a nuanced, precise vocabulary is what jargon is all about. It's why carpenters have at least a dozen names for different kinds of nails, and in the field of neuro-oncology, there are more than 120 types of brain and central nervous system tumors.

Because poker players are in a constant struggle to keep in-the-moment fluctuations in perspective, their jargon has a variety of terms for the concept that "bad outcomes can have an impact on your emotions that compromise your decision-making going forward so that you make emotionally charged, irrational decisions that are likely to result in more bad outcomes that will then negatively impact your decision-making going forward and so on." The most common is *tilt*. Tilt is the poker player's worst enemy, and the word instantly communicates to other poker players that you were emotionally unhinged in your decision-making because of the way things turned out.* If you blow some recent event out of proportion and react in a drastic way, you're on tilt.

The concept of tilt comes from traditional pinball machines. To keep players from damaging the machines by lifting them to alter the course of the ball, the manufacturers placed sensors inside that disabled the machine if it was violently jostled. The flippers stopped working, the lights went off, and the word "tilt" flashed at numerous places on the layout. The origin of tilt in pinball is apt because what's going on in our brain in moments of tilt is like a shaken pinball machine. When the emotional center of the brain starts pinging, the limbic system (specifically the amygdala) shuts down the prefrontal cortex. We light up . . . then we shut down our cognitive control center.

There are emotional and physiological signs of tilt. In poker, you can hear a poker player on tilt from several tables away. Every several hands, you hear a raised voice in an incredulous tone: "Seriously? Again?" or "I don't know why I bother playing. I should just hand over all my money." (Imagine the inflection of exasperation and a lot of swearing.) Along with these verbal cues, there are physiological signs of tilt. We can feel our cheeks flush and our heart race. Our respiration speeds up.

Tilt, of course, is not just limited to poker. Any kind of outcome has the potential for causing an emotional reaction. We can be tempted to make a reactive, emotional decision in a

---

*Tilt doesn't just result from bad outcomes, although that is the more likely impetus. Poker players also talk about winner's tilt, where a series of good outcomes distorts decision-making, particularly in causing a player to play as if their win rate is not a momentary fluctuation from the mean but will continue at that rate in the future. In the euphoric, in-the-moment feeling of a big uptick, winners can make irrational in-game decisions or overestimate their level of skill and accomplishment and commit themselves to play for higher stakes.

disagreement with a relationship partner, or because of bad service in a restaurant, or a comment in the workplace, or making a sale only to have it canceled, or having an idea dismissed. We've all had this experience in our personal and professional lives: blowing out of proportion a momentary event because of an in-the-moment emotional reaction.

By recognizing in advance these verbal and physiological signs that ticker watching is making us tilt, we can commit to develop certain habit routines at those moments. We can pre-commit to walk away from the situation when we feel the signs of tilt, whether it's a fight with a spouse or child, aggravation in a work situation, or losing at a poker table. We can take some space till we calm down and get some perspective, recognizing that when we are on tilt we aren't *decision fit*. Aphorisms like "take ten deep breaths" and "why don't you sleep on it?" capture this desire to avoid decisions while on tilt. We can commit to asking ourselves the 10-10-10 questions or things like, "What's happened to me in the past when I've felt this way?" or "Do I think it's going to help me to be in this state while I'm making decisions?" Or we can gain perspective by asking how or whether this will have a real effect on our long-term happiness.

If you are part of a truthseeking pod, that pod can incorporate questions designed to sniff out tilt and reduce the number of decisions we execute while on tilt. We can incorporate vigilance around ticker watching when evaluating each other's decisions, including the most obvious question: "Do you think maybe you are/were on tilt?" We can follow that with time-traveling questions like, "Do you think this will really matter in the long run?" If we make the concept of tilt and its negative impact on decision quality part of the discussion, it creates accountability around tilt to the group. Ignoring the signals of emotional decision-making raises the prospect of having to answer for it. That, in turn, will get us positive reinforcement from the group for recognizing the signs of tilt and avoiding decision-making in that state. It also trains good habits of mind so we can run these processes on our own, acting as our own decision buddy.

At the very beginning of my poker career, I heard an aphorism from some of the legends of the profession: "It's all just one long poker game." That aphorism is a reminder to take the long view, especially when something big happened in the last half hour, or the previous hand—or when we get a flat tire. Once we learn specific ways to recruit past and future versions of us to remind ourselves of this, we can keep the most recent upticks and downticks in their proper perspective. When we take the long view, we're going to think in a more rational way.

Ulysses contracts: time traveling to precommit

The most famous traveler of antiquity, the Homeric hero Odysseus, was also a mental time traveler. One of the legendary trials on his journey home involved the island of the Sirens. Sailors passing the island became so entranced by the Sirens' song that they would steer toward the shore, crashing to their deaths on the rocky shoal around the island. Aware of the fate that befell any sailor who heard the song, Odysseus told his crew to tie his hands to the mast and fill their ears with beeswax as they approached the island. They could then steer safely, unaffected by the song they could not hear, while he would get to hear the Sirens' song without imperiling the ship.

The plan worked perfectly. This action—past-us preventing

present-us from doing something stupid—has become known as a Ulysses contract. (Most translations of Homer use the hero's ancient Greek name, Odysseus. The time-travel strategy uses the hero's ancient Roman name, Ulysses.)

It's the perfect interaction between past-you, present-you, and future-you. Ulysses recognized that his future-self (along with his crew) would become entranced by the Sirens and steer toward the rocks. So he had his crew fill their ears with wax and tie his hands to the mast, literally binding his future-self to better behavior. One of the simplest examples of this kind of contract is using a ride-sharing service when you go to a bar. A past version of you, who anticipated that you might decide irrationally about whether you are okay to drive, has bound your hands by taking the car keys out of them.

Most illustrations of Ulysses contracts, like the original, involve *raising* a barrier against irrationality. But these kinds of precommitment contracts can also be designed to lower barriers that interfere with rational action. For example, if we are trying to eat healthier, we might identify that an irrational decision point occurs when we go to the mall with someone, agree to meet them in a couple hours, and spend idle time in the food court. A barrier-*inducing* Ulysses contract could involve us not going to the mall at all or budgeting our time tightly so we have just enough time to accomplish our intended purpose. A barrier-*reducing* contract would be to precommit to carry healthy snacks in our bag, so we can increase the probability, if we're doing any idle eating, that we can make a better choice since we have drastically reduced the effort it takes to grab a healthier snack.

Ulysses contracts can come in varying levels of how much your hands are bound, ranging from physically preventing acting on a decision to just committing in advance to certain actions without any barriers save the commitment itself. Regardless of the level of binding, precommitment contracts trigger a decision-interrupt. At the moment when we consider breaking the contract, when we want to cut the binding, we are much more likely to stop and think.

When you are physically prohibited from deciding, you are interrupted in the sense that you are prevented from acting on an irrational impulse; the option simply isn't there. That's the brute-force way to do this kind of time traveling. Past-Ulysses interrupted present-Ulysses's decision by taking the decision, literally, out of his hands.

In most situations, you can't make a precommitment that's 100% tamper-proof. The hurdles aren't necessarily high, but they nevertheless create a decision-interrupt that may prompt us to do the bit of time travel necessary to reduce emotion and encourage perspective and rationality in the decision. A lawyer attending a settlement negotiation can make a precommitment, with the client or other lawyers on their team, as to the lowest amount they would accept in a settlement (or the highest amount they would agree to pay to settle). Home buyers, understanding that in the moment they might get emotionally attached to a home, can commit in advance to their budget. Once they decide on a house they want to buy, they can decide in advance what the maximum amount they'd be willing to pay for it is so that they don't get caught up in the moment of the bidding.

Throwing out all the junk food in our house makes it impossible for midnight-us to easily, mindlessly, down a pint of ice cream. But as long as we have a car or food delivery services, that kind of food is still available somewhere. It just takes a lot more effort to get it. The same is true if we ask the waiter not to put the bread basket on the table at the restaurant. We can still, obviously, get bread, but now we have to ask the waiter to bring it. In fact, even Ulysses had to rely on his crew to ignore him if, upon hearing the Sirens' song, he signaled them to free him.

Ulysses contracts can help us in several ways to be more rational investors. When we set up an automatic allocation from our pay into a retirement account, that's a Ulysses contract. We could go through the trouble of changing the allocation, but setting it up initially gives our goal-setting, System 2–self a chance to precommit to what we know is best for our long-term future. And if we want to change the allocation, we have to take some specific steps to do so, creating a decision-interrupt.

Investment advisors do this with clients, determining in advance, as they are discussing the client's goals, the conditions under which they would buy, sell, hold, or press their positions on particular stocks. If the client later wants to make an emotional decision in the moment (involving, for example, a sudden rise or drop in the value of an investment), the advisor can remind the client of the discussion and the agreement.

In all these instances, the precommitment or predecision doesn't completely bind our hands to the mast. An emotional, reactive, irrational decision is still physically possible (though, to various degrees, more difficult). The precommitments, however, provide a stop-and-think moment before acting, triggering the potential for deliberative thought. Will that prevent an emotional, irrational decision every time? No. Will we sometimes still decide in a reflexive or mindless way? Of course. But it will happen less often.

Decision swear jar

We all know about the concept of a swear jar: if someone swears, they put a dollar in the jar. The idea behind it is that it will make people mindful about swearing and reduce how much they do it. A "decision swear jar" is a simple kind of precommitment contract that we can apply to many of the key concepts of this book. For the decision swear jar, we identify the language and thinking patterns that signal we are veering from our goal of truthseeking. When we find ourselves using certain words or succumbing to the thinking patterns we are trying to avoid because we know they are signs of irrationality, a stop-and-think moment can be can be created. You can think about this as a way to implement accountability.

We have discussed several patterns of irrationality in the way we lodge beliefs and field outcomes. From these, we can commit to vigilance around words, phrases, and thoughts that signal that we might be not be our most rational selves. Your list of those warning signs will be specific to you (or your family, friends, or enterprise), but here is a sample of the kinds of things that might trigger a decision-interrupt.

- Signs of the illusion of certainty: "I know," "I'm sure," "I knew it," "It always happens this way," "I'm certain of it," "you're 100% wrong," "You have no idea what you're talking about," "There's no way that's true," "0%" or "100%" or their equivalents, and other terms signaling that we're presuming things are more certain than we know they are. This also includes stating things as absolutes, like "best" or "worst" and "always" or "never."
- Overconfidence: similar terms to the illusion of certainty.

- Irrational outcome fielding: "I can't believe how unlucky I got," or the reverse, if we have some default phrase for credit taking, like "I'm at the absolute top of my game" or "I planned it perfectly." This includes conclusions of luck, skill, blame, or credit. It includes equivalent terms for irrationally fielding the outcomes of others, like, "They totally had that coming," "They brought it on themselves," and "Why do they always get so lucky?"

- Any kind of moaning or complaining about bad luck just to off-load it, with no real point to the story other than to get sympathy. (An exception would be when we're in a truth-seeking group and we make explicit that we're taking a momentary break to vent.)

- Generalized characterizations of people meant to dismiss their ideas: insulting, pejorative characterizations of others, like "idiot" or, in poker, "donkey." Or any phrase that starts by characterizing someone as "another typical _____." (Like David Letterman said to Lauren Conrad, he dismissed everyone around him as an idiot, until he pulled himself into deliberative mind one day and asked, "What are the odds that *everyone* is an idiot?")

- Other violations of the Mertonian norm of universalism, shooting the message because we don't think much of the messenger. Any sweeping term about someone, particularly when we equate our assessment of *an idea* with a sweeping personality or intellectual assessment of the person delivering the idea, such as "gun nut," "bleeding heart," "East Coast," "Bible belter," "California values"—political or social issues. Also be on guard for the reverse: accepting a message because of the messenger or praising a source immediately after finding out it confirms your thinking.

- Signals that we have zoomed in on a moment, out of proportion with the scope of time: "worst day ever," "the day from hell."
- Expressions that explicitly signal motivated reasoning, accepting or rejecting information without much evidence, like "conventional wisdom" or "if you ask anybody" or "Can you prove that it's not true?" Similarly, look for expressions that you're participating in an echo chamber, like "everyone agrees with me."
- The word "wrong," which deserves its own swear jar. The Mertonian norm of organized skepticism allows little place in exploratory discussion for the word "wrong." "Wrong" is a conclusion, not a rationale. And it's not a particularly accurate conclusion since, as we know, nearly nothing is 100% or 0%. Any words or thoughts denying the existence of uncertainty should be a signal that we are heading toward a poorly calibrated decision.
- Lack of self-compassion: if we're going to be self-critical, the focus should be on the lesson and how to calibrate future decisions. "I have the worst judgment on relationships" or "I should have known" or "How could I be so stupid?"
- Signals we're being overly generous editors when we share a story. Especially in our truthseeking group, are we straying from sharing the facts to emphasize our version? Even outside our group, unless we're sharing a story purely for entertainment value, are we assuring that our listener will agree with us? In general, are we violating the Mertonian norm of communism?
- Infecting our listeners with a conflict of interest, including our own conclusion or belief when asking for advice or

informing the listener of the outcome before getting their input.

- Terms that discourage engagement of others and their opinions, including expressions of certainty and also initial phrasing inconsistent with that great lesson from improvisation—"yes, and . . ." That includes getting opinions or information from others and starting with "no" or "but . . ."

This is by no means a complete list, but it provides a flavor of the kinds of statements and thinking that should trigger vigilance on our part.

Once we recognize that we should watch out for particular words, phrases, and thoughts, when we find ourselves saying or thinking those things, we are breaking a contract, a commitment to truthseeking. These terms are signals that we're succumbing to bias. Because if we are cutting the binding when we catch ourselves saying or thinking these things, it can trigger a moment of reflection, interrupting us in the moment. Popping out of the moment like that can remind us of why we took the trouble to list terms that signal potential decision traps.

The swear jar is a simple example of a Ulysses contract in action: we think ahead to a hazard in our decision-making future and devise a plan of action around that, or at least commit that we will take a moment to recognize we are veering away from truthseeking. Better precommitment contracts result from better anticipation of what the future might look like, what kinds of decisions we want to avoid, and which ones we want to promote. That takes thoughtful reconnaissance.

Reconnaissance: mapping the future

Operation Overlord, the Allied forces operation to retake German-occupied France starting in Normandy, was the largest seaborne invasion in military history. It involved planning and logistics on an unprecedented scale. What if the forces were delayed at the start by bad weather? What if the airborne landing force had trouble communicating by radio due to the terrain? What if significant numbers of paratroopers were blown off course? What if currents interfered with the beach landings? What if the forces on the different beaches remained separated? Countless things could go wrong, with tens of thousands of lives at stake and, potentially, the outcome of the war.

All those things *did* go wrong, along with many other challenges encountered on D-Day and immediately thereafter. The Normandy landings still succeeded, though, because they prepared for as many potential scenarios as possible. Reconnaissance has been part of advance military planning for as long as horses have been used in battle. The modern military, of course, has evolved from sending scouts by horse and reporting back to the main forces to planes, drones, satellites, and other high-tech equipment gathering information about what to expect in battle.

The Navy SEAL team that caught and killed Osama bin Laden wouldn't have entered his compound without knowing what they would find beyond the walls. What buildings were there? What was their layout and purpose? What differences might it make if they conducted the raid in different kinds of weather or different times of day? What other people would be present and what risks would they pose? What would they do if bin Laden wasn't there? What was the team trying to commit to, given what they knew about each of those things (and, of course, numerous others)? Just as they relied on reconnaissance, we shouldn't plan our future without doing advance work on the range of futures that could result from any given decision and the probabilities of those futures occurring.

For us to make better decisions, we need to perform reconnaissance on the future. If a decision is a bet on a particular future based on our beliefs, then before we place a bet we should consider in detail what those possible futures might look like. Any decision can result in a set of possible outcomes.

BETTING ON A FUTURE

BELIEF ⟶ BET ⟶ (SET OF OUTCOMES)

Thinking about what futures are contained in that set (which we do by putting memories together in a novel way to imagine how things might turn out) helps us figure out which decisions to make.

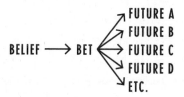

Figure out the possibilities, then take a stab at the probabilities. To start, we imagine the range of potential futures. This is also known as scenario planning. Nate Silver, who compiles and interprets data from the perspective of getting the best strategic use of it, frequently takes a scenario-planning approach. Instead of using data to make a particular conclusion, he sometimes takes the approach of discussing all the scenarios the data *could* support. In early February 2017, he described the merits of scenario planning: "When faced with highly uncertain conditions, military units and major corporations sometimes use an exercise called scenario planning. The idea is to consider a broad range of possibilities for how the future might unfold to help guide long-term planning and preparation."

After identifying as many of the possible outcomes as we can, we want to make our best guess at the probability of each of those futures occurring. When I consult with enterprises on building decision trees and determining probabilities of different futures, people frequently resist having to make a guess at the probability of future events mainly because they feel like they can't be certain of what the likelihood of any scenario is. But that's the point.

The reason why we do reconnaissance is *because* we are uncertain. We don't (and likely can't) know how often things will turn out a certain way with exact precision. It's not about approaching our future predictions from a point of perfection. It's about acknowledging that we're already making a prediction about the future every time we make a decision, so we're better off if we make that explicit. If we're worried about guessing, we're *already* guessing. We are already guessing that the decision we execute will result in the highest likelihood of a good outcome given the options we have available to us. By at least trying to assign probabilities, we will naturally move away from the default of 0% or 100%, away from being sure it will turn out one way and not another. Anything that moves us off those extremes is going to be a more reasonable assessment than not trying at all. Even if our assessment results in a wide range, like the chances of a particular scenario occurring being between 20% and 80%, that is still better than not guessing at all.

This kind of reconnaissance of the future is something that experienced poker players are very familiar with. Before making a bet, poker players consider each of their opponents' possible responses (fold, call, raise), and the likelihood and desirability of each. They also think about what they will do in response (if some or all of the opponents don't fold). Even if you don't know much about poker, it should make sense that a player is better off considering these things *before* they bet. The more expert the player, the further into the future they plan. Before making that decision to bet, the expert player is anticipating what they'll do following each response, as well as how the action they take now affects their future decisions on the hand. The best players think beyond the current hand into subsequent hands: how do the actions of this hand affect how they and their opponents make decisions on future hands? Poker players really live in this probabilistic world of, "What are the possible futures? What are the probabilities of those possible futures?" And they get very comfortable with the fact that they don't know exactly because they can't see their opponent's cards.

This is true of most strategic thinking. Whether it involves sales strategies, business strategies, or courtroom strategies, the best strategists are considering a fuller range of possible scenarios, anticipating and considering the strategic responses to each, and so on deep into the decision tree.

This kind of scenario planning is a form of mental time travel we can do on our own. It works even better when we do it as part of a scenario-planning group, particularly one that is open-minded to dissent and diverse points of view. Diverse viewpoints allow for the identification of a wider variety of scenarios deeper into the tree, and for better estimates of their probability. In fact, if two people in the group are really far off on an estimate of the likelihood of an outcome, that is a great time to have them switch sides and argue the other's position. Generally, the answer is somewhere in the middle and both people will end up moderating their positions. But sometimes one person has thought of a key influencing factor the other hasn't and that is revealed only because the dissent was tolerated.

In addition to increasing decision quality, scouting various futures has numerous additional benefits. First, scenario planning reminds us that the future is inherently uncertain. By making that explicit in our decision-making process, we have a more realistic view of the world. Second, we are better prepared for how we are going to respond to different outcomes that might result from our initial decision. We can anticipate positive or negative developments and plan our strategy, rather than being reactive. Being able to respond to the changing future is a good thing; being surprised by the changing future is not. Scenario planning makes us nimbler because we've considered and are prepared for a wider variety of possible futures. And if our reconnaissance has identified situations where we are susceptible to irrationality, we can try to bind our hands with a Ulysses contract. Third, anticipating the range of outcomes also keeps us from unproductive regret (or undeserved euphoria) when a particular future happens. Finally, by mapping out the potential futures and probabilities, we are less likely to fall prey to resulting or hindsight bias, in which we gloss over the futures that did not occur and behave as if the one that did occur must have been inevitable, because we have memorialized all the possible futures that could have happened.

Scenario planning in practice

A few years ago, I consulted with a national nonprofit organization, After-School All-Stars (ASAS), to work with them on incorporating scenario planning into their budgeting.* ASAS, founded in 1992 by Arnold Schwarzenegger, provides three hours of structured after-school programming for over 70,000 underserved youth in eighteen cities across the United States. They depend heavily on grants for funding and were struggling with budget planning, given the uncertainty in the grant award process. To help them with planning, I asked for a list of all their grant applications and how much each grant was worth. They provided me with a list of all their outstanding grant applications and the award amounts applied for. I told them that I didn't see how much each grant was worth in the information they provided. They pointed to the column of the award amounts sought. At that point, I realized we were working from different ideas about how to determine worth. The misunderstanding came from the disconnect between the *expected value* of each grant and the amount they would be awarded *if they got the grant.*†

Coming up with the expected value of each grant involves a simple form of scenario planning: imagining the two possible futures that could result from the application (awarded or declined) and the likelihood of each future. For example, if they

---

*I joined the ASAS board of directors in 2009. The consulting was part of my work as a board member.

†I was asking them, for each grant, to calculate the expected value, which is the average long-run value calculated by multiplying the probability of each possible outcome by the likelihood each outcome will occur and taking the sum of those values.

applied for a $100,000 grant that they would win 25% of the time, that grant would have an expected value of $25,000 ($100,000 × .25). If they expected to get the grant a quarter of the time, then it wasn't worth $100,000; it was worth a quarter of $100,000. A $200,000 application with a 10% chance of success would have an expected value of $20,000. A $50,000 grant with a 70% chance of success would be worth $35,000. Without thinking probabilistically in this way, determining a grant's worth isn't possible— it leads to the mistaken belief that the $200,000 grant is worth the most when, in fact, the $50,000 grant is. ASAS recognized that uncertainty was causing them problems (to the point where they felt enslaved by it in their budgeting), but they hadn't wrapped uncertainty into their planning or resource-allocation process. They were flying by the seat of their pants.

After I worked with the national office, ASAS made estimating the likelihood of getting each grant part of their planning. The benefits they got from scenario planning were immediate and substantial:

- They created a more efficient and productive work stack. Before doing this exercise, they naturally put a higher priority on applications seeking larger dollar amounts, executing those first, putting more senior staff on them, and being more likely to hire outside grant writers to get those applications completed. By shifting to thinking about the probability of getting each grant, they were now able to prioritize by how much the grant was actually worth to the organization in making these decisions. Thereafter, the higher *value* grants went to the top of the stack rather than just the grants with the higher potential awards.

- They could budget more realistically. They had greater confidence in advance estimates of the amount of money they could expect to receive.

- Because coming up with an expected value required estimating the likelihood of getting the grant, they increasingly focused on improving the accuracy of their estimates. This prompted them to close the loop by going back to the grantors. They had previously, after rejections, followed up with grantors. Because they were now focusing on checking and calibrating their probabilities, they expanded this to the grants they won. Overall, their post-outcome reviews focused on understanding what worked, what didn't work, what was luck, and how to do better, improving both their probability estimates and the quality of their grant applications.

- They could think about ways to increase the probability of getting grants and commit to those actions.

- They were less likely to fall prey to hindsight bias because they had considered in advance the probability of getting or not getting the grant.

- They were less likely to fall prey to resulting because they had evaluated the decision process in advance of getting or not getting the grant.

- Finally, because of all the benefits ASAS received from incorporating scenario planning into budgeting and grant applications, they expanded the implementation of this type of scenario planning across departments, making it part of their decision-making culture.

Grant prospecting is similar to sales prospecting, and this process can be implemented for any sales team. Assign probabilities for closing or not closing sales, and the company can do better at establishing sales priorities, planning budgets and allocating resources, evaluating and fine-tuning the accuracy of its predictions, and protecting itself against resulting and hindsight bias.

A more complex version of scenario planning occurs when the number of possible futures multiplies and/or we go deeper into the tree, considering what we will do next in response to how things turn out and what the set of outcomes of that next decision is and so on.

Consider the scenario planning involved in Seahawks coach Pete Carroll's much-criticized Super Bowl decision, trailing by four, twenty seconds remaining, one time-out, second-and-goal at the Patriots' one-yard line. Carroll has two general choices, run or pass, and they in turn lead to multiple scenarios.

If Carroll calls for a run, these are the possible futures: (a) touchdown (immediate win); (b) turnover-fumble (immediate loss); (c) tackle short of the goal line; (d) offensive penalty; and (e) defensive penalty. Futures (c)–(e) branch into additional scenarios. The most likely failure scenario, by far, is that the runner is tackled before reaching the end zone. Seattle could stop the clock with its final time-out, but if they run the ball again and do not score, time will expire.

If Carroll calls for a pass, the possible futures are (a) touchdown (immediate success); (b) turnover-interception (immediate failure); (c) incomplete pass; (d) sack; (e) offensive penalty; and (f) defensive penalty. Again, the first two futures essentially end the game and the others branch off into additional play calling and additional outcomes.

The main difference between passing and running is that calling a pass likely gives Seattle a total of three plays to score, instead of two if Carroll calls a running play. An unsuccessful run would require that Seattle use their final time-out to stop the clock so they could run a second play. An incomplete pass would stop the clock and leave Seattle with a time-out and the chance to call those same two running plays. An interception, which negates the possibility of a second or third offensive play, is only a 2%–3% probability, a small price to pay for three chances to score rather than two. (A turnover caused by a fumble on a running play is 1%–2%.)*

Notice that the option of the extra play doesn't reveal itself without this kind of scouting of the future. Even after the fact, with lots of time to analyze the decision, very few commentators saw this advantage.

The important thing is that we do better when we scout all these futures and make decisions based on the probabilities and desirability of the different futures. ASAS couldn't guarantee it would get awarded every grant it applied for, but it could, through good process, make better decisions about which grants to prioritize and how much revenue to expect from the basket of grant

---

*NFL teams have the advantage of advanced analytics, but a fan with basic knowledge of the game can plug in general probabilities. (These don't include adjustment for New England's defense or data specific to short-yardage situations.) If Wilson drops back to pass, he is about 8% to get sacked (significant loss of yardage, use of the final time-out), 55% to complete the pass (touchdown), 35% to throw incomplete (stopping the clock for two additional plays, which can include an unsuccessful running play because of the remaining time-out), and 2% to throw an interception.

If Wilson hands off to Marshawn Lynch, he either gains a yard and scores, is stopped short of the goal, or fumbles. Lynch fumbles 1%–2% of the time. After that, advanced analytics are necessary (and may be based on small samples). But we can guess. On fourth-down running plays (presumably short-yardage situations), in 13 career attempts he has 2 touchdowns and 7 first downs. For his career, at the time of this writing, on third- or fourth-and-short rushing plays, he has 121 attempts, 11 touchdowns, and 70 first downs.

proposals they submitted. Despite the outcry, I'd like to think that Pete Carroll didn't lose much sleep over his decision to call for Wilson to pass.

Reconnaissance of the future dramatically improves decision quality and reduces reactivity to outcomes. So far, we have talked about thinking ahead to what the future might look like. But it turns out that better decision trees, more effective scenario planning, results from working backward rather than forward.

Backcasting: working backward from a positive future

All methods of imagining the future are not created equal. You know that Chinese proverb, "A journey of a thousand miles starts with a single step"? Turns out, if we were contemplating a thousand-mile walk, we'd be better off imagining ourselves looking back from the destination and figuring how we got there. When it comes to advance thinking, standing at the end and looking backward is much more effective than looking forward from the beginning.

The distorted view we get when we look into the future from the present is similar to the stereotypical view of the world by Manhattan residents, poked fun at by the famous *New Yorker* cover. The cover was a drawing of a map from the perspective of a person from New York. In that view, half the map covers a few blocks of the city. While you can see all the buildings on Ninth Avenue and even vehicles and people, the Hudson River and New Jersey are just horizontal strips. The entire United States occupies the same amount of space as the distances between Ninth and Tenth avenues. Beyond a strip of the Pacific Ocean are three tiny lumps, labeled "China," "Japan," and "Russia."

When we forecast the future, we run the risk of a similar distortion. From where we stand, the present and the immediate future loom large. Anything beyond that loses focus.

Imagining the future recruits the same brain pathways as remembering the past. And it turns out that remembering the future is a better way to plan for it. From the vantage point of the present, it's hard to see past the next step. We end up over-planning for addressing problems we have right now. Implicit in that approach is the assumption that conditions will remain the same, facts won't change, and the paradigm will remain stable. The world changes too fast to assume that approach is generally valid. Samuel Arbesman's *The Half-Life of Facts* makes a book-length case for the hazards of assuming the future is going to be like the present.

Just as great poker players and chess players (and experts in any field) excel by planning further into the future than others, our decision-making improves when we can more vividly imagine the future, free of the distortions of the present. By working backward from the goal, we plan our decision tree in more depth, because we start at the end.

When we identify the goal and work backward from there to "remember" how we got there, the research shows that we do better. In a *Harvard Business Review* article, decision scientist Gary Klein summarized the results of a 1989 experiment by Deborah Mitchell, J. Edward Russo, and Nancy Pennington. They "found that prospective hindsight—imagining that an event has already occurred—increases the ability to correctly identify reasons for future outcomes by 30%."

A huge urban planning project requires enormous amounts

of money, materials, commitment—and the vision to work backward from a distant future goal. When Frederick Law Olmsted designed Central Park, for example, he recognized that a lot of the charm of the park, and a lot of enjoyment that people would get from it, would take decades, as the landscape changed and matured. People walking through Central Park when it opened to the public in 1858 would have seen a lot of barren land. Even in 1873, when construction was substantially completed, there was a lot of undergrown foliage. The trees, shrubs, and plants were clearly recent transplants. None of those visitors would recognize Central Park today. But Olmstead would because he was starting from what it would develop into.

The most common form of working backward from our goal to map out the future is known as backcasting. In backcasting, we imagine we've already achieved a positive outcome, holding up a newspaper with the headline "We Achieved Our Goal!" Then we think about how we got there.

Let's say an enterprise wants to develop a three-year strategic plan to double market share, from 5% to 10%. Each person engaged in the planning imagines holding up a newspaper whose headline reads "Company X Has Doubled Its Market Share over the Past Three Years." The team leader now asks them to identify the reasons they got there, what events occurred, what decisions were made, what went their way to get the enterprise to capture that market share. This enables the company to better identify strategies, tactics, and actions that need to be implemented to get to the goal. It also allows it to identify when the goal needs to be tweaked. Backcasting makes it possible to identify when there are low-probability events that must occur to reach the goal. That could lead to developing strategies to increase the chances those events occur or to recognizing the goal is too ambitious. The company can also make precommitments to a plan developed through backcasting, including responses to developments that can interfere with reaching the goal and identifying inflection points for re-evaluating the plan as the future unfolds.

In planning a trial strategy after taking a new case, a trial lawyer can imagine the headline of winning at trial. What favorable rulings did the lawyer get along the way? How did the most favorable testimony play out? What kind of evidence did the judge allow or throw out? What points did the jury respond to?

If our goal is to lose twenty pounds in six months, we can plan how to achieve that by imagining it's six months from now and we've lost the weight. What are the things we did to lose the weight? How did we avoid junk food? How did we increase the amount of exercise we were doing? How did we stick to the regimen?

Imagining a successful future and backcasting from there is a useful time-travel exercise for identifying necessary steps for reaching our goals. Working backward helps even more when we give ourselves the freedom to imagine an *unfavorable* future.

Premortems: working backward from a negative future

If you know medical terms or watch forensic-crime dramas on TV, you are familiar with a postmortem: that's where a medical examiner determines the cause of death. A premortem is an investigation into something awful, but *before* it happens. We all like to bask in an optimistic view of the future. We generally are biased to overestimate the probability of good things happening.

Looking at the world through rose-colored glasses is natural and feels good, but a little naysaying goes a long way. A premortem is where we check our positive attitude at the door and imagine not achieving our goals.

Backcasting and premortems complement each other. Backcasting imagines a positive future; a premortem imagines a negative future. We can't create a complete picture without representing both the positive space and the negative space. Backcasting reveals the positive space. Premortems reveal the negative space. Backcasting is the cheerleader; a premortem is the heckler in the audience.

Imagining a headline that reads "We Failed to Reach Our Goal" challenges us to think about ways in which things could go wrong that we otherwise wouldn't if left to our own (optimistic, team-player) devices. For the company with the three-year plan to double market share, the premortem headline is "Company Fails to Reach Market Share Goal; Growth Again Stalls." Members of the planning team now imagine delays in new products, loss of key executives or sales or marketing or technical personnel, new products by competitors, adverse economic developments, paradigm shifts that could lead customers to do without the product or rely on alternatives not on the market or in use, etc.

A lawyer trying a case now considers favorable evidence being disallowed, undiscovered evidence undermining the case, drawing an unsympathetic judge, and the jury disliking or distrusting the main witnesses.

When we set a weight-loss goal and put a plan to reach that goal in place, a premortem will reveal how we felt obligated to eat cake when it was somebody's birthday, how hard it was to resist the bagels and cookies in the conference room, and how hard it was to find time for the gym or how easy it was to find excuses to procrastinate going. There has been a massive amount written about visualizing success as a way to achieve our goals. Because that's such a common element in self-help strategies, conducting a premortem (with its negative visualization) may seem like a counterproductive way to succeed.

Despite the popular wisdom that we achieve success through positive visualization, it turns out that incorporating *negative visualization* makes us *more* likely to achieve our goals. Gabriele Oettingen, professor of psychology at NYU and author of *Rethinking Positive Thinking: Inside the New Science of Motivation*, has conducted over twenty years of research, consistently finding that people who imagine obstacles in the way of reaching their goals are more likely to achieve success, a process she has called "mental contrasting." Her first study, of women enrolled in a weight-loss program, found that subjects "who had strong positive fantasies about slimming down . . . lost twenty-four pounds *less* than those who pictured themselves more negatively. Dreaming about achieving a goal apparently didn't help that goal come to fruition. It impeded it from happening. The starry-eyed dreamers in the study were less energized to behave in ways that helped them lose weight."

She repeated these results in different contexts. She recruited college students who claimed to have an unrequited crush. She then prompted one group to imagine positive scenarios of initiating a relationship, and another group to imagine negative scenarios of how that would play out. The results were similar to those in the weight-loss study: five months later, the subjects indulging in the positive scenario planning were less likely to initiate the relationship. She found the same results when studying job seekers, students before a midterm exam, and patients undergoing hip replacement surgery.

Oettingen recognized that we need to have positive goals, but we are more likely to execute on those goals if we think about the negative futures. We start a premortem by imagining why we failed to reach our goal: our company hasn't increased its market share; we didn't lose weight; the jury verdict came back for the other side; we didn't hit our sales target. Then we imagine why. All those reasons why we didn't achieve our goal help us anticipate potential obstacles and improve our likelihood of succeeding.

A premortem is an implementation of the Mertonian norm of organized skepticism, changing the rules of the game to give permission for dissent. Being a team player in a premortem isn't about being the most enthusiastic cheerleader; it's about being the most productive heckler. "Winning" isn't about the group feeling good because everyone confirms their (and the organization's) narrative that things are going to turn out great. The premortem starts with working backward from an unfavorable future, or failure to achieve a goal, so competing for favor, or feeling good about contributing to the process, is about coming up with the most creative, relevant, and actionable reasons for why things didn't work out.

The key to a successful premortem is that everyone feels free to look for those reasons, and they are motivated to scour everything—personal experience, company experience, historical precedent, episodes of *The Hills*, sports analogies, etc.—to come up with ways a decision or plan can go bad, so the team can anticipate and account for them.

Conducting a premortem creates a path to act as our own red team. Once we frame the exercise as "Okay, we failed. Why did we fail?" that frees everyone to identify potential points of failure they otherwise might not see or might not bring up for fear of being viewed as a naysayer. People can express their reservations without it sounding like they're saying the planned course of action is wrong. Because of that, a planning process that includes a premortem creates a much healthier organization because it means that the people who do have dissenting opinions are represented in the planning. They don't feel like they're shut out or not being heard. Everyone's voice now has more value. The organization is less likely to discourage dissent and thereby lose the value of diverse opinions. Those who have reservations are less likely to have resentment or regret build if things don't work out; their voices were represented in the strategic plan.

Incorporating this type of imagining of the negative space into a truthseeking group reinforces a new habit routine of visualizing and anticipating future obstacles. As always, when a group we are part of reinforces this kind of thinking, we are more likely in our own thinking to consider the downside of our decisions.

Imagining both positive and negative futures helps us build a more realistic vision of the future, allowing us to plan and prepare for a wider variety of challenges, than backcasting alone. Once we recognize the things that can go wrong, we can protect against the bad outcomes, prepare plans of action, enable nimble responses to a wider range of future developments, and assimilate a negative reaction in advance so we aren't so surprised by it or reactive to it. In doing so, we are more likely to achieve our goals.

Of course, when we backcast and imagine the things that went right, we reveal the problems if those things *didn't* go right. Backcasting doesn't, therefore, ignore the negative space so much as it overrepresents the positive space. It's in our optimistic nature (and natural in backcasting) to imagine a successful future. Without a premortem, we don't see as many paths to the future in which we don't reach our goals. A premortem forces us to build out that side of the tree where things don't work out. In the process, we are likely to realize that's a pretty robust part of the tree.

Remember, the likelihood of positive and negative futures must add up to 100%. The positive space of backcasting and the negative space of a premortem still have to fit in a finite amount of space. When we see how much negative space there really is, we shrink down the positive space to a size that more accurately reflects reality and less reflects our naturally optimistic nature.

We make better decisions, and we feel better about those decisions, once we get our past-, present-, and future-selves to hang out together. This not only allows us to adjust how optimistic we are, it allows us to adjust our goals accordingly and to actively put plans in place to reduce the likelihood of bad outcomes and increase the likelihood of good ones. We are less likely to be surprised by a bad outcome and can better prepare contingency plans.

It may not feel so good during the planning process to include this focus on the negative space. Over the long run, however, seeing the world more objectively and making better decisions will feel better than turning a blind eye to negative scenarios. In a way, backcasting without premortems is a form of temporal discounting: if we imagine a positive future, we feel better *now*, but we'll more than compensate for giving up that immediate gratification through the benefits of seeing the world more accurately, making better initial decisions, and being nimbler about what the world throws our way.

Once we make a decision and one of those possible futures actually happens, we can't discard all that work, even—or especially—if it included work on futures that did not occur. Forgetting about an unrealized future can be dangerous to good decision-making.

Dendrology and hindsight bias
(or, Give the chainsaw a rest)

One of the goals of mental time travel is keeping events in perspective. To understand an overriding risk to that perspective, think about time as a tree. The tree has a trunk, branches at the top, and the place where the trunk meets the branches. The trunk is the past. A tree has only one, growing trunk, just as we have only one, accumulating past. The branches are the potential futures. Thicker branches are the equivalent of more probable futures, thinner branches are less probable ones. The place where the top of the trunk meets the branches is the present. There are many futures, many branches of the tree, but only one past, one trunk.

As the future becomes the past, what happens to all those branches? The ever-advancing present acts like a chainsaw. When one of those many branches happens to be the way things turn out, when that branch transitions into the past, present-us cuts off all those other branches that didn't materialize and obliterates them. When we look into the past and see only the thing that happened, it seems to have been inevitable. Why wouldn't it seem inevitable from that vantage point? Even the smallest of twigs, the most improbable of futures—like the 2%–3% chance Russell Wilson would throw that interception—expands when it becomes part of the mighty trunk. That 2%–3%, in hindsight, becomes 100%, and all the other branches, no matter how thick they were, disappear from view.

That's hindsight bias, an enemy of probabilistic thinking.

Judge Frank Easterbrook, a leading jurist and member of the U.S. Court of Appeals for the Seventh Circuit, warned about the danger in the legal system of assessing probabilities *after* one of the potential futures has occurred. *Jentz v. ConAgra Foods* involved a "hot" grain bin owned by ConAgra and the company it hired (named West Side) to investigate and deal with the cause of the burning smell, smoke, and raised temperatures from the bin. After failing to solve the problem, West Side's foreman told ConAgra to call the fire department. He then told some of his employees to remove tools from a tunnel to the bin that could impair firefighters' access.

While the workers were in the tunnel, the bin exploded, severely injuring the West Side employees. Those injured sued ConAgra and West Side. The jury awarded $180 million in compensatory and punitive damages. In addressing the punitive damages against West Side, Judge Easterbrook, writing for the court, pointed out that Illinois law required a "gross deviation" from the standard of care to award punitive damages. Finding no evidence in the record of any foreseeable likelihood of explosion at the time the foreman ordered the workers to remove tools from the tunnel, he concluded, "The verdict appears to be a consequence of hindsight bias—the human tendency to believe that whatever happened was bound to happen, and that everyone must have known it. If [the foreman] believed that an explosion was imminent, then he is a monster; but of that there is no evidence. Hindsight bias is not enough to support a verdict."

Once we know there was an explosion, it's difficult to imagine the actions of the parties when the explosion was only one of several possible futures. The members of the jury had a conflict of interest. When they heard the story of the men entering the tunnel to retrieve the tools, they knew the outcome. The jury lopped off the other branches of the tree, all the other ways things could have turned out given the situation in the grain-storage bin and, in hindsight, all they could see was a confluence of circumstances with an inevitable tragedy at the end.

Imagine how things would be different for the protagonists throughout this book if more of us acted like Judge Easterbrook.

Steve Bartman could have used a stadium full of Cubs fans with Judge Easterbrook's perspective. They would have recognized that the Cubs losing the game was only one of many ways it could have turned out. At the moment Bartman and others around him reached for the foul ball, the branch of the future where Steve Bartman touches the ball was a small one, and the chance of the Cubs losing after that was the tiniest of twigs, requiring a number of unlikely on-field developments (like the pitching ace giving up hit after hit, and the great-fielding shortstop committing a rare error on an inning-ending double play). Just as the foreman ordering workers into the tunnel didn't cause the explosion, Bartman touching the ball didn't cause the loss. He just got an unlucky result, based on all the things that happened over which he had no control after the foul ball touched his hands.

Pete Carroll and the world of Monday Morning Quarterbacks could have used the judge's reminder that we tend to assume that, once something happens, it was bound to happen. If we don't try to hold all the potential futures in mind *before* one of them happens, it becomes almost impossible to realistically evaluate decisions or probabilities *after*.

This turned out to be a big part of the problem for the CEO in the wake of firing his president. Although he had initially characterized the decision as one of his worst, when we reconstructed the tree, essentially picking the branches up off the ground and reattaching them, it was clear that he and his company had made a series of careful, deliberative decisions. Because they led to a negative result, however, the CEO had been consumed with regret. When he looked back at his decisions, he couldn't see all those branches and their likelihoods. He could only see the trunk. All he saw was a bad result.

The CEO removed all those other branches with a chainsaw and ran them through a wood-chipper. They disappeared and he acted as if they never existed. That's what hindsight bias is, and we're all running amok through the forest with a chainsaw once we get an outcome. Once something occurs, we no longer think of it as probabilistic—or as *ever* having been probabilistic. This is how we get into the frame of mind where we say, "I should have known" or "I told you so." This is where unproductive regret comes from.

By keeping an accurate representation of what could have happened (and not a version edited by hindsight), memorializing the scenario plans and decision trees we create through good planning processes, we can be better calibrators going forward. We can also be happier by recognizing and getting comfortable with the uncertainty of the world. Instead of living at extremes, we can find contentment with doing our best under uncertain circumstances, and being committed to improving from our experience.

Reaction to the 2016 election provides another strong demonstration of what happens when we lop branches off the tree. Hillary Clinton had been favored going into the election, and her probability of winning, based on an accumulation of the polls, was somewhere between 60% and 70%, according to FiveThirty Eight.com. When Donald Trump won, pollsters got the Pete Carroll treatment, maybe no one more than Nate Silver, founder of FiveThirtyEight.com and a thoughtful analyzer of polling data. ("Nate Silver was wrong." "The pollsters missed it." "Just like Brexit, the bookies blew it." Etc.) The press spun this as a certain win for Clinton, despite the Trump branch of the tree being no mere twig at 30%–40%. By the day after the election, the Clinton branch had been severed, only the Trump branch remained, and how could pollsters and the polling process have been so blind?

One of the things poker teaches is that we have to take satisfaction in assessing the probabilities of different outcomes given the decisions under consideration and in executing the bet we think is best. With the constant stream of decisions and outcomes under uncertain conditions, you get used to losing a lot. To some degree, we're all outcome junkies, but the more we wean ourselves from that addiction, the happier we'll be. None of us is guaranteed a favorable outcome, and we're all going to experience plenty of unfavorable ones. We can always, however, make a good bet. And even when we make a bad bet, we usually get a second chance because we can learn from the experience and make a better bet the next time.

Life, like poker, is one long game, and there are going to be a lot of losses, even after making the best possible bets. We are going to do better, and be happier, if we start by recognizing that we'll never be sure of the future. That changes our task from trying to be right every time, an impossible job, to navigating our way through the uncertainty by calibrating our beliefs to move toward, little by little, a more accurate and objective representation of the world. With strategic foresight and perspective, that's manageable work. If we keep learning and calibrating, we might even get good at it.

ACKNOWLEDGMENTS

The list of people who made it possible for me to write this book is long. It starts, of course, with my family: my father Richard, and my late mother Deedy, who inspired in me a love of games, a love of teaching, and a love of writing—a good brew for creating this book; my brother Howard, for being a great brother and for his obvious influence in my poker career and my dedication to treating the art of decision-making as a science, and vice versa—many of the ideas in this book originated from conversations with him; and my sister Katy, for being a supportive sister, an inspiring writer and poet who I hope to impress the littlest bit, and for doing a careful read and edit of the book, encouraging me every step of the way.

Levine Greenberg Rostan Literary Agency and Portfolio collaborated on the business of getting this book published. It took a lot to get me into this project, and a lot more to get this book out of me. Wonderful people in both organizations did so much to help me and enhance the final product:

Jim Levine, my literary agent and hand-holder, who got me through the proposal writing and has been there every step of the way. Jim believed in the project from the beginning, helped me work through many different ways to attack the material, and patiently guided me through many iterations of the proposal. His enthusiasm for this book never wavered, and kept me sane through my own periods of self-doubt. And to Matthew Huff, Jim's assistant, who has been there since the very first meeting and offered invaluable help in the proposal-writing process.

Niki Papadopoulos, my editor and therapist, who made this book immeasurably better in so many ways, not the least of which by suggesting a format that forced an organization of ideas that I could not have achieved otherwise. I'm forever grateful. And to Leah Trouwborst for, along with Niki, providing encouragement, editorial guidance, and occasional therapy. And to Vivian Roberson for keeping the production trains running on time.

Everyone in these acknowledgments (and many others) encouraged me to write this book. I'd like to single out, for specific contributions in this regard, Dan Ariely, who also introduced me to Jim Levine, and Charles Duhigg, who also kindly shared his book proposal for *The Power of Habit*, which was an invaluable guide to writing my own proposal. Dan and Charles played significant roles from the time this project was in its infancy. Both gave generously of their time and attention, and encouraged me to believe that poker provided valuable insight into decision-making.

Glen Clarkson's encouragement has also been remarkable. He has tried to get me to write this book forever. I insisted on writing about poker strategy first. He was a noodge in the most positive sense of the term, and he was right.

Among the people who inspired me in my education, several stand out:

Lila Gleitman, my advisor at Penn, who inspired in me a love of the study of learning and has been a role model for scientific endeavor—intrepid, funny, smart, insightful, and passionate about her work. She taught me to think like a scientist and, at eighty-eight, is still the most inspiring person I know. She has also been incredibly generous in the time since she was my advisor, especially given that I left the program before getting my PhD. She was happy for the life I created after leaving and never once made me feel bad for not finishing. And to the memory of her husband Henry, who was also my mentor, a master of experimental design, and a character who looms so large in my intellectual development.

Barbara Landau, who got me interested in and excited about psychology at Columbia. I am grateful for the four years I was able to spend as her research assistant while an undergrad. She also pushed me to continue my studies at Penn, where she had studied with Lila and Henry Gleitman.

Jon Baron, who taught my first seminar on decision-making. Bob Rescorla, for sharing his fascination with conditioning and guiding me in the depths of learning about learning. And all the professors at Columbia and Penn that taught me and nurtured in me the interest and curiosity to explore science, psychology, behavior, learning, and decision-making.

Even after I took a leave of absence from school to play poker—for twenty years—I never left the subjects that captivated me: how we learn and what we do with the product of our learning. I am grateful to so many people I met along the way in poker. I appreciate the poker community for welcoming a young girl into the game, and helping me find mentors, friends, and unforgettable characters who enriched my time in the game. And I am grateful to the game of poker itself, which offered me something to be passionate about, rewarding me for discoveries about its complexity, at the same time reminding me that, for every layer I peeled off, there were always more layers beneath it.

My appreciation for poker would not be complete without especially thanking Erik Seidel for innumerable reasons, including showing me what it means to really strive to be a rational thinker.

Particular thanks to David Grey, for sharing his story about Ira the Whale; Phil Hellmuth, for uttering one of the best quotes in poker history; and John Hennigan, for sharing his story about moving to Des Moines on a bet. These superlative players and many others also bestowed their expertise and friendship, a truly wonderful gift. I was lucky to watch and learn from, in addition, remarkable players including Chris Ferguson, Doyle Brunson, Chip Reese, Gus Hansen, Huckleberry Seed, Ted Forrest, Andy Bloch, Mori Eskandani, Phil Ivey, Bobby Buckler, Allen Cunningham, Danny Robison, and Chau Giang. (These and so many other wonderful players I encountered over the years weren't just remarkable in their skills: they were remarkable in their variety of approaches toward the similar goal of making good decisions.)

This book would not exist without the input and feedback I received from all the companies, conferences, professional groups, and executives who have hired me over the years, giving me an opportunity to workshop my ideas through keynotes, retreats, consulting, and coaching. That started with Roger Lowe, who took a chance on inviting a poker player to speak to options traders about how poker could inform decision-making. Without his outside-the-box request back in 2002, this book might never have happened. Those nascent ideas I expressed at that retreat were the small beginnings of what bloomed over time into this book.

During the time it took to write this book, countless friends in publishing, academics, and business shared their expertise, knowledge, and passion, engaging me in discussions, answering my questions, and leading me to further information:

Colin Camerer, who took time out to talk to a stranger.

Stuart Firestein, for reminding me as I wavered about whether to write this book that uncertainty is an interesting, exciting topic. He continues to be an inspiration to me and a great friend. His joyfulness and enthusiasm are contagious, even if they are impossible to duplicate.

Olivia Fox Cabane, for encouraging me and enthusiastically believing uncertainty is an interesting topic to write about.

Victoria Gray, for introducing me to so many brilliant scholars through Adventures of the Mind (including George Dyson and Stuart Firestein) and for being such a great friend.

Jon Haidt, whom I first met when we were first-year graduate students at Penn, for taking time out after being swamped after the 2016 election to get on the phone with me, and for reminding me to delve back into John Stuart Mill.

Maria Konnikova, who helped me through the process of writing this book and has shown me a fresh perspective on how poker can inspire. We both share a crush on Erik Seidel's intellect.

Dave Lenowitz, for his intellectual curiosity and willingness to share ideas.

Robert MacCoun, for several great conversations on the topic of outcome blindness.

Gary Marcus, for engaging me in some long conversations on subjects that helped form the ideas of the book. I first met Gary when we were in grad school, when I was a student of Lila's and he was a student of Steven Pinker's. We reconnected years later after I started working on this book, and the conversations I have been lucky to have with him about memory and time were invaluable.

Gabriele Oettingen and her husband Peter Gollwitzer, psychology professors at NYU, who were kind enough to have a very long lunch with me to talk about mental contrasting. That conversation was invaluable to this book.

Gerry Ohrstrom, for reintroducing me to Gary Marcus, who in turn introduced me to Gabriele Oettingen and Peter Gollwitzer.

Joseph Sweeney, whose love of learning and devouring of material in this space led to many long lunch conversations that informed this book and made it better in so many ways.

Philip Tetlock, for a conversation that became three of the most informative hours of my life; also for encouraging me to reacquaint myself with Robert Merton's scientific norms.

Joseph Kable, for kindly having lunch with me to talk about the brain circuitry recruited in imagining the future.

Thank you to all my friends and colleagues at How I Decide, an educational nonprofit foundation I cofounded with the mission to equip youth with better decision-making and critical thinking skills (www.howidecide.org). Thanks to the all the dedicated folks who do the heavy lifting, executive director Dave Lenowitz and all the staff: Dan Donaldson, Dylan Gordon, Jillian Hardgrove, Adriana Massara, Ramin Mohajer, and Joseph Sweeney. And thank you to all the members of the board and advisory council. In addition to so many individual contributions from these wonderful people to the book, their hard work and dedication have been a constant inspiration for me to do my best at understanding and teaching decision-making skills.

Thanks to the following people who read early portions or drafts of this material and offered their comments: Jim Doughan, Paul Schoemaker, T. C. Scornavacchi, Todd Simkin, and Joseph Sweeney.

A special thanks to Michael Craig—who gave me extraordinary and invaluable editorial help. Without him this book would never have happened. I am grateful to him for his professional help and for being a good friend.

I am indebted for the help of Jenifer Sarver, who literally runs my professional life and keeps the trains running on time; I'd fall apart without her. I'm also thankful for Luz Stable's vital role in helping me juggle my business responsibilities while writing this book.

I appreciate that my friends graciously put up with my being in a black hole during the writing of this book and patiently waited for me to stick my head back up. I canceled plans more times than I can count and the understanding I got back will not be forgotten.

This book truly would not have happened without Eric, who puts up with me and inspires me, both in the writing of this book and in every other way. Thank you to my stepchildren, who have made my life so much fuller, and have always been patient and understanding.

Just as I benefited greatly from the foundation and continuous help provided by my parents and my siblings, my most important influence continues to be my wonderful, exceptional children. They put up with me. They put up with this book. Teaching them has been the goal of my life, and yet it's impossible to even contemplate all the things they've taught me. They are awesome and inspire me every day.

NOTES

INTRODUCTION : WHY THIS ISN'T A POKER BOOK

1 On several occasions in the book, I refer to tournament poker results. In addition to cash games, poker can be played in a tournament format. In tournaments, players pay an entry fee and receive tournament chips, good only within the competition. They play at assigned tables, at stakes designed to rise on a pre-established schedule, and are eliminated when they lose all their chips. The tournament winner ends up with all the chips, but prize money is awarded based on order of finish. My source for tournament titles and earnings is the Hendon Mob Database (pok erdb.thehendonmob.com), which includes results from over 300,000 events going back to the first World Series of Poker in 1970.

CHAPTER 1: LIFE IS POKER, NOT CHESS

5 **Pete Carroll and the Monday Morning Quarterbacks:** I refer throughout the book to Pete Carroll's play-call at the end of the Super Bowl and the reaction. The critical stories referred to by headlines are Chris Chase, "What on Earth Was Seattle Thinking with Worst Play Call in NFL History?," *USA Today*, February 1, 2015, http://ftw.usato day.com/2015/02/seattle-seahawks-last-play-interception-marshawn -lynch-super-bowl-malcolm-butler-play-clal-pete-carroll; Mark Maske, "'Worst Play-Call in Super Bowl History' Will Forever Alter Percep-tion of Seahawks, Patriots," *Washington Post*, February 2, 2015, https://

www.washingtonpost.com/news/sports/wp/2015/02/02/worst-play
-call-in-super-bowl-history-will-forever-alter-perception-of-seahawks
-patriots; Alex Marvez, "Dumbest Call in Super Bowl History Could Be
Beginning of the End for Seattle Seahawks," FoxSports.com, February
2, 2015, http://www.foxsports.com/nfl/story/super-bowl-seattle-seahawks
-pete-carroll-darrell-bevell-russell-wilson-dumbest-call-ever-020215;
Jerry Brewer, "Seahawks Lost Because of the Worst Call in Super Bowl
History," *Seattle Times*, February 1, 2015, http://old.seattletimes.com
/html/seahawks/2025601887_brewer02xml.html; and Nicholas Da-
widoff, "A Coach's Terrible Super Bowl Mistake," *New Yorker*, February
2, 2015, http://www.newyorker.com/news/sporting-scene/pete-carroll
-terrible-super-bowl-mistake.

The stories explaining the potentially sound rationale for the play-
call are Brian Burke, "Tough Call: Why Pete Carroll's Decision to Pass
Was Not as Stupid as It Looked," Slate.com, February 2, 2015, http://
www.slate.com/articles/sports/sports_nut/2015/02/why_pete_carroll
_s_decision_to_pass_wasn_t_the_worst_play_call_ever.html, and Benjamin Morris, "A Head Coach Botched the End of the Super Bowl, and
It Wasn't Pete Carroll," FiveThirtyEight.com, February 2, 2015, https://
fivethirtyeight.com/features/a-head-coach-botched-the-end-of-the
-super-bowl-and-it-wasnt-pete-carroll. The description of Pete Carroll's appearance on the *Today* show came from Chris Wesseling, "Pete
Carroll Concedes 'Worst Result of a Call Ever," NFL.com, February 5,
2015, http://www.nfl.com/news/story/0ap3000000469003/article/pete
-carroll-concedes-worst-result-of-a-call-ever.

The game information and statistics are from Pro-Football-Reference
.com, though many of them also appeared in accounts and analyses of the
game.

Three years later, in Super Bowl LII, Philadelphia Eagles coach
Doug Pederson made a similarly daring play-call. Near the end of the
first half, on fourth-and-goal at the New England one-yard line and
leading by three, Pederson declined the conventional choice of a short
field-goal attempt. In going for the touchdown, he also relied on a trick
play, "the Philly Special," which called for quarterback Nick Foles to
catch a pass in the end zone from tight end Trey Burton. Unlike Carroll's call, Pederson's call resulted in a touchdown. Resulting won the
day again as ESPN credited Pederson with "nothing less than the gut-
siest coaching job in Super Bowl history." See Dan Graziano, "Guts and
Glory: Eagles Coach Doug Pederson Had Game for the Ages," ESPN,
February 5, 2018, http://www.espn.com/nfl/story/_/id/22326781/inside

-philly-special-gutsiest-play-calling-super-bowl-history-doug-peder
son-philadelphia-eagles.

11 **Quick or dead: our brains weren't built for rationality:** For a good
overview on our problems processing data, including assuming causation
when there is only a correlation and cherry-picking data to confirm the
narrative we prefer, see the *New York Times* op-ed by Gary Marcus and
Ernest Davis, "Eight (No, Nine!) Problems with Big Data," on April 6,
2014.

In addition to the sources mentioned in this section and additional
materials cited in the Selected Bibliography and Recommendations for
Further Reading, Colin Camerer was nice enough to spend two hours
on the phone talking with me about this subject. I highly recommend
watching his outstanding TEDx Talk, "Neuroscience, Game Theory,
Monkeys," which includes a fun look at where chimpanzees are actually
better at game theory than humans.

18 **Dr. Strangelove:** I met historian George Dyson (son of Freeman Dyson)
at a mentoring conference for youth called Adventures of the Mind. The
conference was held at the Institute for Advanced Study. During my
speech, I mentioned—as I do in practically every speech—John von
Neumann and told the students that this site was hallowed ground for
me because it's where von Neumann worked. George heard me say that
and later e-mailed me a scan of one of von Neumann's gambling markers.

The information about von Neumann, in addition to the sources
mentioned in the section (which are cited in the Selected Bibliography
and Recommendations for Further Reading), are from the following
sources: Boston Public Library, "100 Most Influential Books of the Century," posted on TheGreatestBooks.org; Tim Hartford, "A Beautiful
Theory," *Forbes*, December 10, 2006; Institute for Advanced Study,
"John von Neumann's Legacy," IAS.edu; Alexander Leitch, "von Neumann, John," *A Princeton Companion* (1978); Robert Leonard, "From
Parlor Games to Social Science: von Neumann, Morgenstern, and the
Creation of Game Theory 1928–1944," *Journal of Economic Literature*
(1995).

The quotes from reviews that greeted *Theory of Games* are from Harold W. Kuhn's introduction to the sixtieth anniversary edition.

The influences behind the title character in *Dr. Strangelove* either are
alluringly vague or differ based on who's telling (or speculating). John
von Neumann shared a number of physical characteristcs with the character and is usually cited as an influence. Others named as influences
include Wernher von Braun, Herman Kahn, Edward Teller, and Henry

Kissinger. Except for Kissinger, who was a relatively obscure Harvard professor when the film was made, these are all conceivable models.

The influence of John von Neumann on game theory, and of game theory on modern economics, is unquestioned. At least eleven Nobel laureates in economics have been cited for their work connected with or influenced by game theory. NobelPrize.org has cited the following eleven winners of the Prize in Economic Sciences (formally called "The Sveriges Riksbank Prize in Economic Sciences in Memory of Alfred Nobel"), by year, field, and contribution: (1) John C. Harsanyi, (2) John F. Nash Jr., and (3) Reinhard Selten (1994, game theory, "for their pioneering analysis of equilibria in the theory of non-cooperative games"); (4) Robert J. Aumann and (5) Thomas C. Schelling (2005, game theory, "for having enhanced our understanding of conflict and cooperation through game theory analysis"); (6) Leonid Hurwicz, (7) Eric S. Maskin, and (8) Roger B. Myerson (2007, microeconomics, "for having laid the foundations of mechanism design theory"); (9) Alvin E. Roth and (10) Lloyd S. Shapley (2012, applied game theory, "for the theory of stable allocations and the practice of market design"); and (11) Jean Tirole (2014, industrial organization, microeconomics, "for his analysis of market power and regulation").

20 **Poker vs. chess:** My brother Howard came from a chess background, but the movement of players from chess into poker is relatively rare. In my opinion, the lack of uncertainty in chess compared with the great uncertainty in poker is a barrier to transitioning from one to the other. In contrast, during my time in poker there was a lot of crossover between backgammon and poker. Many of the greatest poker players are also world-class backgammon players: Chip Reese, Huckleberry Seed, Jason Lester, Gus Hansen, Paul Magriel, Dan Harrington, and Erik Seidel. The greater crossover with backgammon likely comes from the more prominent element of uncertainty that backgammon and poker share. Poker players have to navigate the luck in the deal of the cards. Backgammon players have to navigate the luck in the roll of the dice.

23 **A lethal battle of wits:** The scene between Westley and Vizzini from *The Princess Bride* should be instantly familiar to generations of movie fans. The quotes from the lethal battle of wits are actually from the novel, though the scenes are nearly identical in both formats. The only notable difference is one instance where author-screenwriter William Goldman and director Rob Reiner expertly adapted Vizzini's overconfidence to the appropriate medium. When Vizzini introduces the man in black to his indescribable intellect, movie-Vizzini gets right to the point, reciting the names of antiquity's greatest minds and concluding, by comparison:

"MORONS!" In the novel, Goldman has Vizzini deliver a pompous, gasbaggy speech. This is the speech in its entirety: "There are no words to contain all my wisdom. I am so cunning, crafty and clever, so filled with deceit, guile and chicanery, such a knave, so shrewd, cagey as well as calculating, as diabolical as I am vulpine, as tricky as I am untrustworthy . . . well, I told you there were not words invented yet to explain how great my brain is, but let me put it this way: the world is several million years old and several billion people have at one time or another trod upon it, but I, Vizzini the Sicilian, am, speaking with pure candor and modesty, the slickest, sleekest, sliest and wiliest fellow who has yet come down the pike."

When talking about 4 coin flips versus 10,000, I was speaking relatively. There has actually been a lot of work done on how many times you need to flip a coin to determine if the coin is fair. If you are interested, you can read an explanation in *Wikipedia*, s.v. "Checking Whether a Coin Is Fair," accessed June 1, 2017, https://en.wikipedia.org/wiki /Checking_whether_a_coin_is_fair.

30 **Redefining wrong:** For the quotes about how, in setting odds in advance of the Brexit vote, the bookmakers got it "wrong," see Jon Sindreu, "Big London Bets Tilted Bookmakers' 'Brexit' Odds," *Wall Street Journal*, June 26, 2016, https://www.wsj.com/articles/big-london-bets-tilted -bookmakers-brexit-odds-1466976156, and Alan Dershowitz, "Why It's Impossible to Predict This Election," *Boston Globe*, September 13, 2016, https://www.bostonglobe.com/opinion/2016/09/13/why-impossible -predict-this-election/Y7B4N39FqasHzuiO81sWEO/story.html. If you are interested in more details about the confusion that follows when you declare someone "right" or "wrong" about a prediction, I wrote on the topic right after the Brexit vote and again before the presidential election. "Bookies vs. Bankers on Brexit: Who's Gambling Now?," Huff ingtonPost.com, July 13, 2016, http://www.huffingtonpost.com/entry /bookies-vs-bankers-on-brexit-whos-gambling-now_us_57866312e4b 0cbf01e9ef902, and "Even Dershowitz? Mistaking Odds for Wrong When the Underdog Wins," *Huffington Post*, September 21, 2016, http:// www.huffingtonpost.com/annie-duke/even-dershowitz-mistaking_b _12120592.html.

Nate Silver and his website, FiveThirtyEight.com, bore the brunt of the criticism for pollsters and forecasters after the 2016 presidential election. Silver's site updated, in real time, polling and forecasting data on the election and had (depending on the date) the probability of a Clinton victory at approximately 60%–70%. If you Google (without the quotation marks) "Nate Silver got it wrong election," 465,000 results come up. *Politico*'s November 9 headline was "How Did Everyone Get It So

Wrong?," http://www.politico.com/story/2016/11/how-did-everyone-get
-2016-wrong-presidential-election-231036. Gizmodo.com jumped on
Silver even before the election, in a November 4 article by Matt Novak
titled "Nate Silver's Very Very Wrong Predictions About Donald Trump
Are Terrifying," http://paleofuture.gizmodo.com/nate-silvers-very-very
-wrong-predictions-about-donald-t-1788583912, including the declaration, "Silver has no f**king idea."

CHAPTER 2: WANNA BET!

49 **Hearing is believing:** The quote about baldness is from Susan Scutti,
   "Going Bald Isn't Your Mother's Fault; Maternal Genetics Are Not to
   Blame," *Medical Daily*, May 18, 2015, http://www.medicaldaily.com/going
   -bald-isnt-your-mothers-fault-maternal-genetics-are-not-blame
   -333668. There are numerous lists of such common misconceptions,
   such as Emma Glanfield's "Coffee Isn't Made from Beans, You Can't
   See the Great Wall of China from Space and Everest ISN'T the World's
   Tallest Mountain: The Top 50 Misconceptions That Have Become
   Modern Day 'Facts,'" *Daily Mail*, April 22, 2015, http://www.dailymail
   .co.uk/news/article-3050941/Coffee-isn-t-beans-t-Great-Wall-China
   -space-Everest-ISN-T-worlds-tallest-mountain-Experts-unveil
   -life-s-50-misconceptions-modern-day-facts.html; *Wikipedia*, s.v. "List
   of Common Misconceptions," accessed June 27, 2017, https://en.wikipedia
   .org/wiki/List_of_common_misconceptions.

56 **"They saw a game":** The quotes from the school newspapers are as they
   appeared in Hastorf and Cantril's paper.

67 **Redefining confidence:** When you express uncertainty to someone
   who knows about communicating that way, the mutual recognition is
   like a light switch turning on. When I was early in the process of writing
   this book, I had lunch with Stuart Firestein. We had barely exchanged
   pleasantries when the waiter came to take our order. The waiter was not
   a native English speaker, and I have a lot of dietary restrictions that are
   difficult enough to communicate to someone who shares my first language. When the waiter walked away, I said, "Well, that's seventy-three
   percent." Stuart started laughing, because he immediately knew what I
   meant. "I think it's lower than that," he said. "Maybe somewhere in the
   forties that he's going to get your order right." My declaration of uncertainty invited the discussion about whether my lunch order would be
   correct. That seems like a small thing, but when you express uncertainty
   in this way, you will invite debate about more significant topics.

CHAPTER 3: BET TO LEARN: FIELDING THE UNFOLDING FUTURE

85 **Working backward is hard: the SnackWell's Phenomenon:** In discussing classical stimulus-response experiments, I'm referring to the legendary work by B. F. Skinner. The Selected Bibliography and Recommendations for Further Reading includes a citation to one of his principal experiments, as well as to an article by psychologist Ogden Lindsley describing some of Skinner's work.

89 **"If it weren't for luck, I'd win every one":** The Institute for Advanced Study's web page on John von Neumann's legacy includes von Neumann's quote about the trees passing him at 60 mph, and how one of them stepped into his path. William Poundstone, who told several von Neumann stories in *Prisoner's Dilemma*, also mentioned JvN's driving habits.

There are several versions of transcripts and videos of the Iowa Republican presidential primary debate on January 28, 2016, such as Team Fix, "7th Republican Debate Transcript, Annotated: Who Said What and What It Meant," *Washington Post*, January 28, 2016, https://www.washingtonpost.com/news/the-fix/wp/2016/01/28/7th-republican-debate-transcript-annotated-who-said-what-and-what-it-meant.

96 **People watching:** Yogi Berra has proven a fertile source for quotes on such a variety of subjects that it's reasonable to wonder whether he actually said all the things attributed to him. Because he wrote a book using this astute observation as its title, I feel I'm on safe ground considering this an actual quote, or at least one Berra adopted as his own. Note the title of Yogi's 2008 book (written with Dave Kaplan): *You Can Observe a Lot by Watching: What I've Learned about Teamwork from the Yankees and Life.*

Published information about the Bartman play and its aftermath is plentiful, and the game and the play are available on YouTube. The behavior of the fans at Wrigley Field and the quotes appear in Alex Gibney's 2014 ESPN Films documentary, *Catching Hell*.

102 **Other people's outcomes reflect on us:** For some of the places in which Dawkins has written about natural selection proceeding by competition among the phenotypes of genes, see *Current Problems in Sociobiology* and *The Greatest Show on Earth*, cited in the Selected Bibliography and Recommendations for Further Reading.

For an examination of whether people would choose to earn $70,000 in 1900 or in 2010, see (and listen to) "Would You Rather Be Rich in

1900, or Middle-Class Now?," NPR.org, October 12, 2010, http://www
.npr.org/sections/money/2010/10/12/130512149/the-tuesday-podcast
-would-you-rather-be-middle-class-now-or-rich-in-1900.

105 **Reshaping habit:** Ivan Pavlov's work is well known and summarized in every form of media. I included, in the Selected Bibliography and Recommendations for Further Reading, one of countless possible ways to learn more about Pavlov's ubiquitous experiments, a book by Daniel Todes titled *Pavlov's Physiology Factory: Experiment, Interpretation, Laboratory Enterprise*.

If you don't watch golf on television, golf analyst and former PGA Tour pro John Maginnes described the "blame the green" stare in "Maginnes On Tap," Golf.SwingBySwing.com, February 13, 2013, http://golf.swingbyswing.com/article/maginnes-on-tapgolfers-in-hollywood.
Phil Mickelson's practice drill of making one hundred straight three-foot putts has been described by legendary golf teacher David Pelz, who has worked with Mickelson. "Dave Pelz and the 3 Foot Putting Circle," GolfLife.com, June 13, 2016, http://www.golflife.com/dave-pelz-3-foot-putting-circle.

CHAPTER 4: THE BUDDY SYSTEM

119 **"Maybe you're the problem, do you think?":** You can see for yourself David Letterman's uncomfortable interview of Lauren Conrad from the *Late Show with David Letterman* on October 27, 2008, on YouTube. The web response to the interview came from the following sources: Ryan Tate, "David Letterman to Lauren Conrad: 'Maybe You're the Problem,'" Gawker.com, October 28, 2008, http://gawker.com/5069699/david-letterman-to-lauren-conrad-maybe-youre-the-problem; Ayman, "Lauren Conrad on David Letterman," Trendhunter.com, October 30, 2008, https://www.trendhunter.com/trends/lauren-conrad-interview-david-letterman; and "Video: Letterman Makes Fun of Lauren Conrad & 'The Hills' Cast," Starpulse.com, October 29, 2008, http://www.starpulse.com/video-letterman-makes-fun-of-lauren-conrad-the-hills-cast-1847865350.html. (Warning: these websites may not still be operating or hosting their prior content.)

127 **Not all groups are created equal:** My point in bringing up the group approach of Alcoholics Anonymous is to demonstrate the obvious value people can get in working on difficult habits by enlisting a group, illustrated in part by the story of founders Bill W. and Dr. Bob. My knowledge of the details of AA is based on commonly available public sources. These start with AA's website (aa.org), which includes the Big Book, the Twelve Steps, its archives and history, and its eLibrary.

I first met Erik Seidel when I went off to New York for college. How-ard was part of a study group of exceptional poker players in New York, including Erik Seidel, Dan Harrington, Steve Zolotow, and Jason Les-ter. These players all went on to successful poker careers, including earning seven World Series of Poker bracelets and combined tourna-ment earnings of nearly $18 million—that's *excluding* Seidel's eight bracelets and $34.5 million; it was a remarkable study pod. I met these players when I visited Howard at the Mayfair Club, where they played backgammon and then poker, the place where they all grew up together as poker players.

137 **The group ideally exposes us to a diversity of viewpoints:** The Dis-sent Channel is codified in the Department of State's Foreign Affairs Manual, 2 FAM 071-075.1, https://fam.state.gov/fam/02fam/02fam0070 .html. Its history and origins were described in several news stories about uses of the Dissent Channel in the Obama and Trump adminis-trations. See Joseph Cassidy, "The Syria Dissent Channel Message Means the System Is Working," *Foreign Policy*, June 19, 2016; Jeffrey Gettleman, "State Dept. Dissent Cable on Trump's Ban Draws 1,000 Signatures," *New York Times*, January 31, 2017; Stephen Goldsmith, "Why Dissenting Viewpoints Are Good for Efficiency," *Government Technology*, July 26, 2016; Neal Katyal, "Washington Needs More Dissent Channels," *New York Times*, July 1, 2016; and Josh Rogin, "State Department Dissent Memo: 'We Are Better Than This Ban'," *Washington Post*, January 30, 2017. For a list of the four awards for constructive dissent, see "Con-structive Dissent Awards," AFSA.org, http://www.afsa.org/constructive -dissent-awards.

The CIA's acknowledgment of the red-team approach in the raid on Osama bin Laden was also mentioned in Neal Katyal's *New York Times* op-ed, above.

141 **Federal judges: drift happens:** The details of the growing homogene-ity in the chambers of Supreme Court justices comes from Adam Lip-tak's September 6, 2010, *New York Times* article, "A Sign of the Court's Polarization: Choice of Clerks." Justice Thomas's hiring practices are described in the same article. The measure of his ideological distance from the other justices can be found in Oliver Roeder's January 30, 2017, FiveThirtyEight.com article, "How Trump's Nominee Will Alter the Supreme Court." Roeder's article introduced me to the data from a pa-per Lee Epstein and colleagues wrote in the *Journal of Law, Economics, and Organization*. Justice Thomas's remark about his hiring practices, including his adaptation of the famous line often attributed to Mark Twain about teaching a pig to sing, has been widely reported, including

in David Savage's profile, "Clarence Thomas Is His Own Man," in the *Los Angeles Times*, July 3, 2011.

149 **Wanna bet (on science)?**: Several studies about corporate prediction markets mention the companies studied or those known to be testing prediction markets. See Cowgill, Wolfers, and Zitzewitz, "Using Prediction Markets to Track Information Flows." Some studies also refer to some of the companies anonymously. For an example of a study doing both, see Cowgill and Zitzewitz, "Corporate Prediction Markets, Evidence from Google, Ford, and Firm X." Both citations appear in the Selected Bibliography and Recommendations for Further Reading.

CHAPTER 5: DISSENT TO WIN

153 **CUDOS to a magician**: I wish I had the space or the excuse to share more details from Robert K. Merton's remarkable life. See the following stories celebrating his fascinating life: Jason Hollander, "Renowned Columbia Sociologist and National Medal of Science Winner Robert K. Merton Dies at 92," *Columbia News*, February 25, 2003, http://www.co lumbia.edu/cu/news/03/02/robertKMerton.html; and Michael Kaufman, "Robert K. Merton, Versatile Sociologist and Father of the Focus Group, Dies at 92," *New York Times*, February 24, 2003, http://www.nytimes .com/2003/02/24/nyregion/robert-k-merton-versatile-sociologist-and -father-of-the-focus-group-dies-at-92.html.

155 **Mertonian communism: more is more**: For an account of John Madden's attendance at Vince Lombardi's eight-hour seminar on one play, see Dan Oswald's *HR Hero* blog post, "Learn Important Lessons from Lombardi's Eight-Hour Session," March 10, 2014. The documentary *Lombardi* was produced by NFL Films and HBO and initially appeared for broadcast on HBO on December 11, 2010.

172 **Communicating with the world beyond our group**: "Yes, and . . ." is so fundamental to group improvisation that it might be easier to list improv texts that *don't* start with this rule. If you don't have any improv texts handy, an excellent, practical description of "yes, and . . ." appears in Tina Fey's autobiography, *Bossypants*.

CHAPTER 6: ADVENTURES IN MENTAL TIME TRAVEL

180 **Night Jerry**: I learned a great deal about the neural pathways involved in imagining the future and remembering the past from a conversation with Joe Kable, psychology professor at Penn and primary investigator at the Kable Lab at the university. One of Joe's studies is cited in the Selected Bibliography and Recommendations for Further Reading, though you

should consider it just an introduction to his body of work. In addition to his work, I recommend, as a good overview for readers trying to learn more about the subject, the *Neuron* paper by Schacter and colleagues, cited in the Selected Bibliography and Recommendations for Further Reading.

Our collective retirement-savings shortfall has been widely reported. For some excellent overviews of the behavioral issues involved in retirement planning and the size of the shortfall, see Dale Griffin, "Planning for the Future: On the Behavioral Economics of Living Longer," Slate .com, August 2013, http://www.slate.com/articles/health_and_science /prudential/2013/08/_planning_for_the_future_is_scary_but_why_is _that.html; Mary Josephs, "How to Solve America's Retirement Savings Crisis," *Forbes*, February 6, 2017, https://www.forbes.com/sites/maryjo sephs/2017/02/06/how-to-solve-americas-retirement-savings -crisis/#163d6e9015ae; and Gillian White, "The Danger of Borrowing Money from Your Future Self," *Atlantic*, April 21, 2015, https://www .theatlantic.com/business/archive/2015/04/the-danger-of-borrowing -money-from-your-future-self/391077.

For a description of the Merrill Edge app, see Bank of America's February 26, 2014, news release, "New Merrill Edge Mobile App Uses 3D Technology to Put Retirement Planning in Your Hands," http:// newsroom.bankofamerica.com/press-releases/consumer-banking/new -merrill-edge-mobile-app-uses-3d-technology-put-retirement-planni.

190 **A flat tire, the ticker, and a zoom lens:** For an interview with Professor Howard, including his fascination with flat-tire stories, see his conversation with Somik Raha, "A Conversation with Professor Ron Howard: Waking Up," Conversations.org, October 17, 2013.

For an examination of Warren Buffett's market prowess and Berkshire Hathaway's stock performance over the last fifty years, see Andy Kiersz, "Here's How Badly Warren Buffett Has Beaten the Market," *Business Insider*, February 26, 2016. The graph of Berkshire's long-term price compared with the S&P 500 was re-created from stock data from Yahoo! Finance and a study in *Financial Analysts Journal* by Meir Statman and Jonathan Scheid, "Buffett in Foresight and Hindsight."

197 **Tilt:** A list of basic surfing terms can be found on http://www.surfing -waves.com/surf_talk.htm and https://www.swimoutlet.com/guides/differ ent-wave-types-for-surfing. For an overview of all the different kinds of nails, go to any hardware store, or see http://www.diynetwork.com /how-to/skills-and-know-how/tools/all-about-the-different-types-of-nails. The number of types of brain tumors was reported on http://braintumor

.org/brain-tumor-information/understanding-brain-tumors/tumor-types.

208 **Reconnaissance: mapping the future:** There are innumerable descriptions of the planning and execution of the D-Day invasion at Normandy, so you can look practically anywhere to see this monumental example of scenario planning in practice. One such introduction to the subject is an interview that appeared in the *Daily Beast* with naval historian Craig Symonds, in connection with the release of his 2014 book on the subject. See Marc Wortman, "D-Day Historian Craig Symonds Talks about History's Most Amazing Invasion," TheDailyBeast.com, June 5, 2014, and, of course, Symonds's book, *Neptune: Allied Invasion of Europe and the D-Day Landings.*

Also, see Nate Silver, "14 Versions of Trump's Presidency, from #MAGA to Impeachment," FiveThirtyEight.com, February 3, 2017.

218 **Backcasting: working backward from a positive future:** For stories describing Olmsted's genius in the design of Central Park and his use of backcasting, see David Allan, "Backcasting to the Future," CNN.com, December 16, 2015, and Nathaniel Rich, "When Parks Were Radical," *Atlantic*, September 2016, https://www.theatlantic.com/magazine/archive/2016/09/better-than-nature/492716.

221 **Premortems: working backward from a negative future:** In addition to Gabriele Oettingen's books and published work with her husband Peter Gollwitzer (see citations in the Selected Bibliography and Recommendations for Further Reading), I recommend that you look at her website based on an application of mental contrasting known by the acronym WOOP (Wish, Outcome, Obstacle, Plan), WoopMyLife.org. WOOP provides numerous practical ways to implement mental contrasting.

SELECTED BIBLIOGRAPHY
AND RECOMMENDATIONS
FOR FURTHER READING

Allan, David. "Backcasting to the Future." CNN.com, December 16, 2015. http://www.cnn.com/2015/10/22/health/backcasting-to-the-future.

Arbesman, Samuel. *The Half-Life of Facts: Why Everything We Know Has an Expiration Date.* New York: Current, 2012.

Ariely, Dan. *Predictably Irrational: The Hidden Forces That Shape Our Decisions.* Rev. exp. ed. New York: Harper Collins, 2009.

Babcock, Linda, and George Loewenstein. "Explaining Bargaining Impasse: The Role of Self-Serving Biases." *Journal of Economic Perspectives* 11, no. 1 (Winter 1997): 109–26.

Bailenson, Jeremy, and Laura Carstensen. "Connecting to the Future Self: Using Web-Based Virtual Reality to Increase Retirement Saving." Stanford Freeman Spogli Institute for International Studies, 2009–2011. http://fsi.stanford.edu/research/connecting_to_the_future_self_using _webbased_virtual_reality_to_increase_retirement_saving.

Baumeister, Roy, Jennifer Campbell, Joachim Krueger, and Kathleen Vohs. "Does High Self-Esteem Cause Better Performance, Interpersonal Success, Happiness, or Healthier Lifestyles?" *Psychological Science in the Public Interest* 4, no. 1 (May 2003): 1–44.

Berra, Yogi, and David Kaplan. *You Can Observe a Lot by Watching: What I've Learned about Teamwork from the Yankees and Life.* Hoboken, NJ: Wiley, 2008.

Bi, Chongzeng, and Daphna Oyserman. "Left Behind or Moving Forward? Effects of Possible Selves and Strategies to Attain Them among Rural Chinese Children." *Journal of Adolescence* 44 (2015): 245–58.

Boston Public Library. "The 100 Most Influential Books of the Century." TheGreatestBooks.org. http://thegreatestbooks.org/lists/42.

Boyer, Pascal. "Evolutionary Economics of Mental Time Travel?" *Trends in Cognitive Sciences* 12, no. 6 (June 30, 2008): 219–24.

Brockman, John, ed. *Thinking: The New Science of Decision-Making, Problem-Solving, and Prediction.* New York: Harper Perennial, 2013.

Bronowski, Jacob. *The Ascent of Man.* London: British Broadcasting Corporation, 1973.

Cabane, Olivia Fox. *The Charisma Myth: How Anyone Can Master the Art and Science of Personal Magnetism.* New York: Portfolio/Penguin, 2012.

Cabane, Olivia Fox, and Judah Pollack. *The Net and the Butterfly: The Art and Practice of Breakthrough Thinking.* New York: Portfolio/Penguin, 2017.

Cain, Susan. *Quiet: The Power of Introverts in a World That Can't Stop Talking.* New York: Crown, 2012.

Camerer, Colin. "Neuroscience, Game Theory, Monkeys." Filmed January 2013, posted on TED.com. https://www.ted.com/talks/colin_camerer_neuroscience_game_theory_monkeys#t-1912.

Campbell, W. Keith, and Constantine Sedikides. "Self-Threat Magnifies the Self-Serving Bias: A Meta-Analytic Integration." *Review of General Psychology* 3, no. 1 (1999): 23–43.

Cassidy, Joseph. "The Syria Dissent Channel Message Means the System Is Working." *Foreign Policy*, June 19, 2016. http://foreignpolicy.com/2016/06/19/syria-obama-assad-state-department.

Cavagnaro, Daniel, Gabriel Aranovich, Samuel McClure, Mark Pitt, and Jay Myung. "On the Functional Form of Temporal Discounting: An Optimized Adaptive Test." *Journal of Risk and Uncertainty* 52, no. 3 (June 2016): 233–54.

Chen, M. Keith, Venkat Vakshminarayanan, and Laurie Santos. "How Basic Are Behavioral Biases: Evidence from Capuchin Monkey Trading Behavior." *Journal of Political Economy* 114, no. 3 (June 2006): 517–37.

Cherones, Tom, dir. *Seinfeld.* Season 5, Episode 3, "The Glasses." Written by Larry David, Jerry Seinfeld, Tom Gammill, and Max Pross. Aired September 30, 1993, on NBC.

Cialdini, Robert. *Influence: The Psychology of Persuasion.* Rev. ed. New York: HarperCollins, 2009.

Cowgill, Bo, Justin Wolfers, and Eric Zitzewitz. "Using Prediction Markets to Track Information Flows: Evidence from Google," January 2009. http://users.nber.org/~jwolfers/papers/GooglePredictionMarketPaper.pdf.

Cowgill, Bo, and Eric Zitzewitz. "Corporate Prediction Markets: Evidence from Google, Ford, and Firm X." *Review of Economic Studies* 82, no. 4 (April 2, 2015): 1309–41.

Dalio, Ray. *Principles: Life and Work.* New York: Simon & Schuster, 2017.

Dawkins, Richard. *The Greatest Show on Earth: The Evidence for Evolution.* New York: Free Press, 2010.

Dawkins, Richard, "Replicators and Vehicles." In *Current Problems in Sociobiology,* edited by King's College Sociobiology Group, 45–64. Cambridge: Cambridge University Press, 1982.

Dawkins, Richard. *The Selfish Gene.* 40th anniv. ed. Oxford: Oxford Landmark Science, 2016. First published 1976 by Oxford University Press (Oxford).

Ditto, Peter, Brittany Liu, Cory Clark, Sean Wojcik, Eric Chen, Rebecca Grady, and Joanne Zinger. "At Least Bias Is Bipartisan: A Meta-Analytic Comparison of Partisan Bias in Liberals and Conservatives." April 13, 2017. Available at SSRN: https://ssrn.com/abstract=2952510.

Dreber, Anna, Thomas Pfeiffer, Johan Almenberg, Siri Isaksson, Brad Wilson, Yiling Chen, Brian Nosek, and Magnus Johannesson. "Using Prediction Markets to Estimate the Reproducibility of Scientific Research." *Proceedings of the National Academy of Sciences* 112, no. 50 (December 2015): 15343–47.

Duarte, Jose, Jarret Crawford, Charlotta Stern, Jonathan Haidt, Lee Jussim, and Philip Tetlock. "Political Diversity Will Improve Social Psychological Science." *Behavioral and Brain Sciences* 38 (January 2015): 1–58.

Duhigg, Charles. *The Power of Habit: Why We Do What We Do in Life and Business.* Ed. with new afterword. New York: Random House, 2014.

Duhigg, Charles. *Smarter Faster Better: The Secrets of Being Productive in Life and Business.* New York: Random House, 2016.

Dyson, George. *Turing's Cathedral: The Origins of the Digital Universe.* New York: Pantheon, 2012.

Easterbook, Frank, Circuit Judge. *Jentz v. ConAgra Foods, Inc.,* 767 F.3d 688 (7th Cir. 2014).

Ellenberg, Jordan. *How Not to Be Wrong: The Power of Mathematical Thinking.* New York: Penguin, 2014.

Epstein, Lee, Andrew Martin, Jeffrey Segal, and Chad Westerland. "The Judicial Common Space." *Journal of Law, Economics, & Organization* 23, no. 2 (May 2007): 303–25.

Ersner-Hershfield, Hal, G. Elliott Wimmer, and Brian Knutson. "Saving for the Future Self: Neural Measures of Future Self-Continuity Predict Temporal Discounting." *Social Cognitive and Affective Neuroscience* 4, no. 1 (2009): 85–92.

Fey, Tina. *Bossypants.* New York: Reagan Arthur Books, 2011.

Feynman, Richard. "Cargo Cult Science." *Engineering and Science* 37, no. 7 (June 1974): 10–13.

Feynman, Richard. *The Pleasure of Finding Things Out: The Best Short Works of Richard P. Feynman.* New York: Perseus Publishing, 1999.

Firestein, Stuart. *Ignorance: How It Drives Science.* New York: Oxford University Press, 2012.

Firestein, Stuart. "The Pursuit of Ignorance." Filmed February 2013, posted on TED.com. https://www.ted.com/talks/stuart_firestein_the_pursuit_of_ignorance/transcript.

Fischhoff, Baruch. "Hindsight ≠ Foresight: The Effect of Outcome Knowledge on Judgment under Uncertainty." *Journal of Experimental Psychology: Human Perception and Performance* 1, no. 3 (August 1975): 288–99.

Frederick, Shane, George Loewenstein, and Ted O'Donoghue. "Time Discounting and Time Preference: A Critical Review." *Journal of Economic Literature* 40, no. 2 (June 2002): 351–401.

Gibney, Alex, dir. *Catching Hell.* Written by Alex Gibney, produced by Alison Ellwood, Libby Geist, and Matt McDonald. Aired on February 20, 2014, on ESPN. http://www.espn.com/video/clip?id=13883887.

Gilbert, Daniel. "How Mental Systems Believe." *American Psychologist* 46, no. 2 (February 1991): 107–19.

Gilbert, Daniel. *Stumbling on Happiness.* New York: Alfred A. Knopf, 2006.

Gilbert, Daniel, Romin Tafarodi, and Patrick Malone. "You Can't Not Believe Everything You Read." *Journal of Personality and Social Psychology* 65, no. 2 (August 1993): 221–33.

Gino, Francesca. "What We Miss When We Judge a Decision by the Outcome." *Harvard Business Review*, September 2, 2016. https://hbr.org/2016/09/what-we-miss-when-we-judge-a-decision-by-the-outcome.

Gladwell, Malcolm. *Outliers: The Story of Success.* New York: Little, Brown, 2008.

Goldman, William. *Adventures in the Screen Trade: A Personal View of Hollywood and Screenwriting.* New York: Warner Books, 1983.

Goldman, William. *The Princess Bride: S. Morgenstern's Classic Tale of True Love and High Adventure—The Good Parts.* Boston: Houghton Mifflin Harcourt, 1973.

Goldsmith, Stephen. "Why Dissenting Viewpoints Are Good for Efficiency." *Government Technology*, July 26, 2016. http://www.govtech.com/opinion/why-dissenting-viewpoints-are-good-for-efficiency.html.

Golman, Russell, David Hagmann, and George Loewenstein. "Information Avoidance." *Journal of Economic Literature* 55, no. 1 (March 2017): 96–135.

Haidt, Jonathan. *The Happiness Hypothesis: Finding Modern Truth in Ancient Wisdom.* New York: Basic Books, 2006.

Haidt, Jonathan. *The Righteous Mind: Why Good People are Divided by Politics and Religion.* New York: Pantheon Books, 2012.

Harford, Tim. "A Beautiful Theory." *Forbes*, December 10, 2006. http://www.forbes.com/2006/12/10/business-game-theory-tech-cx_th_games06_1212harford.html.

Hastorf, Albert, and Hadley Cantril. "They Saw a Game: A Case Study." *Journal of Abnormal and Social Psychology* 49, no. 1 (January 1954): 129–34.

Haynes, Tara, Raymond Perry, Robert Stupnisky, and Lia Daniels. "A Review of Attributional Retraining Treatments: Fostering Engagement and Persistence in Vulnerable College Students." In *Higher Education: Handbook of Theory and Research* 24, edited by John Smart, 227–72, Springer Netherlands, 2009.

Heider, Fritz. *The Psychology of Interpersonal Relations.* Hillsdale, NJ: Lawrence Erlbaum Assocs., 1958.

Hershfield, Hal. "You Make Better Decisions If You 'See' Your Senior Self." *Harvard Business Review*, June 2013, 30–31.

Hershfield, Hal, Daniel Goldstein, William Sharpe, Jesse Fox, Leo Yeykelis, Laura Carstensen, and Jeremy Bailenson. "Increasing Saving Behavior Through Age-Progressed Renderings of the Future Self." *Journal of Marketing Research* 48 (November 2011): S23–S37.

Holmes, Jamie. *Nonsense: The Power of Not Knowing.* New York: Crown, 2015.

Institute for Advanced Study. "John von Neumann's Legacy." https://www .ias.edu/people/vonneumann/legacy.

Jiang, Wei, Hualin Wan, and Shan Zhao. "Reputation Concerns of Independent Directors: Evidence from Individual Director Voting." *Review of Financial Studies* 29, no. 3 (December 2015): 655–96.

Johnson, Hollyn, and Colleen Seifert. "Sources of the Continued Influence Effect: When Misinformation in Memory Affects Later Inferences." *Journal of Experimental Psychology: Learning, Memory, and Cognition* 20, no. 6 (November 1994): 1420–36.

Johnson-Laird, Philip. "Mental Models and Probabilistic Thinking." *Cognition* 50, no. 1 (June 1994): 189–209.

Kable, Joseph, and Paul Glimcher. "The Neural Correlates of Subjective Value During Intertemporal Choice." *Nature Neuroscience* 10, no. 12 (December 2007): 1625–33.

Kahan, Dan, David Hoffman, Donald Braman, Daniel Evans, and Jeffrey Rachlinsky. "'They Saw a Protest': Cognitive Illiberalism and the Speech-Conduct Distinction." *Stanford Law Review* 64 (2012): 851–906.

Kahan, Dan, Ellen Peters, Erica Dawson, and Paul Slovic. "Motivated Numeracy and Enlightened Self-Government." *Behavioural Public Policy* 1, no. 1 (May 2017): 54–86.

Kahneman, Daniel. *Thinking, Fast and Slow.* New York: Farrar, Straus and Giroux, 2011.

Kahneman, Daniel, and Amos Tversky. "Prospect Theory: An Analysis of Decision Under Risk." *Econometrica: Journal of the Econometric Society* 47, no. 2 (March 1979): 263–91.

Katyal, Neil. "Washington Needs More Dissent Channels." *New York Times*, July 1, 2016. https://www.nytimes.com/2016/07/02/opinion/washington -needs-more-dissent-channels.html.

Katz, David, and Stephanie Meller. "Can We Say What Diet Is Best for Health?" *Annual Review of Public Health* 35 (March 2014): 83–103.

Kearns, Cristin, Laura Schmidt, and Stanton Glantz. "Sugar Industry and Coronary Heart Disease Research: A Historical Analysis of Internal Industry Documents." *JAMA Internal Medicine* 176, no. 11 (November 1, 2016): 1680–85.

Kestemont, Jenny, Ning Ma, Kris Baetens, Nikki Clément, Frank Van Overwalle, and Marie Vandekerckhove. "Neural Correlates of Attributing Causes to the Self, Another Person and the Situation." *Social Cognitive and Affective Neuroscience* 10, no. 1 (March 2014): 114–21.

Kiersz, Andy. "Here's How Badly Warren Buffett Has Beaten the Market." *Business Insider*, February 26, 2016. http://www.businessinsider.com/warren -buffett-berkshire-hathaway-vs-sp-500-2016-2.

Kirwan, C. Brock, Stefania Ashby, and Michelle Nash. "Remembering and Imagining Differentially Engage the Hippocampus: A Multivariate fMRI Investigation." *Cognitive Neuroscience* 5, no. 3–4 (October 2014): 177–85.

Klein, Gary. "Performing a Project Premortem." *Harvard Business Review*, September 2007, 18–19.

Konnikova, Maria. *The Confidence Game: Why We Fall for It . . . Every Time.* New York: Penguin, 2016.

Konnikova, Maria. *Mastermind: How to Think Like Sherlock Holmes.* New York: Penguin, 2013.

Kriss, Peter, George Loewenstein, Xianghong Wang, and Roberto Weber. "Behind the Veil of Ignorance: Self-Serving Bias in Climate Change Negotiations." *Judgment and Decision Making* 6, no. 7 (October 2011): 602–15.

Krusemark, Elizabeth, W. Keith Campbell, and Brett Clementz. "Attributions, Deception, and Event Related Potentials: An Investigation of the Self-Serving Bias." *Psychophysiology* 45, no. 4 (July 2008): 511–15.

Kuhn, Harold, Introduction to *Theory of Games and Economic Behavior*. 60th anniv. ed. Princeton, NJ: Princeton University Press, 2004.

Kuhn, Manford. "The Reference Group Reconsidered." *Sociological Quarterly* 5, no. 1 (January 1964): 5–19.

Lederer, Richard. *Anguished English*. Rev. exp. upd. ed. Layton, UT: Wyrick & Co., 2006. First published in 1987.

Leitch, Alexander. *A Princeton Companion*. Princeton, NJ: Princeton University Press, 1978. http://etcweb.princeton.edu/CampusWWW/Companion /von_neumann_john.html.

Leonard, Robert. "From Parlor Games to Social Science: Von Neumann, Morgenstern, and the Creation of Game Theory 1928–1944." *Journal of Economic Literature* 33 (June 1994): 730–61.

Lerner, Jennifer, and Philip Tetlock. "Accounting for the Effects of Accountability." *Psychological Bulletin* 125, no. 2 (March 1999): 255–75.

Lerner, Jennifer, and Philip Tetlock. "Bridging Individual, Interpersonal, and Institutional Approaches to Judgment and Decision Making: The Impact of Accountability on Cognitive Bias." In *Emerging Perspectives on Judgment and Decision Research*, edited by Sandra Schneider and James Shanteau, 431–57. Cambridge: Cambridge University Press, 2003.

Letterman, David. *The Late Show with David Letterman*. Season 16, Episode 30. Produced by Eric Stangel and Justin Stangel. Aired October 27, 2008, on CBS.

Levitin, Daniel. *A Field Guide to Lies: Critical Thinking in the Information Age.* New York: Dutton, 2016.

Levitt, Steven, and Stephen Dubner. *Freakonomics: A Rogue Economist Explores the Hidden Side of Everything.* Rev. ed. New York: Harper Collins, 2006.

Libby, Robert, and Kristina Rennekamp. "Self-Serving Attribution Bias, Overconfidence, and the Issuance of Management Forecasts." *Journal of Accounting Research* 50, no. 1 (March 2012): 197–231.

Lillard, Lee, and Robert Willis. "Cognition and Wealth: The Importance of Probabilistic Thinking." Unversity of Michigan Retirement Research Center, Working Paper WP 2001-007, 2001. https://deepblue.lib.umich.edu/bitstream/handle/2027.42/50613/wp007.

Lindsley, Ogden. "Precision Teaching's Unique Legacy from B. F. Skinner." *Journal of Behavioral Education* 1, no. 2 (June 1991): 253–66.

Liptak, Adam. "A Sign of the Court's Polarization: Choice of Clerks." *New York Times*, Politics, September 6, 2010. http://www.nytimes.com/2010/09/07/us/politics/07clerks.html.

Loewenstein, George, Samuel Issacharoff, Colin Camerer, and Linda Babcock. "Self-Serving Assessments of Fairness and Pretrial Bargaining." *Journal of Legal Studies* 22, no. 1 (January 1993): 135–59.

Loewenstein, George, Daniel Read, and Roy Baumeister, eds. *Time and Decision: Economic and Psychological Perspectives on Intertemporal Choice.* New York: Russell Sage Foundation, 2003.

Ludwig, David. "Lowering the Bar on the Low-Fat Diet." *Journal of the American Medical Association* 316, no. 20 (November 22, 2016): 2087–88.

Lyubomirsky, Sonja. *The How of Happiness: A Scientific Approach to Getting the Life You Want.* New York: Penguin, 2007.

———*The Myths of Happiness: What Should Make You Happy, but Doesn't, What Shouldn't Make You Happy, but Does.* New York: Penguin, 2013.

————"Why are Some People Happier Than Others? The Role of Cognitive and Motivational Processes in Well-Being." *American Psychologist* 56, no. 3 (March 2001): 239–49.

MacCoun, Robert. "Blaming Others to a Fault?" *Chance* 6, no. 4 (September 1993): 31–34.

MacCoun, Robert, and Saul Perlmutter. "Blind Analysis as a Correction for Confirmatory Bias in Physics and in Psychology." In *Psychological Science Under Scrutiny: Recent Challenges and Proposed Solutions*, edited by Scott Lilienfeld and Irwin Waldman, chap. 15. Oxford: Wiley Blackwell, 2017.

————"Hide Results to Seek the Truth: More Fields Should, Like Particle Physics, Adopt Blind Analysis to Thwart Bias." *Nature* 52 (October 8, 2015): 187–90.

Marcus, Gary. *Kluge: The Haphazard Evolution of the Human Mind.* Boston: Houghton Mifflin, 2008.

Marcus, Gary, and Ernest Davis. "Eight (No, Nine!) Problems with Big Data," *New York Times*, April 6, 2014. https://www.nytimes.com/2014/04 /07/opinion/eight-no-nine-problems-with-big-data.html.

Mauboussin, Michael. *The Success Equation: Untangling Skill and Luck in Business, Sports, and Investing.* Boston: Harvard Business Review Press, 2012.

McGandy, Robert, D. Mark Hegsted, and Fredrick Stare. "Dietary Fats, Carbohydrates and Atherosclerotic Vascular Disease." *New England Journal of Medicine* 277, no. 4 (1967): 186–92, 245–47.

Merton, Robert K., "The Normative Structure of Science." 1942. Reprinted in *The Sociology of Science: Theoretical and Empirical Investigations*, edited by Norman Storer, 267–78. Chicago: University of Chicago Press, 1973.

Mezulis, Amy, Lyn Abramson, Janet Hyde, and Benjamin Hankin. "Is There a Universal Positivity Bias in Attributions? A Meta-Analytic Review of Individual, Developmental, and Cultural Differences in the Self-Serving Attributional Bias." *Psychological Bulletin* 130, no. 5 (September 2004): 711–47.

Mill, John Stuart, *On Liberty.* London: Walter Scott Publishing, 1859. Released on Project Gutenberg, 2011. https://www.gutenberg.org/files/34901 /34901-h/34901-h.htm.

Miller, Dale, and Michael Ross. "Self-Serving Biases in the Attribution of Causality: Fact or Fiction." *Psychological Bulletin* 82, no. 2 (March 1975): 213–25.

Mischel, Walter. *The Marshmallow Test: Why Self Control Is the Engine of Success.* New York: Little, Brown, 2014.

Mitchell, Deborah, J. Edward Russo, and Nancy Pennington. "Back to the Future: Temporal Perspective in the Explanation of Events." *Journal of Behavioral Decision Making* 2, no. 1 (January 1989): 25–38.

Morewedge, Carey, Lisa Shu, Daniel Gilbert, and Timothy Wilson. "Bad Riddance or Good Rubbish? Ownership and Not Loss Aversion Causes the Endowment Effect." *Journal of Experimental Social Psychology* 45, no. 4 (July 2009): 947–51.

Mullally, Sinead, and Eleanor Maguire. "Memory, Imagination, and Predicting the Future: A Common Brain Mechanism?" *The Neuroscientist* 20, no. 3 (June 2014): 220–34.

Munnell, Alice, Wenliang Hou, and Anthony Webb. "NRRI Update Shows Half Still Falling Short." *Center for Retirement Research at Boston College*, no. 14–20, December 2014. http://crr.bc.edu/briefs/nrri-update-shows-half-still-falling-short.

Murray, Bridget. "What Makes Mental Time Travel Possible?" *APA Monitor on Psychology* 34, no. 9 (October 2003): 62.

Myerson, Roger. *Game Theory: Analysis of Conflict*. Cambridge, MA: Harvard University Press, 1991.

Neiss, Michelle, Constantine Sedikides, and Jim Stevenson. "Self-Esteem: A Behavioural Genetic Perspective." *European Journal of Personality* 16, no. 5 (September 2002): 351–67.

Nisbett, Richard. *Mindware: Tools for Smart Thinking*. New York: Farrar, Straus and Giroux, 2015.

NobelPrize.org. "Economic Sciences Laureates: Fields." https://www.nobelprize.org/nobel_prizes/economic-sciences/fields.html.

Nyberg, Lars, Alice Kim, Reza Habib, Brian Levine, and Endel Tulving. "Consciousness of Subjective Time in the Brain." *Proceedings of the National Academy of Sciences* 107, no. 51 (December 21, 2010): 22356–59.

Oettingen, Gabriele. *Rethinking Positive Thinking: Inside the New Science of Motivation*. New York: Current, 2014.

Oettingen, Gabriele, and Peter Gollwitzer. "Strategies of Setting and Implementing Goals." In *Social Psychological Foundations of Clinical Psychology*, edited by James Maddox and June Price Tangney, 114–35. New York: Guilford Press, 2010.

Open Science Collaboration. "Estimating the Reproducibility of Psychological Science." *Science* 349, no. 6251 (August 28, 2015): 943 and aac4716-1–8.

Oswald, Dan. "Learn Important Lessons from Lombardi's Eight-Hour Session." *HR Hero* (blog), March 10, 2014. http://blogs.hrhero.com/oswaldletters/2014/03/10/learn-important-lessons-from-lombardis-eight-hour-session.

Oyserman, Daphna, Deborah Bybee, Kathy Terry, and Tamara Hart-Johnson. "Possible Selves as Roadmaps." *Journal of Research in Personality* 38, no. 2 (April 2004): 130–49.

Oyserman, Daphna, Mesmin Destin, and Sheida Novin. "The Context-Sensitive Future Self: Possible Selves Motivate in Context, Not Otherwise." *Self and Identity* 14, no. 2 (March 2015): 173–88.

Pariser, Eli. *The Filter Bubble: What the Internet Is Hiding from You.* New York: Penguin, 2011.

Paulos, John. *Innumeracy: Mathematical Illiteracy and Its Consequences.* New York: Hill & Wang, 1989.

Pollan, Michael. *In Defense of Food: An Eater's Manifesto.* New York: Penguin, 2008.

Pollan, Michael, "History of Nutritionism" in "Michael Pollan and 'In Defense of Food: The Omnivore's Solution,'" Otis Lecture at Bates College, Lewiston, Maine, October 27, 2008. http://www.bates.edu/food/foods-importance/omnivores-solution/history-of-nutritionism.

Pollan, Michael. *The Omnivore's Dilemma: A Natural History in Four Meals.* New York: Penguin, 2006.

Poundstone, William. *Prisoner's Dilemma.* New York: Anchor, 1993.

Raha, Somik. "A Conversation with Professor Ron Howard: Waking Up." Conversations.org, October 17, 2013. http://www.conversations.org/story.php?sid=373.

Rees, Tim, David Ingledew, and Lew Hardy. "Attribution in Sport Psychology: Seeking Congruence Between Theory, Research and Practice." *Psychology of Sport and Exercise* 6 (2005): 189–204.

Reiner, Rob, dir. *The Princess Bride.* Written by William Goldman, produced by Andrew Scheinman and Rob Reiner. 1987.

Rhee, Nari. "The Retirement Savings Crisis: Is It Worse Than We Think?" Washington, DC: National Institute on Retirement Security, June 2013. http://www.nirsonline.org/storage/nirs/documents/Retirement%20Savings%20Crisis/retirementsavingscrisis_final.pdf.

Rich, Nathaniel. "When Parks Were Radical." *Atlantic*, September 2016. https://www.theatlantic.com/magazine/archive/2016/09/better-than-nature/492716.

Roeder, Oliver. "How Trump's Nominee Will Alter the Supreme Court." FiveThirtyEight.com, January 30, 2017. https://fivethirtyeight.com/features/how-trumps-nominee-will-alter-the-supreme-court.

Rosati, Alexandra, Jeffrey Stevens, Brian Hare, and Marc Hauser. "The Evolutionary Origins of Human Patience: Temporal Preferences in Chimpanzees, Bonobos, and Human Adults." *Current Biology* 17, no. 19 (October 2007): 1663–68.

Ross, H. Laurence. "Drinking and Driving: Beyond the Criminal Approach." *Alcohol Health & Research World* 14, no. 1 (January 1990): 58–63.

Ross, Lee, and Richard Nisbett. *The Person and the Situation: Perspectives of Social Psychology*. New York: McGraw-Hill, 1991; London: Pinter & Martin, 2011.

Ross, Michael, and Fiore Sicoly. "Egocentric Biases in Availability and Attribution." *Journal of Personality and Social Psychology* 37, no. 3 (March 1979): 322–36.

Santos, Laurie, and Alexandra Rosati. "The Evolutionary Roots of Human Decision Making." *Annual Review of Psychology* 66 (January 2015): 321–47.

Savage, David. "Clarence Thomas Is His Own Man." *Los Angeles Times*, Nation, July 3, 2011. http://articles.latimes.com/2011/jul/03/nation/la-na-clarence-thomas-20110703/2.

Schacter, Daniel, Donna Addis, Demis Hassabis, Victoria Martin, R. Nathan Spreng, and Karl Szpunar. "The Future of Memory: Remembering, Imagining, and the Brain." *Neuron* 76, no. 4 (November 21, 2012): 677–94.

Schessler-Jandreau, Imke. "Fat America: A Historical Consideration of Diet and Weight Loss in the US." *21st ICC 2008* (2009): 88–93.

Schoemaker, Paul, and Philip Tetlock. "Superforecasting: How to Upgrade Your Company's Judgment." *Harvard Business Review*, May 2016, 72–78.

Sedikides, Constantine, W. Keith Campbell, Glenn Reeder, and Andrew Elliot. "The Self-Serving Bias in Relational Context." *Journal of Personality and Social Psychology* 74, no. 2 (February 1998): 378–86.

Sedikides, Constantine, John Skowronski, and Lowell Gaertner. "Self-Enhancement and Self-Protection Motivation: From the Laboratory to an Evolutionary Context." *Journal of Cultural and Evolutionary Psychology* 2, no. 1–2 (August 2004): 61–79.

Shapiro, Ouisie, writer. *Lombardi*. Produced by Keith Cossrow and Joe Lavine for HBO Sports and NFL Films. Aired December 11, 2010, on HBO. http://www.hbo.com/sports/lombardi.

Shepperd, James, Wendi Malone, and Kate Sweeny. "Exploring Causes of the Self-Serving Bias." *Social and Personality Psychology Compass* 2, no. 2 (March 2008): 895–908.

Shermer, Michael. *The Believing Brain: From Ghosts and Gods to Politics and Conspiracies—How We Construct Beliefs and Reinforce Them as Truths*. New York: Times Books, 2011.

Silver, Nate. "14 Versions of Trump's Presidency, from #MAGA to Impeachment." FiveThirtyEight.com, February 3, 2017. http://fivethirtyeight.com/features/14-versions-of-trumps-presidency-from-maga-to-impeachment.

Silver, Nate. *The Signal and the Noise: Why So Many Predictions Fail—But Some Don't*. New York: Penguin, 2012.

Simmons, Joseph, Leif Nelson, and Uri Simonsohn. "False-Positive Psychology: Undisclosed Flexibility in Data Collection and Analysis Allows

Presenting Anything as Significant." *Psychological Science* 22, no. 11 (November 2011): 1359–66.

Sirois, Fuschia, and Timothy Pychyl. "Procrastination and the Priority of Short-Term Mood Regulation: Consequences for Future Self." *Social and Personality Psychology Compass* 7, no. 2 (February 2013): 115–27.

Skinner, B. F. "A Case History in Scientific Method." *American Psychologist* 11, no. 5 (May 1956): 221–33.

Stanovich, Keith. *What Intelligence Tests Miss: The Psychology of Rational Thought.* New Haven, CT: Yale University Press, 2009.

Statman, Meir, and Jonathan Scheid. "Buffett in Foresight and Hindsight." *Financial Analysts Journal* 58, no. 4 (July 2002): 11–18.

Stephan, Elena, Constantine Sedikides, Daniel Heller, and Daniella Shidlovski. "My Fair Future Self: The Role of Temporal Distance and Self-Enhancement in Prediction." *Social Cognition* 33, no. 2 (April 2015): 149–68.

Stevens, Jeffrey. "Evolutionary Pressures on Primate Intertemporal Choice." *Proceedings of the Royal Society of London, Series B: Biological Sciences* 281, no. 1786 (July 7, 2014): 1–6.

Stroebele, Nanette, John De Castro, Jennifer Stuht, Vicki Catenacci, Holly Wyatt, and James Hill. "A Small-Changes Approach Reduces Energy Intake in Free-Living Humans." *Journal of the American College of Nutrition* 28, no. 1 (February 2009): 63–68.

Suddendorf, Thomas, and Janie Busby. "Making Decisions with the Future in Mind: Developmental and Comparative Identification of Mental Time Travel." *Learning and Motivation* 36, no. 2 (May 2005): 110–25.

Suddendorf, Thomas, and Michael Corballis. "The Evolution of Foresight: What Is Mental Time Travel, and Is It Unique to Humans?" *Behavioral and Brain Sciences* 30, no. 3 (June 2007): 299–351.

Sunstein, Cass, and Reid Hastie. *Wiser: Getting Beyond Groupthink to Make Groups Smarter.* Boston: Harvard Business Review Press, 2015.

Sunstein, Cass, David Schkade, Lisa Ellman, and Andres Sawicki. *Are Judges Political? An Empirical Analysis of the Federal Judiciary.* Washington, DC: Brookings Institution Press, 2006.

Symonds, Craig. *Neptune: Allied Invasion of Europe and the D-Day Landings.* Oxford: Oxford University Press, 2014.

Taleb, Nassim. *Fooled by Randomness: The Hidden Role of Chance in Life and in the Markets.* New York: Random House, 2004.

Tetlock, Philip, and Dan Gardner. *Superforecasting: The Art and Science of Prediction.* New York: Crown, 2015.

Thaler, Richard. *Misbehaving: The Making of Behavioral Economics.* New York: W. W. Norton, 2015.

————"Some Empirical Evidence on Dynamic Inconsistency." *Economics Letters* 8, no. 3 (January 1981): 201–07.

Thaler, Richard, and Cass Sunstein. *Nudge: Improving Decisions About Health, Wealth, and Happiness*. Upd. ed. New York: Penguin, 2009.

Todes, Daniel. *Pavlov's Physiology Factory: Experiment, Interpretation, Laboratory Enterprise*. Baltimore: Johns Hopkins University Press, 2002.

Tomlin, Damon, David Rand, Elliot Ludvig, and Jonathan Cohen. "The Evolution and Devolution of Cognitive Control: The Costs of Deliberation in a Competitive World." *Scientific Reports* 5 (June 16, 2015).

Tversky, Amos, and Daniel Kahneman. "Loss Aversion in Riskless Choice: A Reference-Dependent Model." *Quarterly Journal of Economics* 106, no. 4 (November 1991): 1039–61.

Von Neumann, John, and Oskar Morgenstern. *Theory of Games and Economic Behavior*. 60th anniv. ed. Princeton, NJ: Princeton University Press, 1944, 2004.

Wachowski, Lana, and Wachowski, Lilly, dirs. *The Matrix*. Written by Lana Wachowski and Lilly Wachowski, produced by Joel Silver. 1999.

Wagenaar, Alexander, and Susan Farrell. "Alcohol Beverage Control Policies: Their Role in Preventing Alcohol-Impaired Driving. In *Surgeon General's Workshop on Drunk Driving: Background Papers*, 1989, 1–14.

Walsh, Jeffrey. "Operant Conditioning: Schedules of Reinforcement." Khan Academy.org. https://www.khanacademy.org/test-prep/mcat/behavior/learning-slug/v/operant-conditioning-schedules-of-reinforcement.

Wansink, Brian, and Jeffery Sobal. "Mindless Eating: The 200 Daily Food Decisions We Overlook." *Environment and Behavior* 39, no. 1 (January 2006): 106–23.

Warner, John, and Saul Pleeter. "The Personal Discount Rate: Evidence from Military Downsizing Programs." *American Economic Review* 91, no. 1 (March 2001): 33–53.

West, Richard, Russell Meserve, and Keith Stanovich. "Cognitive Sophistication Does Not Attenuate the Bias Blind Spot." *Journal of Personality and Social Psychology* 103, no. 3 (September 2002): 506–19.

Welch, Suzy. *10-10-10: A Life-Transforming Idea*. New York: Scribner, 2009.

Wilson, Anne, Roger Buehler, Heather Lawford, Colin Schmidt, and An Gie Yong. "Basking in Projected Glory: The Role of Subjective Temporal Distance in Future Self-Appraisal." *European Journal of Social Psychology* 42, no. 3 (April 2012): 342–53.

Wilson, Timothy, and Patricia Linville. "Improving the Academic Performance of College Freshmen: Attribution Therapy Revisited." *Journal of Personality and Social Psychology* 42, no. 2 (February 1982): 367–76.

Woodward, Bob, and Scott Armstrong. *The Brethren: Inside the Supreme Court.* Reissue ed. New York: Simon & Schuster, 2011.

Wortman, Marc. "D-Day Historian Craig Symonds Talks about History's Most Amazing Invasion." TheDailyBeast.com, June 5, 2014. http://www.thedailybeast.com/d-day-historian-craig-symonds-talks-about-historys-most-amazing-invasion.

Zemeckis, Robert, dir. *Back to the Future: Part II.* Written by Robert Zemeckis and Bob Gale, produced by Neil Canton and Bob Gale. 1989.

Zinberg, Michael, dir. *WKRP in Cincinnati.* Season 1, Episode 7, "Turkeys Away." Written by Bill Dial. Aired October 30, 1978, on CBS.

INDEX

Annie Duke has devoted her life to the study of decision-making under pressure. During her career as a professional poker player, she won over $4 million in tournaments, earned a World Series of Poker bracelet, and is the only woman to have won the WSOP Tournament of Champions and the NBC National Heads-Up Poker Championship. Retired from poker since 2012, she is now a corporate speaker and consultant on decision strategy, merging her poker expertise and her graduate-level research in psychology at the University of Pennsylvania. She has authored five books, is a cofounder of HowIDecide.org, serves on the board of After-School All-Stars, and is a trustee of the Franklin Institute. She has also won a televised championship in rock-paper-scissors. A mom of four, she lives outside Philadelphia.